Ending Wars,
Consolidating Peace:
Economic Perspectives

Edited by Mats Berdal and Achim Wennmann

D1417211

Ending Wars, Consolidating Peace: Economic Perspectives

Edited by Mats Berdal and Achim Wennmann

IISS The International Institute for Strategic Studies

The International Institute for Strategic Studies
Arundel House | 13–15 Arundel Street | Temple Place | London | WC2R 3DX | UK

First published September 2010 by **Routledge**
4 Park Square, Milton Park, Abingdon, Oxon, OX14 4RN

for **The International Institute for Strategic Studies**
Arundel House, 13–15 Arundel Street, Temple Place, London, WC2R 3DX, UK
www.iiss.org

Simultaneously published in the USA and Canada by **Routledge**
270 Madison Ave., New York, NY 10016

Routledge is an imprint of Taylor & Francis, an Informa Business

© 2010 The International Institute for Strategic Studies

DIRECTOR-GENERAL AND CHIEF EXECUTIVE John Chipman
EDITOR Tim Huxley
MANAGER FOR EDITORIAL SERVICES Ayse Abdullah
ASSISTANT EDITOR Janis Lee
COVER/PRODUCTION John Buck

The International Institute for Strategic Studies is an independent centre for research, information and debate on the problems of conflict, however caused, that have, or potentially have, an important military content. The Council and Staff of the Institute are international and its membership is drawn from almost 100 countries. The Institute is independent and it alone decides what activities to conduct. It owes no allegiance to any government, any group of governments or any political or other organisation. The IISS stresses rigorous research with a forward-looking policy orientation and places particular emphasis on bringing new perspectives to the strategic debate.

The Institute's publications are designed to meet the needs of a wider audience than its own membership and are available on subscription, by mail order and in good bookshops. Further details at www.iiss.org.

Printed and bound in Great Britain by Bell & Bain Ltd, Thornliebank, Glasgow

All rights reserved. No part of this book may be reprinted or reproduced or utilised in any form or by any electronic, mechanical, or other means, now known or hereafter invented, including photocopying and recording, or in any information storage or retrieval system, without permission in writing from the publishers.

British Library Cataloguing in Publication Data
A catalogue record for this book is available from the British Library

Library of Congress Cataloging in Publication Data

ADELPHI series
ISSN 0567-932X

ADELPHI 412–413
ISBN 978-0-415-61387-3

Contents

ACKNOWLEDGEMENTS

Dedicated to the memory of Karen Ballentine, who made a great contribution to the study of the economic aspects of peacebuilding.

This book grew out of a two-year research programme at The International Institute for Strategic Studies on 'Economics and Conflict Resolution'. The editors wish to thank The Portland Trust for its generous support of this research programme. We would also like to thank participants in two roundtable meetings – held in Washington DC and London in 2009 – for their intellectual contribution to the programme.

Mats Berdal and Achim Wennmann, London, August 2010

Introduction

Mats Berdal

> 'For every complex problem, there is a solution that is
> simple, neat, and wrong.'
> Attributed to H.L. Mencken

The record of international efforts to assist countries emerging
from war in the post-Cold War era is, by any measure, distinctly
uneven. A major reason for this, as several of the contributions to this volume make clear, lies in the recurring failure
of those charged with peacebuilding and reconstruction activities – however benign and well-meaning their intentions – to
treat societies emerging from violence and war on their own
terms. In part, this failure is linked to an all-too-common lack
of understanding and sensitivity towards the cultural and
historical specificities of war-torn societies. At least as important, however, has been the failure of outsiders to recognise the
dynamic and complex ways in which the conditions of war and
violent conflict themselves affect and reshape societies, and,
in doing so, how they generate distinctive political, economic
and development challenges that do not lend themselves to
'templated' solutions or 'business-as-usual' approaches to

economic recovery. While zones of protracted conflict are often described in terms of anarchy and lawlessness, individuals and communities are never *merely* 'passive victims in the face of state failure and collapse'.[1]

Of necessity, many will strive to find ways of surviving and coping during conflict, sometimes displaying great ingenuity, entrepreneurial skill and initiative in the process. Others will develop a vested interest in the continuation of armed conflict, not just for the purposes of survival but also for the cover it usefully provides for predatory and criminal activity, a point developed more fully by James Cockayne in the present volume. The result of these adaptations, by a range of local and external actors, to the realities of war and conflict is a distinctive political economy based on violence that persists into the 'post-war' period. And precisely because it persists, it needs to be understood as ground reality by those engaged in peacebuilding and reconstruction. That reality is not, however, fixed or static. As an earlier and pioneering *Adelphi Paper* on the economic functions of violence in civil wars put it, war-to-peace transitions are rarely smooth or clear cut but involve instead 'a realignment of political interests and a readjustment of economic strategies rather than a clean break from violence to consent, from theft to production, or from repression to democracy'.[2] In such circumstances, peacebuilders would indeed 'be naïve to assume that positive outcomes are the automatic result of good intentions'.[3]

What these considerations make clear is that progress in the peacebuilding field is not only a function of political commitment and staying power, appropriately matched by resources, on the part of outsiders. While those factors are often vital to success, they are not sufficient. Indeed, they will count for little if they are not accompanied by analytical and conceptual clarity about the challenges that need to be tackled. It is with respect to this latter requirement – that is, for a deeper under-standing of war-torn societies and war-to-peace transitions – that this collection of essays seeks to contribute. However, acquiring such an understanding, as several of the contributors emphasise, does not necessarily make the policy challenges and choices confronting peacebuilders any easier. Indeed, in many cases improved understanding only serves to highlight the trade-offs that often exist between short-term objectives aimed at stabilising fragile and delicate 'post-conflict' environ-ments and longer-term objectives relating to the promotion of justice, balanced economic growth and the building of insti-tutions, all critical to 'lasting peace and stability'. In terms of the overall focus of the present volume – that is, the economic dimension of peacebuilding – short-term demands for security and stability may well require some form of engagement with informal, often illiberal, power structures as a necessary step in a longer process designed to 'wean an economy away from violence and crime, and towards peaceful, legitimate economic activity.'[4] However difficult the policy judgements involved, diagnosing the peacebuilding environment and its challenges correctly is nonetheless critical – and this is more than just a trite academic point. All too often, the failure to grasp the underlying political economy of a conflict zone, relying instead on crude, value-laden and simplistic labelling of complex prob-lems, has served to perpetuate and stimulate renewed violence. At the same time, a better analytical grasp of the peacebuilding environment is also a precondition – and this is a further aim of the book – for looking more positively at 'economic issues as a problem solver and bridge builder'.[5]

Linking analysis and policy: the debate on 'state failure'

The point here, one that also serves to bring out the overall intention behind the book, is well illustrated by the debate surrounding, and the international policy response to, 'state failure' and 'state fragility'. It is a subject that is addressed in several of the essays below, notably by Robert Muggah, James Cockayne and Jennifer Hazen. The most explicit treatment of the subject, however, is by Ken Menkhaus who starts out with a depressing paradox: 'despite [the] prominent place failed states have assumed in global security, few international security problems since the end of the Cold War have been so misunderstood as state failure'.[6] In a passage that neatly and clearly brings home the importance of basing policy on sound and empirically sustainable analysis, he notes the dominant assumption that 'the problem of state failure is low capacity':

> ...were the leaders of a failed state given adequate means, this reasoning goes, they would naturally put those resources to use to strengthen their state. Leaders who fail to strengthen the capacity of their government are thus irrational, venal, or both. By reducing state failure to a matter of low capacity, this view lends itself to 'off-the-shelf' technical solutions that, not coincidentally, are ideally suited for conventional foreign aid programmes. More funding, better trained civil servants, a more professionalised and equipped police force, and a healthy dose of democratisation (where not politically inconvenient) have been the main elements of state-building strategies ... Yet two decades of research on the dynamics of weak and failed states suggests that in some circumstances state failure is viewed by local elites as a desired outcome, not a problem to be solved. This reflects a political strategy of survivalism and an economic strategy of personal enrichment that has its own rationale.[7]

A key implication to flow from this is that policymakers need to give much greater analytic attention to the 'interests of key actors in state failure' and, by extension, to key actors and their economic interests in countries emerging from violent conflict.[8] And as evidence from Afghanistan, the Democratic Republic of the Congo and Somalia shows, identification of key actors' interests has highlighted another counter-intuitive phenomenon: resistance to strong central *government* (and thus to the kind of state-building policies typically promoted by outsiders) does not preclude interest in and commitment to local *governance* systems, including systems of law and order. In such circumstances it may be both prudent and more realistic for outsiders to target aid, encourage entrepreneurial initiative and stimulate economic activity, including programmes aimed at employment generation and direct support for businesses, at the local level. Support for informal structures and local initiative is, crucially, also likely to benefit from greater legitimacy in the eyes of the local community. Although one should be cautious about idealising *all* locally driven initiatives and informal governance arrangements (many of which have proved to be violent and predatory), the wider point remains valid: without a proper understanding of how war and conflict transform socio-economic relationships and shape distinctive political economies of war and peace, the policies of outsiders risk producing perverse and unintended consequences. Specific policies and judgements about peacebuilding priorities must proceed from an understanding of those risks. This key point emerges clearly from James Cockayne's analysis of the new challenges facing peace-builders – both moral and practical in nature – that have crystallised as a result of the growing 'convergence of crime, corruption and conflict' in many of the world's conflict zones. Where that convergence occurs, he concludes, 'peace-builders must ... differentiate between violent groups based on whether they adopt a predatory, parasitic or symbiotic fund-raising strategy, before considering which tools and incentives may be available to wean such organisations away from violence, and the spoils it brings.'[9]

Learning lessons and identifying appropriate policies

Encouragingly, though there is still a long way to go, there are signs that donors and key institutions are beginning to take some of the aforementioned lessons on board, including the need to engage with the political economy of war-torn societies. In particular, there appears to be a general recognition, at the rhetorical level at any rate, that specific economic policies and initiatives must not be allowed to undermine the overall aims of political stabilisation and peace consolidation. Several contributors stress the importance of this realisation and spell out its policy implications, noting that what may be ideal or optimal in terms of economic development may well prove politically destabilising and conflict-generating, especially in the short term. As James Boyce notes in his chapter on the role of aid and the need to build fiscal capacity in post-conflict countries: 'when the distributional impacts of expenditure and revenue policies are ignored in favour of a single-minded focus on economic growth and efficiency, a result can be the exacerbation of social tensions that jeopardise the peace'.[10] Similarly, while stressing that 'sound, robust institutions – at both national and local level – provide the backbone of resource-revenue management and peacebuilding', Päivi Lujala, Siri Aas Rustad and Philippe Le Billon accept that in the short run it may sometimes 'be necessary to postpone the application of the principles of "good governance" … as institution-building efforts may destabilise the peace negotiations'.[11]

These observations – and the volume as a whole – highlight the tensions and the competing logic that often exist in 'post-conflict' settings between the pursuit of economic priorities *narrowly* conceived, and the requirements of peacebuilding and political stability. Those tensions are real and cannot be wished away. Even so, an important premise of the book is that the economic challenges presented by societies emerging from war must also be seen, once they have been properly contexualised and understood, as positive opportunities. As such, carefully designed policies aimed at economic recovery and at the transformation of political economies of violence, are not only crucial in their own right but can also provide powerful incentives for cooperation and peaceable behaviour among erstwhile belligerents.

CHAPTER ONE

Peace Processes, Business and New Futures after War

Achim Wennmann

Introduction

The economic issues underlying armed conflicts and the belligerents' motivation to fight are often overlooked by peacemakers.[1] They are usually relegated to the later stage of post-conflict reconstruction as largely technical or humanitarian matters, while political and military issues take centre stage. However, there is a growing recognition in the peace mediation community that such a neat separation between the 'political' peace process, and 'economic' – or 'developmental' – post-conflict peacebuilding is no longer conducive to brokering a lasting peace. Economic issues are associated with conflict economies, natural resources or socio-economic inequalities, and as such they are an intrinsic part of many armed conflicts. The economy also plays a crucial part in vision-based peacemaking, which sets out realistically achievable alternatives to continued war and instability. These issues place economics and development at the heart of peace

Achim Wennmann is a Researcher at the Centre on Conflict, Development and Peacebuilding (CCDP) of the Graduate Institute of International and Development Studies in Geneva, Switzerland.

processes. In the words of Noble Peace Prize Laureate Martti Ahtisaari:

> agreeing about practical and concrete economic condi-tions during peace negotiations is crucial. Maybe one could even claim that finding a mutual understanding on money can really be seen as a manifestation of joint political will for peace.[2]

While there is a recognition that economic issues and political economy concerns are important to peace processes, it is not yet entirely clear what the integration of an economic perspective into peacemaking would really entail in terms of negotiation challenges and the building of new partnerships. What are the opportunities and pitfalls of addressing economic issues in peace processes? How can we construct a credible new vision for the future that will provide jobs, allow mobility and end the shooting? What are the new alliances needed to address economic issues in peace processes and strengthen new futures after war?

There is clearly a need to take a fresh look at the economic dimension of peace processes and explore these questions further.

Economic issues in peace negotiations

Economics has been discussed in various ways in relation to armed conflict and conflict resolution. Historically, the emphasis has been on the use of sanctions as part of economic statecraft and policy makers' 'attempts to exercise power, i.e., to get others to do what they would not otherwise do'.[3] More recently, economics has manifested itself in conflict and fragile countries in terms of political economy challenges, including issues such as patrimonial governance, rent seeking, competition for power and resources, and corruption. In the study of armed conflict, these challenges have been related to the complex web of motives and interactions emerging from the interplay of economic agendas, vested interests in prolonging civil war, widespread poverty and globalisation.[4]

In peace processes economic issues have been mainly related to the backward- and forward-looking aspects of peacemaking. The former harks back to past violence and injustices, as well as economic causes or 'drivers' of conflict (issues such as control over natural resources, the reduction of socio-economic inequalities, or the compensation for victims for past atrocities). Forward-looking peacemaking relates to the crafting of new political, economic or societal orders. In this context, economic issues include frameworks for establishing new economic institutions, employment creation, land reform or creating the conditions for private investments.

The way these issues are addressed affects peace process dynamics. In principle, incompatibilities over economic issues should be easier to solve than, for example, identity disputes. The control over mines, markets or economic infrastructure can be quantified and divided, which is not possible with the hatred associated with ethnic conflicts. Moreover, if armed conflict is really about greed, the only requirement to end a conflict would be to show that belligerents can make more money within the bounds of a functioning state, private sector investment and a lasting peace. Certainly, economic issues are often fundamentally interlinked with broader cultural or identity issues, but looking at economic issues as a problem solver and bridge builder may open opportunities for peace mediation that so far remain unrecognised.

The treatment of economic issues in peace processes has so far had mixed results. The possibility to rationalise and divide economic issues can provide incentives for cooperation, as illustrated by the 2004 Agreement on Wealth Sharing between North and South Sudan. The parties' economic interests overrode some of the political and military priorities, and they found an agreement on a sharing formula: the institutional arrangement to govern the oil sector and the way to handle existing contracts. They also agreed to disagree on the question of who owns the oil by leaving the issue to be addressed at a later stage, thereby preventing an early breakdown of the talks.[5]

In Sri Lanka, talks about development were intended to dissipate tensions between the parties and broaden the constituency for peace before entering into more contentious political or military issues. Talking about development became possible because it mattered to both parties, but as their mutual interests in the topic declined, political and military incompatibilities resurfaced and negotiations were suspended. With hindsight, it has been said that there was no political commitment by the parties to end the conflict, and the topic of development was merely exploited to strengthen support within their constituencies for agendas that were not entirely related to the peace process. The government promised its electorate an economic recovery and, by making development a priority, it hoped to gain votes for the elections; the Liberation Tigers of Tamil Eelam wanted to satisfy the urgent humanitarian and material needs of the populations under their control in Northeastern Sri Lanka, thereby re-enforcing their role as a de-facto authority and strengthening the legitimacy of its claim for regional autonomy.[6]

Another example of 'development for peace' occurred in 2006–07 on the Georgian-controlled side of the disputed breakaway region of South Ossetia, where development initiatives were intended to make remaining within Georgia more attractive, and to exert pressure on the de-facto authorities. Initiatives included infrastructure improvements, new private businesses, and a $10 million European Union grant for the rehabilitation of gas and water distribution, a hydropower plant and waste management. However, these projects were accompanied by the persistence of a political discourse based on an exclusive rather than inclusive Georgian nationalism, which antagonised South Ossetians and undermined the objectives behind the development initiatives.[7]

Economic issues can also be willingly left out of the talks to reduce tension and increase the manageability of a peace process. In Angola, natural-resource management was excluded from the 1992 Lusaka Protocol to facilitate the transition of the National Union for the Total Independence of Angola (UNITA) from an armed group into a political party.[8] In Nepal, socio-economic inequalities received little attention during the peace process despite being understood as 'root causes' by many observers. The Communist Party of Nepal-Maoist wanted first to change the nature of the state from a monarchy to parliamentary democracy and then address economic issues after the peace agreement.[9]

In addition, negotiations on economic issues often occur in the context of formal or informal economies. The issue of natural-resource revenues can effectively be off limits because they are central to the financing of the parties or local political economies. Insisting on their inclusion may even lead to the outright rejection of the entire peace process, as the example of the Democratic Republic of the Congo shows. There, the control of natural resources was considered an unacceptable constraint on the mobilisation and business opportunities of the parties. Had any party insisted on its inclusion, it would have meant the end of the peace process.[10]

The sensitivity of economic agendas has also been illustrated in Aceh where various parts of the Indonesian armed forces had been involved in military business. For them, a peace process and the end of Aceh's 'conflict province' status would have implied the end of business.[11] The first lesson to be drawn from this is that insisting on a ceasefire as a starting point for negotiations in self-financing conflicts can undermine a peace process. Armed groups with strong economic agendas are less likely to engage. They use armed violence as an economic strategy and are, therefore, less inclined to lay down their arms because this would imply eroding their means of business (armed violence) and the conditions upon which it thrives (insecurity). In these circumstances, tacitly allowing the parties to control informal economies may be the best of bad choices and a way for mediators to plant the seed among the parties for a continued dialogue and a long-term transition process.

Charting new futures

Economic issues are also crucial considerations in preparing what comes after a peace agreement. Negotiations can lay the initial foundation for post-conflict political and economic transitions, and craft economic visions that become the foundation for a new society. The objective of these endeavours is to make a life without violence a more credible reality at the time when the parties consider a negotiated exit out of a conflict. In this way, peace processes facilitate the implementation of peace agreements, as well as disarmament, demobilisation and reintegration programmes. They prepare the groundwork for the prevention of future armed conflict by addressing security dilemmas and ensuring that no party has the means to impose itself militarily in the future.[12]

Addressing economic futures in peace processes has a significant political value for peace negotiations. From the perspective of the parties, the economic dimension of peace mediation bridges the period between the signing of a peace agreement and the manifestation of peace dividends. When the parties agree to peace they face immediate demands to lay down their arms, but in return they usually only receive a vague promise of a better future in the long term. The time lag involved, and individual assessments of each party about the likelihood of long-term shared prosperity, affects their political commitment to a peace process. In this context, mediators can attempt to strengthen this commitment by placing post-conflict futures on the table, exploring ways to ensure that a new vision of the future becomes a credible prospect.

Negotiating economic futures remains a difficult challenge because ensuring the positive long-term impact of the economic provisions in peace agreements depends on many variables. For example, the positive contribution of income-sharing provisions on economic recovery in South Sudan has been undermined by other problems such as a lack of security guarantees, persistent distrust between former belligerents, the armed conflict in Darfur, and renewed armed confrontations between the North and the South. Nevertheless, the Government of South Sudan now receives significant sums in revenue payments, totalling $1.5 billion in 2007, $2.9bn in 2008, and $1bn in 2009.[13] In Nepal, economic issues became part of the post-conflict politics between the government and the opposition. In early 2009, the opposition wanted to prevent any government successes in the field of economic development in order to expose the government's incapacity to deliver on promises.[14] In contrast and despite obvious challenges, Aceh's post-conflict economy recovered relatively fast because the December 2004 Tsunami provided unprecedented humanitarian and development attention, and the province had a larger pre-existing economic base than South Sudan.

To overcome the challenges of creating new futures, mediation teams need to forge new partnerships. Peace negotiations and post-conflict economic recovery are often perceived as two distinct operations that are conducted in different contexts and by different institutions. However, making economic futures tangible entails shifting our understanding of peacemaking from a two-stage process before and after a peace agreement, towards an ongoing process in which the resolution of a conflict and the preparation of future political or economic orders go hand in hand. The expertise and skill of the development and business community is important for mediators during a peace process in order to determine realistic economic futures; but the expertise and skill of mediators is equally important for the development and business communities in the post-conflict phase in order to implement a peace process, maintain the transitional pacts between the main stakeholders and prevent the recurrence of conflict.

Constructing new partnerships with economic actors

The character of peace mediation has changed rapidly over the last decades. While historically it was a matter for kings, princes or generals, today it is conducted at various levels by United Nations Envoys, former Heads of State, elders of local communities or specialised peacemaking NGOs. Mediation processes have become so complex that they sometimes involve dozens of actors and as many agendas. Many mediation practitioners, therefore, advocate limiting the number of intermediaries to keep a peace process manageable.

However, reaching out to economic actors may uncover so-far unrecognised opportunities for peace mediation. The private sector and development agencies have been involved in a series of peace processes and helped find an agreement to stop the fighting, and ways to strengthen transitional pacts. As shown below, the private sector has had important roles in the peace processes in South Africa, Mozambique and Northern Ireland.

In Nepal, development agencies provided crucial support to social-service delivery and agricultural job creation during the conflict that helped prevent major displacements and mitigated the conflict's impact. Development actors also facilitated the establishment of communication channels between the parties that supported mediation activities between 2001 and 2005.[15] In Ghana, various development actors have supported the establishment of the National Architecture of Peace, a decentralised network of dispute-resolution forums that have successfully prevented the outbreak of election violence.[16] Business and development agencies are also significant because they have the technical skills to craft realistic expectations in the economy and the future. By bringing these economic actors into the process before the signature of a peace agreement, post-conflict realities can become a real prospect at the moment when belligerents wonder if it is indeed worthwhile to stop fighting.

In recent years, the role of development agencies in conflict and fragile settings has received a lot of attention in the context of Afghanistan, Iraq, or more broadly in fragile and conflict countries. The role of business in peace processes and conflict settings remains less clear. In general, companies face a similar set of decision-making processes as the development community does in assessing their relationship with armed conflict. In a sense, they need to decide whether to adjust their business operations to work *around, in,* or *on* an armed conflict or violence.[17]

Most mainstream companies work *around* the conflict which means that they withdraw or temporarily cease activities in recognition of political and security risks. However, companies can be extremely hesitant to withdraw. As they operate in a competitive market, their own withdrawal represents an opportunity for a competitor to enter the market. The fact that commercial actors are easily substituted highlights the importance of ensuring that companies with a generally reputable record stay on in conflict and fragile settings because the alternative would be to open the door to un-checked profit-makers that purposefully deviate from responsible practice.[18]

Companies can decide to work *in* the conflict and attempt to minimise the effect of the conflict on their operations. For bigger companies, this means paying for protection from private military companies, which can be a substantial cost factor in some contexts. Small- and medium-sized companies are unable to afford protection or spread risks in the same way as large ones can. Armed violence is, therefore, much more problematic for these enterprises than for multinational firms. The fact that companies stay on and adjust activities emphasises the resilience of entrepreneurs in the face of violence. Strengthening this capacity in rural and urban communities is a crucial ingredient for creating employment in the immediate aftermath of war. Small- and medium-sized companies are particularly important because they use bonds between family and community members as a basis of trust to kick-start commercial transactions. In this way, the private sector can contribute to stability, livelihoods and economic recovery from the bottom-up and directly impacts on the people's experience of war-to-peace transitions.

Private-sector peacemaking

Business can also work *on* the conflict and perform various roles in a peace process. These include building bridges between different communities, and between state and society, engaging directly in talks with belligerents, providing good offices and information, acting as pro-peace constituencies, paying for peace processes, assisting in the delivery of humanitarian assistance, strengthening entrepreneurship, building trust, fostering accountability, and limiting access to conflict financing.[19]

In South Africa, business leaders stepped in to drive a social transition after apartheid. In the 1980s, the private sector became recognised as a stabilising agent by managing social conflicts. During the peace process between 1990 and 1994, companies provided resources, leadership and authority, and fostered communication between black and white communities, contributing to a new vision of society. Business leaders managed peace committees and were accepted as an authority because they had the ability to get things done and manage crises.[20]

In Northern Ireland and Israel, the private sector acted as a pro-peace constituency. Business confederations in Northern Ireland and the Republic realised that economic development was contingent upon the ending of sectarian conflict. They called for greater integration of Northern Ireland's economy into the Irish and European economy. Initiatives such as the 'One Island Economy', that fostered the notion to consider the economy of Ireland and Northern Ireland as an integrated economic space, contributed to a shift in the discourse from the nationalist-emotive to the economic-rational. In Israel, the high-tech industry wanted peace in order to integrate Israel into the global economy. However, it only became a unified actor after the 1993 Oslo Accords highlighted the dependence of companies on the overall political environment. After the Accords, Israeli companies reaped peace dividends through better access to Asian markets, new partnerships with international firms and higher levels of FDI.[21]

In the West Bank, companies strengthen private sector entrepreneurship. The Portland Trust helps build local entrepreneurship and create jobs by addressing the chronic housing shortage in the West Bank. Population growth, the declining viability of existing housing and a strong reduction of construction activity provided the background for the

Palestinian Authority to declare affordable housing a priority in 2007. Through a $1bn private-sector-led affordable-housing programme, construction on 5,000 new homes began in Rawebi in January 2010. In order to ensure the long-term viability of the Palestinian construction companies and suppliers involved in the programme – as well as the jobs created – they must offer services at competitive rates and quality, which in turn requires political advances enabling a freer movement of people and goods between Israel and the West Bank.[22]

In Mozambique, direct engagement by a chief executive officer influenced the peace process. The British multinational infrastructure and transport company Lonrho became involved in the peace process after attacks on its installations in 1990. Previously, it had paid off belligerents to protect its £53 million investments, but as the conflict escalated it was no longer immune to attacks. Considering its investment trapped, the company decided to engage directly in the peace process. The company's executive Roland 'Tiny' Rowland acted as an intermediary and made available company resources and aircrafts. It is also said to have contributed around $6–8m to assist in the transition of the *Resistência Nacional Moçambicana* into a political party.[23]

In Sudan, oil companies shifted perceptions of the conflict, and the role of oil in it, from the emotive to the rational. High levels of violence in oil-producing regions prevented the Sudanese government and the Sudan People's Liberation Movement/Army (SPLM/A) from realising the full commercial potential of oil, and put off foreign companies from committing to greater investments in oil exploration. In this context, the Swedish company Lundin Petroleum made the case to all stakeholders that the end of fighting and a peace process was the best strategy to ensure a sustainable oil production and future prosperity. Its board member, Carl Bildt – a former prime minister of Sweden (1991–94) and United Nations Special Envoy for the Balkans (1995–97) – led a series of talks emphasising that 'oil represented an incentive for peace in so far as oil activities could not be pursued in a war context'.[24] This rationale turned out to be effective in Sudan as oil fields have constituted a major battlefield, and neither party was able to fully commercialise the resources without FDI.

Engaging the business community

These examples suggest that the private sector can directly or indirectly participate in peace processes, acting individually or collectively. Despite these multiple functions, private-sector participation has been found to depend on its credibility and legitimacy in the eyes of a substantive part of the host popula-tion, its ability to act as a unified actor, and its attitude and experience towards social engagement.[25] In Colombia, it has also been found that private-sector peacemaking was mainly motivated by self-interest.[26] A major challenge for mediators is, therefore, to assess how to foster a unity of vision within the business sector that the end of an armed conflict is in its own best interests, and that it is worthwhile for them to invest time and money in peacemaking.

The formation of pro-peace constituencies is complicated because the private sector is internally divided and not neces-sarily aware of the magnitude of the costly effects of armed conflict. While different sectors and companies are affected differently by armed violence – some may even gain from inse-curity – existing costing methods are not yet finely tuned enough to associate costs to specific sectors or companies. Neither is there sufficient distinction in the expression of the costs so as to make them more transparent for a specific sector or company. Greater knowledge on the magnitude and distribution of the costly consequences of armed conflict on companies, as well as their potential benefits from peace, would be an important tool to forge a unity of vision in the business sector and convince it that armed conflict or violence loses it money, and that peace is good for business.[27]

The financial stakes are high, as exemplified by Kenya's post-election violence in 2007. The conflict led to a 24% reduction in flower exports – the country's largest foreign exchange earner. Exports from companies located in the violence-affected areas dropped by as much as 38%, mainly as a result of the displacement of workers.[28] In addition, Kenya's tourism sector suffered a 40% decline from 2m visitors in 2007 to 1.2m in 2008. The Kenyan Tourism Board estimated the economic costs to the tourism industry at over 20bn Kenyan Shillings ($270m).[29]

Of course, the inclusion of the private sector in peace processes also creates new challenges for mediators because it involves changing practices and welcoming a different way of thinking and professional culture. One of the challenges for peacemakers is to identify when and how to reach out to the private sector during peace processes. From one perspective, a mediator has no choice but to include domestic or foreign companies because they have the power to affect negotiation dynamics – both positively and negatively. Companies can make their influence felt by providing incentives or threats to the parties at the negotiation table, or other third parties with an interest in the resolution of the conflict.

Given these pressures, mediators have to carefully evaluate on a case-by-case basis how to build relationships with the private sector. In many conflict-affected settings they will face difficulties in distinguishing political and business elites, or 'public' and 'private' roles of individuals; in dealing with private-sector actors, mediators must also determine how to discriminate between different companies wanting to pursue their own economic interest in a particular market. In this

context, competition between different companies may compli-
cate the peace process because they divide – rather than unite
– the parties. In Iraq, competitive pressure between oil companies translated into a quest for influence over different parties
leading to greater division rather than unity among different
levels of state authority.[30] Another difficulty is that companies
do not represent a legitimate actor and their commercial interests are likely to override the common good. In the worst case,
companies can be perceived as unsuitable interlocutors because
they have been complicit in conflict economies, human-rights
abuses or environmental pollution.

Mediators can address some of these problems by engaging
with the private sector informally on the margins of a peace
process. Companies may in fact not expect anything more than
that. In cases where different companies compete against each
other, mediators can facilitate investment alliances and encourage investment projects to be approved with the consent of
local communities. Moreover, mediators can identify local or
international business associations or chambers of commerce
that have a large membership of companies in a specific sector.
By doing this, it is possible to construct sectoral interest groups;
thus transcending the particular economic interest of a specific
company.

There are also instruments that can cushion the risk associated with investments in conflict countries. For example,
joint ventures distribute corporate risk to various stakeholders
as evidenced by most resource-exploration projects being
conducted by consortia; project financing (the organisation
of capital for specific ventures financed jointly by the private
sector or development agencies); political-risk insurance that
covers companies against potential losses. Involvement of the
Multilateral Investment Guarantee Agency, a member of the
World Bank group that provides risk insurance to companies

providing FDI to developing countries, is often an important prerequisite to private insurances in post-conflict areas; and export credits protect national exporters against commercial and political risks.

Mediators may also need to explore how to improve private-public partnership so as to assist companies in freeing up productive and investment capacity to strengthen post-conflict economies. The private sector is often estranged by external peacebuilding efforts that exclusively channel most aid through what it sees as ineffective and corrupt state administrations. Development agencies often find it easier to establish relationships with another state agency and support the long-term vision of state-building as a framework for a productive economy. Direct relationships between development agencies and local or international business could be another avenue to assist a speedy economic recovery in the aftermath of war.

Finally, engaging the private sector in peace processes must also be considered in the context of a changing global economy. In Africa, for example, the potential of private-sector engagement has risen with Chinese investment in the energy and agricultural sectors. However, this has its drawbacks: local producers have been hit by cheap Chinese imports; the Chinese use contract labour rather than local workers; the end product can be poor quality; and African companies find it difficult to access China's market.[31]

These new constellations have not gone unnoticed for peacemaking, as evidenced by the evolution of China's attitude towards conflict resolution in Sudan. China's growing commercial interest is said to have influenced its diplomatic engagement in support of a political settlement in Darfur.[32] In the North-South peace negotiations, China's resistance to pay for oil with currency rather than consumer goods was a major obstacle in the negotiations. The issue could ultimately be resolved through international pressure and the recognition that a general peace agreement was more valuable to its commercial interests than continued instability and war.[33] The integration of China and other emerging economies into the global economy opens new opportunities that should be made to work for war-to-peace transitions.

Conclusion

In a time when governments and companies are spending vast amounts of political and financial capital on peace and peace-building, the failure of peace processes and the renewal of armed conflict have high stakes. Exploring the economic dimensions of peace processes is an attempt to safeguard these investments at an early stage of conflict management. Experience suggests that peace processes do not end with a peace agreement. A negotiated exit out of armed conflict requires a strong transitional pact that must be nurtured and supported as the parties come closer to an agreement and prepare new political or economic orders.

National or international business is no panacea that miraculously transforms warzones into blooming landscapes. As with all other actors involved in conflict zones, its transformative power depends on the way it positions itself and acts within a broader political process. Companies can have the power to affect negotiation dynamics and can provide critical resources, leadership, and authority to advance a peace process. The private sector can also stimulate post-conflict economic growth and opportunities, and become a significant constituency to end armed conflict and violence. Business has a lot to offer for peacemaking: the results-oriented, problem-solving attitude of the private sector, its interpersonal and leadership skills, as well as sector-specific technology, networks and expertise are tremendous assets for peace processes and crafting a new future after war.

CHAPTER TWO

Stabilising Fragile States and the Humanitarian Space

Robert Muggah

There is growing alarm among Western multilateral and bilateral agencies that insecurity, underdevelopment and poor governance in low- and medium-income countries conspire to create the conditions for state fragility. Member states of the Organisation for Economic Cooperation and Development (OECD) and partners ranging from the North Atlantic Treaty Organisation (NATO) and the World Bank contend that the associated symptoms of fragility can be successfully treated with integrated diplomatic, defensive and developmental interventions. Although still only loosely defined in normative terms, a nascent 'stabilisation agenda' is being advanced by a growing number of Western governments as a means of confronting the varied threats presented by fragility. While considered by some of its supporters as a new and urgent priority, stabilisation belies a wider (and historical)

Robert Muggah is Research Director of the Small Arms Survey, Fellow of the Center for Conflict, Peacebuilding and Development (CCDP), and Principle of The SecDev Group. Special thanks are due to Sarah Collinson and Samir Elharawy from the Overseas Development Institute for their input. Credit is also due to the Folke Bernadotte Academy which is supporting the 'States of Fragility' project: http://graduateinstitute.ch/ccdp/projects-statesoffragility.html.

preoccupation among Western elites with containing and 'fixing' those societies that are considered fragile, failing or failed.

The phenomenon of fragility is more easily described than defined. Its causes and characteristics are surprisingly diverse with most descriptions focusing on the extent to which weak governments are unable or unwilling to deliver core services.[1] In their seminal text *Fixing Failed States: A Framework for Rebuilding a Fractured World,* Ashraf Ghani and Clare Lockhart associated fragility with what they described as a 'sovereignty gap': the social distance between elite decision-makers and those on the receiving end of their decisions.[2] Fragility is typically associated with a combination of sharp social and economic inequality, demographic pressures, poor governance and the instability generated by a bewildering array of 'violence entrepreneurs' – from gangs and organised crime syndicates to insurgents and terrorists. Experts on fragility tend to focus on the complex political economy of unstable states which are described as being mired in corruption and informality.[3]

Although the definitional contours of fragility are conceptually and politically contested, there is comparatively little disagreement over its costs and consequences. The World Bank describes 'waves' of fragility as contributing to cross-border spill-over effects through the production of 'refugees, warring groups, contagious diseases and transnational criminal networks that traffic in drugs, arms and people'. Fragility, the OECD argues, triggers failures in the normal growth trajectories of countries – especially ones emerging from war – and can lead to conflict traps, whereby the outbreak of fighting begets prolonged armed conflict by activating cycles of retaliation and vengeance, and by locking elites and commanders into a system where their surest profit comes from violence.[4]

Because fragile countries are, de facto, outside the (formal) global economic system, they are often described as presenting 'the toughest development challenge of our era'.[5] The United Nations, for its part, has described fragility as a threat to international peace and security.

Given global concerns with fragility, what are the parameters, scope and scale of the 'stabilisation' agenda? From the outset, the concern with stabilisation marks a distinctive departure from international conventions guaranteeing the sanctity of sovereignty and the terms under which a state is permitted to intervene militarily to defend an ally from aggression. The doctrine and practice of stabilisation also extends beyond post-9/11 Afghanistan and Iraq to a growing array of so-called fragile countries and settings such as Colombia, Guatemala, Haiti, Sri Lanka, Sudan and Timor Leste. Stabilisation can encompass direct military operations, the provision of security and policing equipment and the training of national personnel, investment in governance capacity, development and forms of government (usually featuring market economies and democratic elections), and the engagement of multinational firms, non-government organisations, and development aid agencies to provide relief assistance and promote infrastructure development. This uneasy alliance of a wide range of actors and interests not only draws attention to the inherent dilemmas of civil–military cooperation, but also the contradictions and ambiguities internal to humanitarian efforts. Increasingly, the practices of stabilisation–especially counter-terrorism, counter-insurgency and counter-narcotics – are coming under scrutiny for the extent to which they contribute (or not) to outcomes such as improved civilian protection. Put succinctly, some critics are questioning whether the ends of stabilisation justify the means.

The fragile hinterland

While the number and severity of armed conflicts around the world appears to be in decline, preoccupation on the part of senior Western policymakers with fragile states and cities is growing. In 2010, around the world, approximately 20–25 countries were affected by armed conflicts of varying intensity.[6] While representing a slight increase on previous years, it is also apparent that the number of armed conflicts under way has declined over the last two decades, continuing a pattern that began in the early 1990s.[7] The overall decline in armed conflict can also be set against a pronounced escalation in peacemaking and peacekeeping activities. With annual global peacekeeping expenditures exceeding $7 billion a year, there were several times more peacekeeping personnel deployed in 2010 as compared to the previous decade.[8]

Alongside archetypal cases of fragility, such as Afghanistan and Somalia, is a range of well-publicised hot-spots attracting the attention of security specialists – from Jamaica's capital, Kingston, to Sa'ana in Yemen. Depending on what measure is used, between 40 and 50 countries were considered fragile in 2010, and tens of billions of dollars in development aid were directed to addressing the causes and consequences of fragility.[9] As made clear in other chapters of this volume, countries emerging from war and ostensibly at peace are hardly immune. Faced with an alarming escalation in homicidal and gang-related violence in its border regions, Mexico – which is not troubled by the same systemic weaknesses as many conflict-affected states – is teetering at the edge of fragility. Western governments and multilateral institutions describe fragility as among the most dangerous security threats to global order. What is more, the OECD observes that fragile states are among the furthest from achieving the Millennium Development Goals (MDGs), a set of 15 internationally agreed targets such as halving extreme poverty, halting the spread of HIV/AIDS and providing universal primary education by 2015).

Little wonder, then, that stabilisation is taken so seriously in senior policy circles of Western governments. A coalition of upper-income countries, notably Australia, Canada, France, the United Kingdom and the United States, is investing in multi-pronged stabilisation and reconstruction missions to re-assert control in what are routinely described as 'ungoverned spaces'. These and other Western governments talk of 'comprehensive', 'integrated' and 'whole-of-government' approaches to contain fragile situations. Some have introduced bureaucratic mechanisms to promote more integration on the ground: the UK's Stabilisation Unit[10], the US Office for the Coordinator of Stabilization and Reconstruction (CSR)[11], and Canada's Stabilization and Reconstruction Task Force (START)[12] are prominent examples. Although a central tenet of kinetic (counter-insurgency) operations, their explicit fusion of politico-military objectives with humanitarian and development initiatives belies a new and controversial willingness to publicly deal with fragile states.

Some non-donor governments are also pursuing their own domestic stabilisation campaigns. Colombia, for example, as part of a wider 'democratic security' agenda, is promoting enhanced civil–military cooperation in order to mobilise development to stabilise insecure areas.[13] Brazil has also started to initiate a combination of strategies to pacify fragile 'ungoverned' shanty towns from Rio de Janeiro to Port-au-Prince.[14] Likewise, in Pakistan and Sri Lanka, the rhetoric of stabilisation is being hitched by central governments to domestic counter-insurgency campaigns. These efforts stray from the liberal peacebuilding assumptions set out by Western donors: they feature a greater reliance on military action and targeted development activities, rather than inclusive political settlements or the promotion of good governance. The character and durability of the stability achieved by these operations unsurprisingly appears to be determined in large part by the interests, means and capabilities underpinning them.

The stabilisation agenda that has coalesced out of this fear of fragility rests on the now-familiar mantra that security and development are mutually reinforcing.[15] This assumption in turn is premised on an interpretation of war which views violence and instability as arising from a lack of development and of the order accorded by functional states.[16] Instability and fragility, are thus defined as the absence of development.[17] If this formulation is accepted – and it is held as gospel in most defence and development circles – then the logical response is to reduce the causes and manifestations of underdevelopment. It follows, then, that the next step is to promote humanitarian and developmental solutions, by force if necessary. Stabilisation is one instrument by which this can be achieved.

The current debate on the strengths and limitations of stabilisation is dominated by the experiences of large-scale interventions in Iraq and Afghanistan. Yet, if understood to include a wide-spectrum agenda to bring 'stability' to countries and cities beset by fragility, then stabilisation is geographically much broader in scope than these two countries. Its parameters extend far beyond Central Asia and the Middle East to encompass well over a dozen countries in South and Central America, the Caribbean, Sub-Saharan Africa, South Asia and the South Pacific. It can also be extended historically to include counter-insurgency and pacification campaigns waged in Malaya, Algeria and Vietnam, as well as aspects of the colonial and post-colonial nation-building enterprise.

It is useful to recall the origins of the contemporary stabilisation agenda. Indeed, stabilisation can be traced back to nineteenth- and early twentieth-century paranoia in metropolitan capitals stemming from disorder in the colonial hinterlands.[18] It also echoes Cold-War-era fears of the (presumed) linkages between poverty and communism and later, liberation theology and incipient nationalist independence movements. In other words, elites at the centre have long been wedded to the idea of stabilising the periphery – whether by force or through less brutal means. As Thucydides predicted in the fifth century BC, 'the events which happened in the past … will at some time or other and in much the same way be repeated in the future'.

The contemporary stabilisation agenda has been bolstered by other, arguably more liberal, debates and policy processes. For example, from the early 1990s a modest group of activist policymakers and scholars called for an explicitly 'people-centered' foreign-policy doctrine in conflict-affected and post-conflict societies.[19] Under the banner of 'human security', they contended that the protection of human rights and promotion of associated liberal values were central to achieving national security and stability. By the end of the 1990s and following a victorious campaign to ban anti-personnel landmines, the human-security concept acquired widespread legitimacy.[20]

Building on the success of the treaty banning the use of landmines, and the NATO-led 'humanitarian intervention' in Kosovo in 1999, a number of Western policymakers followed up with an initiative designed to make state sovereignty contingent on guaranteeing human security. With support from the Canadian government, an International Commission on Intervention and State Sovereignty (ICISS) was assembled and advocated that states held a basic responsibility to protect their citizens from extreme violence. Moreover, when and where states were unable or unwilling to protect citizens, the international community was obligated to step in. Then-Secretary General of the UN Kofi Annan pronounced that states forfeited their rights to sovereignty if they could not guarantee a modicum of stability for their people.

The concepts of human security and responsibility to protect citizens (R2P) were surprisingly influential. By combining a moral responsibility to protect with more narrow national security imperatives, they spoke to an enlightened form of self-interest but also established entry points for softer and harder variations of stabilisation. Unsurprisingly, certain countries – including China, Indonesia, Iran, Russia, Serbia, Sudan, Syria and Zimbabwe – felt that these emerging doctrines were too interventionist, potentially opening the door for interference in their domestic affairs.

Subsequent interventions in Iraq and Afghanistan revealed that these concerns were not entirely unfounded. By linking a country's *internal* fragility with *international* instability, the doctrines of human security and the responsibility to protect potentially advocate a more muscular form of stabilisation (or intervention) on behalf of the supposed victims of fragility. By transforming a fragile state into a 'good governance state', as was attempted in Kosovo, Timor Leste and other countries, stabilisation embraces a wider logic of social engineering. Previously regarded as something of an afterthought, the roles of development and humanitarian assistance have been elevated to a new strategic importance.

The fusion of security and development is reflected in a host of prescriptive manuals and guidelines.[21] Without necessarily testing or challenging their basic assumptions, Western states have moved swiftly to incorporate these texts into their evolving doctrine on stabilisation. The 2009 US National Security Assessment identifies the world's primary threats as stemming from weak and fragile countries rather than strong or authoritarian ones. The most recent *US Army Operations Manual on Stability Operations* – FM 3-07 – published in October 2008, emphasises the need for militaries to move beyond kinetic operations (the use of direct force to achieve a political aim) and purposefully engage civilian experts in promoting stability and reconstruction. It describes how the US must invest in rebuilding local institutions, help restore essential services, and safeguard and 'protect' vulnerable populations – all activities placed at the core of military training, planning and operations. Indeed, reflecting this change of tone, US General Stanley McChrystal emphasised the protection of civilians as core to counter-insurgency strategies in Afghanistan during his leadership of the military campaign there.[22]

The US is joined by other countries in investing in stabilisation and reconstruction. Specifically, Australia's Department of Foreign Affairs and Aid and its overseas assistance agency (AusAid) have developed a crisis prevention, stabilisation and recovery group to guide integrated operations from Timor Leste and Papua New Guinea to Afghanistan. Likewise, AusAid and Canberra's Department of Defence signed a Strategic Partnership Agreement in 2009 that ensures they are equal and natural partners with common goals. Canada's Department of Foreign Affairs and International Trade has also articulated a multi-pronged strategy to enhance its integrated diplomatic, defence and development activities in the Americas, as well as in Afghanistan and Sudan. The UK's Ministry of Defence, Department for International Development (DfID) and Foreign and Commonwealth Office (FCO) have also emphasised the central role of 'humanitarian assistance and development' in stabilisation doctrine and practice.[23]

The specific role and place of humanitarian assistance in stabilisation discourse and practice varies between governments and among their respective departments. This is due as much to their distinctive foreign policies as to their particular bureaucratic architectures. In the case of the US, for example, humanitarian action is openly described as a tool to engage fragile states and an enduring feature of military strategy. This reflects the subordinate position of the US Agency for International Development (USAID) within the State Department and the dominance of the Pentagon in setting strategic and budget priorities. Under the Labour government, the UK's cross-department stabilisation unit took pains to highlight the impartial and independent role of humanitarian aid, again reflecting the specific place of DfID and its separation from the FCO. It is not yet known whether the coalition government, in power since May 2010, will continue this arrangement.

While not adopting the nomenclature of stabilisation *per se*, the United Nations is also shifting its peace support operations towards a logic that shares aspects of the aforementioned stabilisation agenda. Stabilisation operations have been launched with the UN Mission in the Democratic Republic of the Congo (MONUC), and the UN Stabilisation Mission in Haiti (MINUSTAH). The UN's adoption of this agenda is driven as much by internal institutional pressures – to 'act as one' and undertake integrated missions – as by a wider appreciation of external debates on the causes and consequences of fragility.[24] Indeed, UN missions are now guided by a new doctrine that highlights the role of enforcement coupled with peacebuilding. UN peacekeeping principles and guidelines thus call for agencies to 'create a secure and stable environment while strengthening the state's capacity to provide security'.[25]

Stabilising the frontier

Stabilisation does not comprise merely security and humanitarian aid. The troops and aid workers are joined by developers and businessmen seeking to take advantage of the many opportunities that exist in fragile states. State aid and investment also flow to the affected areas. As mentioned already, the OECD

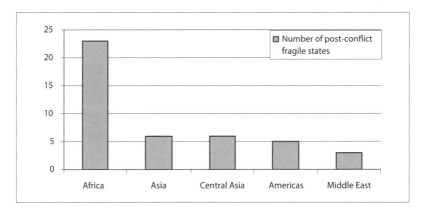

Figure 1. Fragile states by region[28]

Figure 2. Overseas development assistance flows to fragile states ($bn)[29]

	2003	2004	2005	2006	2007	2008
Post-conflict fragile states	17.8	18.3	43.3	36.6	28.72	39
Other developing states	51.2	61	63.74	67.7	74.7	88.3
All developing countries	69.0	79.4	107	104.3	103.4	121.4

counts as many as 50 fragile or failing states (see figure 1). Taken together, these account for more than a billion people.[26] While it would be too simplistic to make the causal claim that poverty necessarily leads to fragility, the flow of OECD-member aid dollars is telling. More than $34bn in development aid was channelled into fragile post-conflict states in 2008 alone (see figure 2). That same year, in a speech about 'securing development', the President of the World Bank Robert Zoellick promised to redouble investment in fragile states over the coming years.[27] This represents a surprising reversal of trends in the 1990s, when only 'good performers' were rewarded with scarce aid dollars.

However, even as aid and investment expand to meet the apparent spread of fragility, it is by no means clear that the archetypal stabilisation missions in Afghanistan and Iraq offer precedents for similar future operations. When planning for the demands of future warfare, military and political leaders acknowledge the need to adapt to multifarious threats, but, though they may accept they will be called on to advance the cause of stabilisation, they are wary of incurring the political and financial costs and strategic overstretch associated with such all-encompassing campaigns. For example, as a joint-operating environment assessment observes as recently as March 2010:

> The next quarter century will challenge US joint forces with threats and opportunities ranging from regular and irregular wars in remote lands, to relief and recon-struction in crisis zones, to cooperative engagement in the global commons ... US military forces will be continually engaged in some dynamic combination of combat, security, engagement, and relief and recon-struction.[30]

A more constrained and targeted stabilisation agenda is foreseeable in an increasingly diverse range of contexts. In addition to bolstering regional and domestic capacities in areas of fragility – through, for example, AFRICOM (the United States armed forces' African Command) and African Standby Forces – Western governments such as Canada, the UK and US are expanding their rosters of civilian experts (i.e., engineers, logisticians, legal specialists, managers) to anticipate stabilisa-tion and reconstruction needs before fragility leads to failure. But as Western governments and their taxpayers grapple with this stabilisation agenda, it is worth asking what *is* new about state fragility. Moreover, what exactly are these stabilisation missions expected to accomplish? And when do they end? Given their radical implications for how donors do business, what are their wider implications for humanitarian action? Perhaps most importantly, are these stabilisation missions improving the safety and security of people who are most vulnerable?

Like fragility, the policy and practice of stabilisation are not easily pinned down. Indeed, the abstract nature of the concept leaves the door open to widely varying interpretations. While the concept has so far been advanced predominantly by Western governments and shaped by their strategic interests and priorities, as noted above it has also progressively taken root in the UN, regional organisations and even in some middle-income countries such as Brazil.[31] Likewise, a number of governments affected by conflict and chronic violence such as Colombia, Pakistan, Sri Lanka and Timor Leste have latched on to the concept to avoid unfortunate labelling (i.e., war- or conflict-affected).

mar

Very generally, the broad parameters of stabilisation interventions include a wide combination of counter-terror, counter-insurgency, humanitarian and development, peace-building and state-building activities pursued in contexts where state authority and legitimacy is contested. They typically consist of both 'hard' and 'soft' forms of intervention – military and civilian – and imply a securitisation of assistance.[32] The practical manifestation of stabilisation activities nevertheless varies from case to case.

min

At a minimum, stabilisation interventions tend to advance a number of parallel and interlocking goals. These include the creation of safe and secure environments, the establishment of a modicum of the rule of law, the achievement of good (or enough) governance and a viable market economy, and the fostering of conditions to allow for governments and aid agencies to promote socio-economic wellbeing and democratic elections. As such, stabilisation represents an attempt to create the conditions for ostensibly liberal Western values to take hold. The means by which these goals are achieved are not always liberal however, and may combine, as noted above, a range of hard and soft measures.

Securing the humanitarian space

When governments put stabilisation doctrine into practice – as in the case of the Provincial Reconstruction Teams (PRTs) in Afghanistan – the lines between what is military and what is humanitarian or developmental inevitably begin to blur. Veteran practitioners worry that from the perspective of affected populations, humanitarian and development agencies are virtually indistinguishable from occupying military forces.[33] Aid recipients in fragile states may (simultaneously) receive assistance from relief agencies, be subjected to hearts and minds campaigns from civil-military teams, suffer from aggressive counter-terrorist operations, or be targeted for their complicity by armed groups. In Afghan towns and remote villages in the Democratic Republic of the Congo's Ituri district news spreads quickly, and the bombing of civilians in one part of the country understandably colours notions of stability offered by Western forces in another.

Ultimately, diverse stabilisation contexts generate opportunities for relief and development actors, albeit with certain constraints. For a variety of reasons, however, the practices and consequences of stabilisation for humanitarian action are generally perceived by relief and development practitioners to be uncertain and contentious.[34] This is due not exclusively to controversies associated with the fusion of military interventions with humanitarian and development activities, but also to ambiguities at the heart of the humanitarian project itself. Indeed, many of the controversies are a byproduct of the continued indecision within the humanitarian community about the place and direction of neutral, impartial and independent assistance.

The 'new' stabilisation agenda has been greeted with mixed responses and even derision by the humanitarian and development sectors. Critics argue that at best, it diverts funds away from poverty-reduction initiatives towards geopolitical interests. At worst, some commentators argue it bolsters counter-insurgency, counter-terrorism and counter-narcotics agendas that may potentially undermine humanitarian goals altogether.[35] Particularly since the US and coalition-led wars in Afghanistan and Iraq, relief agencies complain of an inexorable closure of the humanitarian space. By this, agencies mean both their ability to operate safely and effectively on the ground, as well as the wider social, political and geographic space in which civilians are protected. Yet anxiety in the humanitarian camp at least partly stems from uncertainty concerning the ultimate goals of humanitarian action and whether these ought to be aligned with the transformative aspirations of stabilisation and reconstruction.

Humanitarians are divided over the stabilisation question. On the one side are those who contend that it erodes the neutrality and impartiality of aid agencies and their ability to maintain an apolitical stance in the face of egregious violence. This is typified in a March 2000 report for the UK-based Overseas Development Institute's Humanitarian Policy Group by Nicholas Leader which notes how 'in some, maybe many conflicts the best "political" strategy may be to assert, as loudly and consistently as possible, that one is totally non-political'.[36] On the other, are those who say that stabilisation can protect aid workers and widen the humanitarian space; that it deals with root causes and ultimately expands the availability of life-saving assistance.

Certain humanitarian agencies refuse to be associated with military forces altogether. Specifically, the International Committee of the Red Cross (ICRC) and *Médecins Sans*

Frontières (MSF) are adamant that separation from the armed forces is the only way they can effectively negotiate access with vulnerable populations. The ICRC in particular is unambiguously committed to preserving its neutrality, impartiality and independence. Because it is funded partly from voluntary and personal contributions (as well as from states party to the Geneva Convention and from organisations such as the European Commission), it is in some ways in a better position to set the rules of their engagement. Other organisations such as Care International, Oxfam and World Vision have opted for a more pragmatic but less clear approach. They are convinced that a 'business as usual' model is simply not a viable option in today's fragile hot spots. Some organisations contend that staying clear of politics is impossible and can do more harm than good. Not coincidentally, these same agencies tend to be funded by a wider variety of contributions, including from western donors and private citizens, and are thus in some cases more closely aligned with their agendas.

Most humanitarian agencies are simply trying to make do in the new and uncertain climate of stabilisation. Many already spend in excess of a quarter of their annual budgets on protecting their staff.[37] In most cases, they have tried to insulate their humanitarian operations from those undertaken by the military through the introduction of distinctive symbols and icons. Nevertheless, confusion and competition persist between supporters of stabilisation and humanitarian action. This is at least in part because of continued confusion, and in many cases outright disagreement, over what either sector intends to achieve. And while there are opportunities for cooperation and mutuality of purpose and action, the environment continues to be characterised by mistrust.

Although most humanitarians are decidedly uneasy with the stabilisation agenda, they have yet to clearly articulate a coherent paradigm that incorporates (or rejects) military, political or development action to achieve humanitarian objectives. Rather, the humanitarian agenda continues to be largely defined by the 'apolitical' mantra of core principles, which runs counter to the explicitly political aspirations of stabilisation. This reflects anxiety among many humanitarian actors over what defines their specific humanitarian identity and unity of purpose – itself triggered by military–humanitarian interventions that unsettled the once-clear distinctions between relief workers and 'the rest'.[38]

There is no straightforward positive or negative correlation between stabilisation policies and the protection and maintenance of the humanitarian space. As ever, context determines all. There are at least four types of consequences of stabilisation on the humanitarian space: (i) situations where stabilisation impedes humanitarian agency space but generates certain positive humanitarian outcomes (i.e., Colombia); (ii) circumstances where stabilisation positively shapes agency space but does not result in positive humanitarian outcomes (the former Yugoslavia); (iii) settings where both humanitarian agency space and humanitarian outcomes are compromised (Somalia); and (iv) settings where stabilisation operations simultaneously protect agency space and humanitarian outcomes (Haiti).[39]

Humanitarian agencies have responded in various ways to proponents of stabilisation. Despite restrictive mandates and competencies, many are nevertheless engaged in activities during war and in the post-war period relabelled as recovery and reconstruction. Nevertheless, where military actions are under way, as in Afghanistan, Pakistan and Somalia, efforts by humanitarians may be aligned by default with military actors – both foreign and domestic. In spite of the pains taken to separate military and civilian efforts in these environments, the risks associated with recovery and reconstruction may still be more than many humanitarians are prepared to countenance. When the risks become too high, as they have been in the above-mentioned cases, humanitarian agencies may simply pull out altogether.

Ultimately, the ability of humanitarian agencies to achieve positive outcomes in complex fragile environments will depend on how they navigate their way through rapidly changing policy environments. At the very least, they will have to negotiate strategically with competing institutions involved simultaneously in stabilisation and development. They will need to carry out sophisticated analysis of the objectives of formal and informal partners. Such political engagement does not necessarily demand abandoning their core principles, but it will require a novel way of engaging with new actors.

It might also be possible to anticipate a new humanitarian agenda that explicitly incorporates the ambitions and potential of transformative action on a case-by-case basis. Such a relativist agenda has been resisted by more orthodox relief agencies in the past. Yet in as the cases of Timor Leste, Haiti and some areas of Afghanistan and Pakistan, humanitarian action benefited directly from security-led stabilisation operations from bilateral and multilateral actors. Even so, the humanitarian camp remains concerned over the danger of cooptation, manipulation and politicisation within stabilisation operations. These concerns are likely to amplify should the agenda shift from more wide-spectrum objectives to narrow counter-terrorism, counter-narcotics and counter-insurgency campaigns.

Conclusion

It is difficult to imagine a more complex and demanding set of challenges than those facing stabilisation and reconstruction operations in Afghanistan, Iraq, the Democratic Republic of the Congo, Haiti and Sudan. They may comprise 'wicked problems' without ready solutions.[40] Setbacks and failures on the ground have highlighted the many contradictions within the stabilisation agenda and the limits facing even the most finely coordinated interventions. In some cases, efforts to 'buy' stability through uncertain and risky bargains with local elites have backfired. In others, stabilisation has generated a host of unintended consequences – both positive and negative.

Given the ever-widening contexts in which stabilisation is pursued, it is unsurprising that ambition often outstrips tangible achievements on the ground. One analysis has highlighted a host of structural impediments to rapid stabilisation in post-conflict settings, ranging from the volatility of the environment in which they are pursued, to the way specific actions generate unanticipated knock-on effects and the lack of appropriate competencies among implementing agencies.[41] But it is also the case that so long as there is a preoccupation with so-called 'fragile' and 'failed' states, stabilisation interventions are likely to persist. It remains to be seen, then, whether and in what way the humanitarian sector is prepared to deal with this reality.

For many relief workers toiling away in fragile situations, the stabilisation agenda is described as a pretext for advancing the instrumental political interests of certain Western states.[42] Since their establishment less than a decade ago, the US CRS, the UK Stabilisation Unit and Canada's START have been doing brisk business. Many of their initiatives are described openly as counter-insurgency operations and a bid to win hearts and minds. And while stabilisation has generated some important short-term dividends in places like Haiti and Timor Leste, humanitarian and development personnel are sceptical about whether these missions will make communities and households safer in the long run.

Given these uncertain circumstances, it is entirely predictable that humanitarians may opt to retreat from the stabilisation and reconstruction agenda. They may instead turn to the ethical safe zone of a more conservative interpretation of humanitarianism. As such, they can easily affirm a positive identity as compared to those who may be acting with more dubious credentials and motives. The risk is that by stepping back into more 'principled' humanitarian action, they will also face a return to the moral hazards accompanying short-term material relief and service delivery.

More practically, humanitarian agencies may ultimately confront a forced retreat from zones of fragility owing to insecurity and limited access, especially where international and national actors see little benefit in cooperating. As is now well known, independence, neutrality and impartiality may find little purchase even in those environments where humanitarians choose to 'walk the walk'.[43] By denying the stabilisation and reconstruction agenda altogether, humanitarians risk marginalising themselves from the real world of politics which lies at the heart of many humanitarian crises. They might also continue to risk exposure to manipulation and threats from governments and non-state actors that continue treating them like so many pawns in today's wars.

Assessing Linkages Between Diplomatic Peacemaking and Developmental Peacebuilding Efforts

Ashraf Ghani, Clare Lockhart and Blair Glencorse

Introduction

Although high on the research agenda of donor countries, 'whole-of-government' approaches to state fragility have generated only limited studies and data, particularly at the interface between developmental planning and political diplomacy.[1] Previous studies have emphasised that there 'is little common understanding among agencies ... much less a common government-wide strategic vision'[2] and that there remain 'considerable gaps between what has been agreed in principle and ministerial and agency practice'.[3] One common issue that cuts across all fragile contexts and types of international intervention is the frequent inability of multilateral and bilateral diplomatic and development actors to address problems coherently. Often no effort is made to bring actors together behind

Ashraf Ghani is Chairman of the Institute for State Effectiveness (ISE); **Clare Lockhart** is Director of ISE; **Blair Glencorse** is an Associate at ISE. This chapter is adapted from a working paper by the same authors entitled: 'Recent Experiences in Linking Diplomatic Peacemaking with Development Efforts' written for the OECD-Development Assistance Committee thematic meeting on Diplomacy, Development and Integrated Planning in February 2008. The original paper was generously supported by the Government of Norway and can be downloaded at www.effectivestates.org.

a common aim and ensure that each is prepared to commit the time, resources and mechanisms to support this goal. Diplomacy and development tend to be treated sequentially, with diplomacy giving way to development, rather than simultaneously, with development fully supporting diplomatic efforts from the outset. Moreover, diplomatic and development processes tend to be equated with bureaucratic thought and mechanisms at a policy, or headquarters level, rather than more specifically as they relate to the process of supporting peace and stability on the ground. The parameters for actions and responsibilities are taken as fixed, which creates a distinct disconnect between the international system and the actors within it, and the problems this system is trying to solve. The results of intervention fall far short of expressed intention in many cases. Greater success will require coherent and carefully sequenced efforts to support state-building and peacebuilding in the long term with the necessary human and financial resources.

The relationship between diplomatic and development actors is particularly complex and varies over time and according to context. Interconnected challenges of governance, insecurity and poverty are acute in the world's most unstable countries and regions, and these issues have prompted efforts to increase the coherence of responses from governments and organisations which involve a range of actors, instruments and interventions. However, regardless of whether it is marked by a political settlement or a peace agreement, the cessation of hostilities is only the beginning of a series of simultaneous transitions. The international community cannot operate through the tools and processes as currently conceived, with diplomatic and development personnel working in organisational silos and failing to fully understand, collectively, the nature of their environment, the objective of their intervention, its time horizon, and the resources that need to be mobilised for its realisation. These are critical concerns that determine whether the outcome of international intervention is support for a virtuous circle of stability and prosperity, or for a vicious circle of instability and entrenched poverty.

Current diplomatic interventions

A distinctive pattern of diplomatic activity tends to emerge in conflict-affected states. Initially, diplomatic engagement and close monitoring aim to provide a basis for rapid mobilisation in response to sudden changes, and to reach an agreement to start talks – that is, to facilitate the shift from conflict to discussion. For the sake of analysis, the diplomatic peacemaking and peacebuilding pattern can then be briefly characterised as follows:

Conflict mediation

The intensity and length of conflict mediation efforts vary, depending on specific dynamics on the ground. In certain cases, parties may not be negotiating in good faith, thus perpetuating rather than reducing conflict. Diplomatic actors must therefore seek to discern and distil intentions and information, generate real compromise, effect a movement away from zero-sum thinking, and develop mechanisms that enable political progress. Once parties prove willing to sit at the discussion table, intense diplomatic efforts will be needed to encourage listening and dialogue, build understanding and classification of issues, create ground for negotiation and allow for a compromise settlement.

The peace agreement and deployment of forces

Peace agreements are highly sensitive documents with words that carry tremendous weight. Diplomacy is likely to be vital in creating the context in which agreement is possible, supporting the framing of the agreement itself, and ensuring that the peace agreement lays the foundation for a state-building process and setting political targets against which to measure progress. Diplomatic efforts must be tailored to the specific peace agreement under consideration and must generate consideration of a wide range of issues such as degrees of exclusion and inclusion, decentralisation and the constitution of a legitimate political centre.

The transitional period

A transitional period is geared towards establishing peace and stability, and may involve the use of a transitional government. The process must include outreach and a broadening of the political space. The political transition shifts the focus of diplomacy from preparing for and brokering the peace to building the peace. A carefully sequenced series of targets or milestones for the process, each with its own deadline, is important in order to establish trust between protagonists, and to give the process momentum. Transitional arrangements can then give way to broader and deeper representative approaches that endow the government with legitimacy.

Defining the 'rules of the game'

Any transition entails changes in the basic rules that arrange how the country is to be governed. This is a critical factor in all phases of the journey towards lasting peace, from peacemaking to peacebuilding. This legal restructuring of the institutions of state may involve creating an entirely new constitution or the adaptation of a previous constitution and the transformation of one party to the conflict from rebels to legitimate political actors. These processes should be closely linked to peace agreements, and carefully aligned with existing legal provisions; perhaps most importantly, they should not be rushed.

Current development interventions

The immediate process of post-conflict developmental engagement has taken on mechanical characteristics, with a clear set of steps that seeks to bring about a transition from conflict to peace. The broad pattern of some developmental activities can be briefly characterised as follows:

Continual monitoring

Development actors must be ready to deploy rapidly during transitional periods in fragile states, and to immediately plan for comprehensive development interventions. Continual monitoring is crucial in this regard: since 2005, the Organisation for Economic Cooperation and Development (OECD's) Development Assistance Committee has been carrying out important work in this area including studies on resource flows to fragile states and early warning indicators. Multilateral institutions such as the World Bank have also adapted procedures, policies and human-resource approaches to better measure progress in fragile contexts and provide expedited and exceptional allocations to countries that may require additional financing as a result of conflict.

Post-conflict needs assessment (PCNA)

Typically led by the UN and World Bank, needs assessments provide international actors with some understanding of the situation, focus on what must be done and the grounds for mobilisation. However, PCNAs often lack an agreed overall vision, demonstrate insufficient realism, provide inadequate links between priorities, show insufficient integration of intersecting issues, and fail to generate momentum after key transitional events.[4] While efforts have been made to improve the process, needs assessments tend not to be prioritised strategically and do not take into account a government's ability to manage the sums of money demanded by the development process.

Mobilisation of resources and donor conference

It is critical that a plan for resource mobilisation is in place when peace is reached to avoid losing valuable time in the post-conflict period. A donor conference tends to proceed in three phases: pledging, commitment and disbursement. The conference provides a forum and interface to bring together higher levels of government; it is therefore vital for setting in motion a working relationship between the donors and the government or transitional team. A related issue is the negotiation and forgiveness of debt to allow a range of multilateral and bilateral organisations to re-engage with countries that have arrears on existing loans or grants.

Disarmament, demobilisation and reintegration (DDR)

DDR has tended to be treated as three separate stages of the larger transition from peace to war. Often disarmament and demobilisation is not followed up with effective, sustainable reintegration of the former combatants into communities. The 'rule of gun' cannot be transformed into the rule of law without real economic incentives for young people. This involves not only job-creation programmes and dialogue with the private sector as to how best to generate employment, but also training schemes and vocational courses for the development of new skills, the removal of legal and administrative obstacles to employment, and resocialisation programmes.

Key themes

While it is possible to discern the emergence of this general pattern of diplomatic and development phases in theory, in practice events do not tend to unfold in a linear manner. Rather, the process of moving from conflict to peace involves multiple, complex transitions, human agency and enormous structural difficulties, some of which are outlined above, and all of which may cause deterioration in the situation, and even reversion to conflict. The intensity, shape and timing of approaches vary, but four issues appear to be critical for both diplomatic and development actors to bear in mind throughout the early peacemaking and peacebuilding period: security, resource mobilisation and commitment of funds, regional relations and strategic development.

Security is different from longer-term structural stability. Stability results from agreement among key political forces on the definition of a citizen-oriented system of governance and adherence to agreed rules. The rule of law allows a radical restructuring of the institutions of the state, in which the role of state institutions is transformed and the relationship between state and citizen is prescribed. This process allows power to be reconfigured from a repressive force, often used against citizens, into an instrument for the realisation of citizenship rights, central to the formulation of a new state.

At present, the appeals process for assistance in one country necessarily entails using resources allocated to another. As a result of arrears, multilateral institutions are often prevented from disbursing large amounts of funding to post-conflict governments. A mechanism such as pooled inter-ministerial funding (that is, money specifically reserved for rapid engagement in response to developments in fragile states), would ensure that funding is not committed at the expense of other needy countries. Some important steps are being taken in this regard in donor countries such as Norway, the Netherlands and the United Kingdom. The UN Peacebuilding Fund is the first mechanism devoted to peacebuilding that to some degree avoids the ad-hoc fundraising mechanisms that have previously dominated UN responses.

Regional agreement and support are necessary at all stages of peacemaking and peacebuilding. Conflicts can be reinforced and perpetuated by neighbouring countries, with regional players also acting as 'spoilers'[5] to the prospects for successful transitional arrangements and the emergence of a peaceful, stable state. The diplomatic and development communities can help develop regional approaches to avoid the spill-over effects of regional and related conflicts, by bringing surrounding countries, particularly larger emerging powers, together behind the goals of political, developmental and economic state- and market-building.

The process of strategic development, often embodied in a Poverty Reduction Strategy (PRS), which is prepared in collaboration with the International Monetary Fund (IMF), the World Bank and the country, is valuable because it can generate ownership by the government of the country in question, build national capacity, identify needs through a representative domestic process and articulate development goals over the medium term. However, the process is often not prioritised or truly authored by the partner government. Moreover, international strategies to support the PRS are often not strategic. That is to say, they are produced by amalgamating disparate projects into a single document rather than by a coherent design. A more concrete synergy and strategy could be achieved if both sides agreed on the goals of peace, stability and development, and matched these to suitable funding and support mechanisms, according to a joint government–donor approach.

Linkages between diplomacy and development

A clear and well-defined set of processes and interactions has emerged on both sides in fragile contexts. Diplomatic and development agencies and organisations often have different cultures, capabilities and practices, from which emerge different types of intervention. There can be a fair degree of complementarity when the system as it exists works in tandem, and aspects of the distinct processes and skill sets are leveraged in productive ways. However, the problem in many cases is that the diplomatic phases are not carried out simultaneously with the development phases, which prevents mutually reinforcing patterns emerging and undermines prioritisation of action. Indeed, in some contexts, political-diplomatic actors take the lead and purposely prevent development and humanitarian actors from being brought into the process.

At the same time, the calcification of roles and phases has prevented collaborative thinking, entrenched existing business practices, reduced the opportunity for structural changes to organisational dynamics, enforced disparate operational patterns, ensured different and often competing incentives, and most importantly, prevented coherence behind a common goal. Unity and coherence of purpose, so important for success, are absent. A system has developed which is not aligned with the problems it seeks to resolve on a fundamental level. While the pattern of intervention is clear, the goal, instruments and mechanisms brought to bear are not always appropriate or positive when viewed from the overall goal of building stability in these countries. These outcomes may perpetuate rather than resolve conflict.

Country cases

Progress must be judged ultimately not by the coherence of internal dynamics in donor capitals but by positive changes on the ground. This requires a clear understanding of the tasks, sequence, resources, skills and personnel necessary to provide effective engagement. There is no standard formula for international intervention that fits all contexts and circumstances, but institutional arrangements must take account of the wide range of actors who will be working towards the overarching purpose. The examples below provide a cursory overview of some cases in which progress has been made and problems experienced in this regard.[6]

Liberia

Liberia now benefits from significant international goodwill and is an example of constructive international engagement in many ways. Significant diplomatic–development planning and cooperation have led to a successful sequencing of international intervention since the end of civil war in 2003. The rapid and significant deployment of peacekeeping troops has prevented any type of coup against the government led by Ellen Johnson-Sirleaf; their continued presence has been essential to protect security gains and further support security-sector reform; and the Governance and Economic Management Assistance Program (GEMAP), sanctioned by the UN Security Council after diplomatic negotiations, has provided robust oversight of financial governance since September 2005. International experts have been appointed in key public-finance positions, significantly reducing corruption and improving cash management. The GEMAP represents a ground-breaking example of multilateral and bilateral organisations working across the diplomatic and development arenas to address the serious governance issues that contributed to 23 years of conflict in Liberia.

The sheer number of organisations and bureaucracies involved in the country, however, means that coordination is still difficult and duplication of activities is frequent. Beyond the UN peacekeeping force, there are currently as many as 13 UN agencies, 18 multilateral and bilateral donors, two regional African organisations and 320 international NGOs operating in

Liberia. This manifests itself in a multitude of different projects and strategies, providing ample opportunity for corruption and mismanagement and for overwhelming the government with competing ideas and demands. Diplomatic and development linkages are also coming apart as pressure for positive momentum outstrips the ability to deliver on the developmental side. For example, the UN Security Council (UNSC) lifted sanctions on timber in 2006 and the Forestry Development Authority has since introduced new regulations for logging concessions; but capacity to implement new laws and monitor activities is low. Similarly, the UNSC lifted sanctions on diamond exports in 2007, but the regulatory environment in the mineral sector is weak, capacity is lacking and infrastructure is poor.

Donors must seek to co-produce developmental outcomes in Liberia which support sustainable positive change, rather than engage in a donor–client relationship which only fosters dependency. An updated, comprehensive review of government functionality and a coherent assessment of exactly where donors can exit from activities and technical assistance through which they are currently substituting for the Liberian state, business or civil society, would be productive. This would provide the basis for consolidating the mechanisms and practices of governance that would in turn reinforce loops of reform, thereby making change irreversible and systematised rather than dependent upon competent individuals or reform-minded leadership. A significant risk is that the current reforms remain contained within the present administration, and that ownership of and capacity for positive change does not extend beyond the current leadership.

Nepal

In Nepal, donors have not put in place adequate monitoring mechanisms, at both the diplomatic and developmental levels, to provide early warning signs of conflict. The political terrain in the country has evolved recently from an ad-hoc process of negotiation between stakeholders (including the Maoist rebels and the political parties) with different interests and aims; it has not yet been brought within a framework that could provide stability and direction. While diplomacy has facilitated positive movement, development actors have found it difficult to put in place programmes to build sustainable capacity and support state effectiveness at the various levels of governance in the country. Aid has flowed entirely outside government systems, which has led to competition with the state in terms of the determination and delivery of policy.

While they accept aid harmonisation in principle, most donor organisations are struggling to understand what this would mean in practice. In a context of high structural uncertainty, the mindsets and practices of aid agencies could have unintended consequences for social, political and economic processes in Nepal. The challenge is not just to mobilise aid resources, but to shift the relationship to one of co-producer and strategic partner, based on medium- to long-term goals, that puts the government of Nepal in control. Here, donors are again failing to translate diplomatic and developmental analysis at the strategic level into practical change on the ground. The existence of successful community and village-based programmes in Nepal suggests that carefully designed national programmes could provide a collaborative framework for joint programming that would harness the capabilities of actors and allow the government to improve expenditures. Individual donor programmes reduce the scope for coordination and, as such, these should be the aid modality of last resort.

The test for diplomatic actors is also to understand the role of emerging regional donors. India, which is home to the largest number of Nepali migrants in the world, has a long and open border with Nepal, and is providing significant funds for investment, particularly in infrastructure. China too could offer opportunities for Nepali trade and investment, even though its border is far less accessible. Nepal's location, between two huge and rapidly growing economies, could be of great advantage to its people. This would require creative thinking on the part of the government and the international community, sustained attention by diplomatic and development actors to issues of trade, tariffs, regulation, the creation of an investor-friendly environment and greater participation of Nepali businesses in an expanding regional economy.

Afghanistan

After the September 2001 terrorist attacks on the United States, and the subsequent change of regime enforced by the US-led military intervention, tentative successes were achieved in Afghanistan in terms of some early diplomacy and development efforts. A carefully choreographed series of steps was designed not as an end in itself, but specifically to increase the trust of the population in the capability of the government (in partnership with the international actors) to create a positive future for the country. The Bonn Agreement (officially, the Agreement on Provisional Arrangements in Afghanistan Pending the Re-establishment of Permanent Government Insitutions) was inaugurated in December 2001. It set targets for transferring power to an interim administration and later for the holding of free, democratic elections. It emphasised the establishment of a legitimate, rules-governed and active political process which made clear that victory at one stage would not be permanent, but that winners and losers could reverse their fortunes through engagement in the political process. This latter point was crucial because it prevented the emergence of permanent losers who might then have mobilised against the political process; or permanent winners who could have subverted it. As such, the Bonn Agreement recognised and pledged to support a *process* of legitimisation, by offering assistance to Afghan authorities in rebuilding their governance institutions.

On the development side, donors immediately began to move towards a model of pooled financing via a Multi-Donor Trust Fund that provided budget support for the operations of the government, as well as considering whole-of-government approaches, in order to improve coherence of efforts. The PCNA took place hastily and the costs of reconstruction were seriously underestimated, but an Afghan team was in place to take ownership of the development agenda through the creation of the Afghanistan Development Forum, which was established to meet annually from the beginning of April 2002. This process emphasised a set of tailored, integrated national priority programmes explicitly designed to address drivers of instability.[7] Diplomacy and development efforts subsequently became disconnected, however, because the balance of expenditure between security and development became fundamentally misaligned (thus clearly illustrating the difference between security and stability, as outlined above). Meanwhile, the humanitarian appeal pitted the UN agencies and the government in fundamental competition over the resources that were available for development. More than 50 donor and UN agencies began work on fragmented aid programmes, while 200 NGOs scrambled to implement disparate development projects through parallel delivery mechanisms.

Lack of transparency in the delivery of aid, confused strategic objectives and the failure to create a system for measuring results (in terms of expenditures, cost to the administration, or relative value and efficiency of delivery) also bred disillusionment among ordinary Afghans, whose hearts and minds were so critical to the diplomatic priority of building stability. Only now is concerted thought being applied by the international community to engaging Afghanistan's neighbours in terms of the capacities, skills, networks and markets that exist to underpin a broader, regional peace. The need for agreed systems for diplomatic monitoring of the peace in a war-torn country, based on a clear understanding of the drivers of regional conflict and stability at the developmental level, was underlined by the resurgence of the Taliban. Having been ousted by the 2001 invasion, it gradually regrouped and by 2008 it had spread beyond its rural southern stronghold and was launching attacks and suicide bombings in Kandahar and Kabul. Donor governments have worked to improve inter-agency coherence in Afghanistan and to better synergise development efforts, but implementation remains difficult given the sheer number of actors, priorities and interests on the ground, not to mention the continuing counterinsurgency operation against the Taliban and related security problems.

Synthesis and recommendations

As these brief examples demonstrate, agreement and alignment within the international community on the goal of intervention, and coherence around that goal, are essential. Progress is judged in terms of success in the field, but the international community has created extreme complexity on the ground as a result of misaligned development objectives and ad-hoc practices. But credible steps may be taken to break out of this pattern and free policy-making and implementation from the distinctive organisational frameworks that perpetuate it. These steps must be organised so that they provide optimal support for the twin goals of state- and peacebuilding. Recommendations to this end might include the following:

Ensure that all efforts support the establishment of functioning systems

Adopt state-building as the overarching framework

Diplomatic and development actors must ensure state-building is their collective goal in these contexts despite the fact that, so far, the level of international conceptualisation, expertise and resources specifically dedicated to building effective, sustainable state institutions has been poor.[8] Answering the often urgent call for help from fragile countries has caused practice to surge ahead of analysis, but international actors are now reflecting more carefully on exactly how they should engage in state-building work. This requires a clearer understanding of institutional strengths and weaknesses across the functions of the state, identification of those functions that will be performed across levels of government, and the identification of the links between the state, market and civil society. It is only on this basis that restructuring of the central government can be fully discussed and a coherent state-building and peace-building strategy developed.

Delineate roles while ensuring whole-of-government approaches

There are often far too many international actors in fragile state contexts, but as far as possible, there should be a clear division of labour to support agreed goals, and a delineation of the roles to be performed by the various organisations.[9] Multilateral and bilateral donors can act as direct administrators, facilitators, strategic advisers, catalysts, substitute providers of services, monitors, evaluators and referees, depending on the context. This involves coordination within and between national governments and multilateral organisations. Where coherence is achieved, it will be counterproductive if it leads only to a proliferation of initiatives and a multiplicity of unilateral strategies. Actors in these contexts must instead aspire to 'whole-of-system' approaches, through which the myriad donor approaches are brought together behind common aims.

Consider affordability and feasibility versus desirability

A key issue in all cases is the trade-off between affordability, feasibility and desirability. Historically, needs assessments have included, for example, low-priority issues, issues which were not affordable in financial terms, which could not possibly be implemented by the international community and which did not strictly support the reinforcing loops that produce peace. Diplomatic and development actors must interact closely during peace agreements, needs assessments and post-conflict planning to ensure that priorities match the goal of a stable and peaceful state, and that international promises match the ability to deliver on the ground, as measured by the capacity of the government and the international community either to mobilise or to hire people to implement the agreements.

Use effective mechanisms for coherent international actions

Focus on the implementation of peace agreements

To some extent, all peace agreements have provisional gaps or 'blind spots': the immediate imperative, above all else, is to stop the fighting. However, peace agreements could gain both in realism and coherence if they identified from the outset the different ways to transition from war to peace, and if they included a timeline for achieving that transition. The gains achieved in restoring competitive electoral politics, or the slow momentum in achieving the goal of building inclusive states may be attributable to the degree of focus on implementation. Thus, planning for medium- and longer-term efforts has to happen in the midst of the initial emergency and during early recovery. Attention should not be allowed to fade as soon as a political agreement is reached.

Do not freeze transitional arrangements

A political transition can gain momentum by linking its progress to milestones. A sequence of decisions, creating or reviving formal institutions in the country, can increasingly empower stakeholders. Since a government's legitimacy is limited during a transitional phase, diplomatic emphasis has to be on creating the systems for selecting a legitimate government, and development efforts have to be focused on creating the bonds of trust between government and citizens that can maintain this legitimacy. Settling on a transitional government and allowing the process to stagnate breeds the sense that winners at the transitional phase are permanent, which will encourage losers to exit the political transition and resort to other channels, including the use of violence.

Ensure the necessary duration of international engagement

'Planning retrospectively' from the goal and prioritising tasks

Conflict tends to emerge between donor headquarters and their field offices on political peacebuilding objectives. There can be disagreement over the approaches that are negotiated locally among donor representatives, but which may not adhere to current thought at the policy level. This could be avoided by working backwards from the desired end-state to identifying actors, their critical tasks and the necessary resources, targets and monitoring arrangements, and agreeing on the decisions and responsibilities, with a view to how and when these can be carried out in practice. Realistic, achievable milestones that are tied to specific dates can be critical instruments for creating momentum and reinforcing trust in the process. This facilitates a long-term perspective and engagement over a ten- to 20-year period rather than a short-term horizon of one to three years during the transitional period.

Prevent disengagement

The international community must accept the fact that peacebuilding and state-building take time. When commitment to continual and concerted political, social and political analysis of fragile states falters, or aid programming is halted because of adverse political events, it becomes significantly more difficult to both predict and respond to changes in the diplomatic and development environments. Diplomatic expertise and analysis of situations is critical for early-warning systems, and the correct channels must exist for information flows from diplomatic to development actors, and vice versa. While multilateral organisations, and especially the UN, take the lead in many instances, bilateral partners can and should also step forward to catalyse change, especially when the fragile state government is itself unwilling to fully engage in the multilateral process. Interested parties must be allowed to come into the process early.

Generate the necessary resources for effective states
Identify existing assets

While it is true that in post-conflict countries like Liberia and Nepal, institutional and human capacity has been significantly destroyed or eroded, lessons from state-building in post-conflict environments indicate that significant pockets of capacity persist in these contexts. Government systems, however corrupt and inefficient, remain. The key for the international community is to begin by identifying the critical assets and weaknesses of the state, and understanding elements of national systems that can be used as the basis for development. Diplomats cannot appreciate the viability of a peace agreement or the capacity of a national government to adhere to international treaties if they do not understand the institutional structure of the country in question. Equally, development actors will not be able to create a functioning state that provides political and social stability and economic opportunity if they do not comprehend the capacity that already exists to generate such change.

Use innovative resources

There is a plethora of different channels, beyond aid, through which governments can interact with donor countries. These can provide a far more sustainable basis for economic growth in the long term. This means moving beyond the traditional mindset and framework that consigns diplomatic actions to foreign departments or offices, and development to aid agencies. Diplomatic and development efforts can and should be carried out across a range of donor government organisations that harbour the requisite skills and modalities to support peacemaking and peacebuilding by generating legitimate markets. Comparative analysis indicates that the development of new financial instruments (such as leasing operations, investment guarantees, political risk insurance, domestic venture capital funds and so on), is a prerequisite for helping to create a competitive economy and linking nascent economic actors into the supply and value chains necessary to create growth.

Develop the requisite skills to improve joint planning and implementation

Each of the phases of a transition requires a set of specialised skills and practices, based on a detailed examination of lessons learned. These will enable staff of donor organisations to delineate options within the context of coherent overall strategies so that links between actions, functions and processes are fully understood. Traditional diplomacy does not generate the capacities for peace mediation and consolidation, which require a very distinctive set of abilities, including an understanding of multifunctional states and the dynamics of the market. Bilateral governments may consider targeting senior diplomats for intensive pre-deployment training on issues of peacebuilding and classify such training as essential for career development. Both diplomats and development actors must be able to think in terms of systems, rather than projects or specific concerns, and provide a synthesis of ideas tailored to specific contexts. These people must also be deployed to fragile situations for extended periods; a constant turnover of staff on the donor side hinders continuity of policy and outcomes.

Conclusion

Whole-of-government approaches in conflict-affected countries are necessary, but not sufficient, for stability. Even when coordination does occur, tasks allocated across the international community often do not look integrated from a single partner-country perspective. A donor may focus on a particular partnership (between diplomatic and development departments, for example) but the resulting approach should add up to more than the sum of its parts.

The international community does recognise this fact: the Dili Declaration of April 2010, agreed between the Group of 7+ (countries experiencing conflict or fragility), sets out a new vision for state-building and peacebuilding, for example, that focuses on the so-called '3C' process to build *coherent, coordinated* and *complementary* development interventions in fragile states.[10] But on the ground the reality often remains different as integrated plans often bear little resemblance to each other. The goal of coherence across and between ministry, government and multilateral levels demands system alignment, across multiple organisations, behind clearly defined goals, tasks and resources, with agreed mechanisms for monitoring progress. In this regard, many of the reforms suggested here are by no means easy to initiate, nor can they be carried out quickly. Change can only come about through a series of successive, credible steps that allow diplomatic, development and other donor actors to collectively choreograph rather than individually improvise their approaches. If redistributive power can be transformed into collective will, and independent capabilities channelled into joint action, this will provide focal points from which transitions to peace can grow and expand.

CHAPTER FOUR

The Bretton Woods Institutions, Reconstruction and Peacebuilding

Graciana del Castillo

Introduction

Despite a few success stories, the record of countries that have moved from civil war or other internal chaos to a fragile peace since the end of the Cold War – either through negoti-ated agreements or military interventions – is dismal. Roughly half of them reverted to conflict within a few years.[1] Of the half that managed to keep the peace, the majority ended up highly dependent on foreign aid. Relapses have been costly and often more bloody than previous conflicts, as the experi-ences of Angola and Rwanda in the 1990s, and Afghanistan and Iraq in the 2000s, testify. To make matters worse, failed states have a host of destabilising effects well beyond their borders, a phenomenon that other chapters in this volume explore. While development organisations and NGOs contribute to the economic reconstruction of these countries in many and complex ways, it is the Bretton Woods Institutions (BWI) – the International Monetary Fund (IMF) and the World Bank – that perform *sine qua non* functions in support of reconstruction,

Graciana del Castillo is a Senior Research Scholar at Columbia University, New York.

since it is impossible to consolidate peace in stagnant, jobless economies.[2]

The financial crisis still raging in Europe, together with lack-lustre growth and unprecedented unemployment rates among advanced economies, may cause the needs of small, war-torn countries to seem less urgent. But the political importance of some of these countries and their potential for regional and global disruption are not commensurate with their weight in global production and trade.[3] The period of global recovery may be the perfect time to engage in a broad-based debate with policymakers in countries in transition from war on how the BWIs can assist them in moving effectively through reconstruction towards a sustainable development path.

The BWI have come a long way since the end of the Cold War in terms of the way they support countries in the complex transition from war, but major changes are necessary for peace to have a chance. Because countries in this transition had low levels of development, it became clear that economic reconstruction had to go beyond rehabilitating basic services and infrastructure. It also required the creation of basic macro- and microeconomic policy, institutional and regulatory frameworks necessary for dealing with often-large fiscal and external imbalances and debt arrears. These frameworks were and are essential for reactivating the investment and trade flows that collapsed during conflict. Job creation is key to reintegrating former combatants and other crises-affected groups.

While the BWI are well placed to advise on and finance reconstruction in these countries, they have often been accused of being part of the problem, rather than the solution. Some criticism has been quite dogmatic, generalised and unsubstantiated, and has persisted even when the BWI tried to respond to it. Other detractors have been more rigorous, specific and constructive. The BWI have reacted positively by rectifying some of their shortcomings, although many of them continue to impede effective reconstruction.[4]

Since 2008, following the election of new management (Robert Zoellick as President of the World Bank and Dominique Strauss-Kahn as Managing Director of the IMF), the BWI have been more responsive to their wider membership. They have made important changes to their policies and have overhauled their lending framework in order to adapt and become more effective in supporting member countries. These include the low-income countries that have been greatly affected by surging food and fuel prices as well as contagion from the global financial crisis since 2008. To make the BWI more effective in crises, their resources have been significantly increased.

At the same time, both the World Bank and the IMF have become more sensitive to the specific needs and idiosyncrasies of countries affected by conflict. Changing the status quo has never proved easy and these institutions only move slowly. With the hindsight of two decades of experience since the end of the Cold War, it might now be opportune to examine why conflict-affected countries have either failed to keep the peace, or have become highly aid dependent.[5] Better and more targeted support from the BWI could improve the prospects for recovery and peace in the affected countries. It would also improve the outlook for the general BWI membership that suffers the collateral damage from conflict-prone countries. Such results would clearly be a win-win solution for the BWI membership.

The war-to-peace transition

The political economy of peace

despite the peculiarities of each case, when war ends, countries need to address the root causes of the conflict to make the transition to peace irreversible. In this context, countries have to establish security; create participatory political systems, good governance and respect for the rule of law, human rights and property rights; restore social cohesion following the polarisation caused by war; and embark on economic reconstruction.

These multidimensional challenges are closely interrelated and mutually reinforcing. Failure in any one of these areas often puts the others at risk. Meeting such ambitious goals often has important economic and financial consequences. At the end of the First World War, the economist John Maynard Keynes noted that the deleterious economic consequences of peace can be considerable.[6] Conversely, the rewards can be significant.

The two world wars that led to the establishment of the BWI in 1944 involved several industrial countries with well-educated labour forces and rather homogeneous populations. These countries also had well developed socio-economic, security and political institutions that could be used to support effective economic reconstruction. By contrast, the wars of the last two decades were basically internal conflicts, although they often involved neighbouring countries, such as the conflict in the Democratic Republic of the Congo (DRC). These conflicts resulted from economic and political underdevelopment and were triggered by ethnic, religious, ideological or economic factors, and frequently disputes over access to natural resources. Reconstruction was even more challenging when it took place in failed states or breakaway provinces or territories.

In these countries, going back to what existed before the conflict was not an option. Neither was maintaining the illicit activities and the macroeconomic mismanagement that were prevalent during the war. Reconstruction efforts amid high levels of poverty, low levels of human development and institutional capacity, weak governance and significant international aid have proved particularly challenging, not only to the countries themselves, but also to the BWI.

Much attention has been given in public debate and in academic literature to the political, security and social aspects of the transition to peace,[7] while the political economy of reconstruction has been neglected.[8] This is despite the fact that failure to create functioning economies and to give former combatants and other groups affected by the war an economic stake in the peace process has been a major reason for the dismal record of countries in this transition. A peace dividend, in terms of remunerative and licit jobs, is a prerequisite for countries to keep the peace and to avoid aid dependency.

Reconstruction vs normal development

Although countries undergoing post-conflict reconstruction and those experiencing normal development in the absence of conflict can display similarities,[9] these similarities have led to their conflation, with unfortunate results. In fact, the dismal record mentioned earlier can be directly linked to the failure of donors and partner governments to observe two important distinctions.

Firstly, because economic reconstruction takes place amid the multidimensional transition to peace, it is 'a development-plus' challenge.[10] In addition to the normal challenges of socio-economic development that all poor countries face, these countries must accommodate the extra burden of national reconciliation and infrastructure rehabilitation. Critical activities in this regard include the disarming, demobilising and reintegration (DDR) of former combatants and other groups affected by the conflict into society and into productive activities; the return of refugees and internally displaced groups; demining; and the delivery of emergency aid as well as the rehabilitation of services and infrastructure in the former conflict areas. These extra activities have serious financial implications and need to be given priority in budgetary allocations. This has not often been the case. For example, the failure to create the jobs necessary for the successful reintegration of former combatants and conflict-affected groups strained the peace in El Salvador to breaking point in 1992; it was also a major factor in reviving the Taliban insurgency in Afghanistan in 2006.[11]

Thus, although countries in the transition from war face the development challenges that other countries face, such as alleviating poverty and complying with the Millennium Development Goals (MDGs), these are long-term propositions. In the short run, the challenge of economic reconstruction is primarily to contribute to national reconciliation and the consolidation of peace. This is why the rewards can be high if it succeeds.

Secondly, policymaking in post-crisis settings is fundamentally different from 'business as usual'. In this regard, countries in post-conflict reconstruction share some characteristics with countries coming out of other crises such as natural disasters or deep financial crises.[12] The differences relate to the horizon over which economic policies are planned, the guiding principles, the amount and stability of technical and financial assistance, and the nature and extent of the international community's involvement.

In the aftermath of war or disaster, policymakers react to the emergency, often having no choice but to adopt policies that they know could create distortions later on. Their key objectives at the time when the countries are most vulnerable are to save lives and keep the peace. For example, food aid, which is imperative in the short term, will need to be withdrawn eventually, or it will create disincentives to food production in the medium term.

More importantly, rather than applying the 'equity principle' of normal development, whereby those in need should be treated equally, it is necessary to apply the 'peacekeeping principle'. The latter requires giving preference to the groups most affected by the crisis. Unless these groups – particularly former combatants – have hopes for a stake in the peace process, the chances are that they will revert to war. In this regard, the success of El Salvador contrasts with that of Guatemala, where an ambitious peace agreement signed in 1996 built up expectations that could not be satisfied.

Policymaking during reconstruction is also different from normal development in that foreign assistance often exhibits sharp spikes following crises, whereas it remains at a low, stable level under normal development,With the exception of island economies and a few other countries, aid to developing countries unaffected by crisis is generally less than 3% of their Gross National Income (GNI). By contrast, aid jumped to close to 100% of GNI in Rwanda in 1995 and in the DRC in 2003. Not surprisingly, such large volumes of aid are accompanied by an intrusive political involvement by the international community in the internal affairs of these countries, which would be unacceptable under normal development.

Dealing with such volumes of aid creates serious challenges, partly because in countries coming out of war or natural disaster, the absorptive capacity is low – that is, the capacity to utilise aid effectively is restricted by the country's deficient civil service and institutions – and partly because the opportunities for corruption are considerable. These countries often lack adequate procurement policies. This is why the support of the BWI is so important in reconstruction, including in the administration of trust funds, in ensuring the timely, transparent and accountable disbursement of donors' pledged funds, and in making aid utilisation more effective.

Peace vs development objectives
Countries in the transition to peace have found it particularly difficult to reconcile the need to carry out extra peace-related activities, including DDR programmes which have important

financial consequences, with the financial targets imposed as conditionality in their BWI-supported economic programmes.

However, because there cannot be development without peace, the peace (the political objective) should prevail over development (the economic objective) whenever the two clash, which is frequently. In such cases, the decision on priorities should be made at the highest political level, including the UN Security Council and the UN Secretary-General, and *not* by the United Nations Development Programme (UNDP), the BWIs, or other development and financial institutions. If this prioritisation of peace were accepted, then it follows that optimal or first-best economic policies of classic theory are often not possible, or even desirable. As Zoellick recognised: 'development projects may need to be suboptimal economically – good enough rather than first-best.'[13]

If it is accepted that reconstruction is an intermediate and temporary phase following the country's emergence from war to ensure that a relapse does not occur and the country can move into a normal development path, a strong argument may be made for preferential treatment from the BWI for countries in this phase. Effective reconstruction, with BWI support, would not only ensure that countries keep the peace, but it would also help these countries to be weaned from aid dependency and move faster on to normal development. Once on this path, policymakers would be able to shoot for optimal policies and establish them with a medium- and long-term perspective in mind.[14]

BWI support and the new infrastructure

The BWI play a key role in peace and security.[15] They support countries in the transition to peace through many and interconnected channels, including policy advice, technical assistance and capacity building; financing through their own instruments, programmes and trust funds; administering trust funds that donors set up for different countries; and catalysing resources from other institutions and governments. Both institutions continuously carry out applied research to guide their respective interventions.

There is a basic division of labour between the two organisations, but there are many areas of overlap. The IMF helps to rebuild countries' capacity in the fiscal, monetary, exchange and statistical areas. The World Bank focuses on rebuilding the microeconomic foundations for investment, employment, growth and poverty alleviation. It also organises donors' meetings and administers trust funds (often in collaboration with regional development banks and the UNDP). While the IMF provides budgetary support only, the World Bank also provides project financing. The BWI collaborate in supporting governments, civil society and other development partners in the preparation of Poverty Reduction Strategy Papers (PRSP), which describe the country's macroeconomic, structural and social policies and programmes to promote growth and reduce poverty, as well as associated external financing needs and major sources of financing.

Since a detailed analysis of how such support has evolved over time and the problems associated with some of its features have been presented elsewhere,[16] suffice it to say here that both the IMF and the World Bank have come a long way since the early 1990s, a time when they supported countries emerging from war in the same manner that they supported countries in the normal process of development. Furthermore, both institutions have streamlined the conditions they attach to the provision of support. Conditionality had previously been particularly harsh on countries in the transition from war.[17]

The BWI have also come a long way since the early 1990s when they argued that conflict had a political dimension well beyond their mandate—and hence carried out their economic and development operations with little consideration for politics. There has indeed been a fundamental change in the way the BWI address their respective mandates and an increased recognition by both institutions of the interconnectedness of economic policies, political and security constraints, conflict and poverty alleviation.

The World Bank

In a major speech on 'Securing Development' in January 2009, Robert Zoellick expressed concern about the poor record of conflict-affected countries:

> too often, the development community has treated states affected by fragility and conflict simply as harder cases of development ... Yet, these situations require looking beyond the analytics of both security studies and development—to a different framework of building security, legitimacy, governance, and economy. This is not security as usual or development as usual. Nor is this about what we have come to think of as peacebuilding or peacekeeping. This is about *Securing Development* – bringing security and development together first to smooth the transition from conflict to peace and then to embed stability so that development can take hold over a decade and beyond. Only by securing development can we put down roots deep enough to break the cycle of fragility and violence.[18]

Zoellick concluded: 'Too many perfect economic plans have floundered upon the rocks of political impossibility.' His statement is a clear indication of why these institutions need to respond to political and security constraints.[19] Following this major change in vision and policy, which recognises that reconstruction is not development as usual and calls for an integrated approach to economic, political and security issues,[20] the World Bank is now in the process of analysing conflict to determine how best to support countries whose development is affected by it. Findings and recommendations for action will be presented in the *World Development Report 2011: Conflict, Security and Development*.[21]

It will be interesting to see what effect the report has on the way the World Bank supports countries through its advice and technical assistance, particularly in addressing the critical failure in creating sustainable employment, and the effect it may have in rallying support for a more permanent infrastructure and financing mechanisms to address the specific problems of conflict countries. As Zoellick mentions, support needs to be committed for the long haul; it must also move beyond ad hoc remedies. In particular, funding mechanisms need to ensure continuity and stability of resources over a decade or more. Ways also have to be found to ensure the proper and timely disbursement of funds from the Bank's administered trust funds.

The International Development Association (IDA), the concessional lending arm of the World Bank, has provided almost $6 billion for post-conflict reconstruction assistance to fragile and conflict-affected countries. Middle-income or credit worthy Post-conflict countries borrow from the International Bank for Reconstruction and Development (IBRD) arm of the World Bank that lends at market rates.[22] A few countries that are low-income but credit-worthy, such as Pakistan and Indonesia, have access to a blend of IDA and IBRD resources.[23] Since 2008, The World Bank has also financed fragile and conflict-affected countries through the State and Peace-Building Fund (SPF). The overall goal of the

SPF is to address the needs of state and local governance, and peace-building in war-torn countries.

The IMF

The IMF also carried out its activities in the 1990s as if it could isolate its programmes from political and security constraints. However, the link between economic conditions and political instability that leads to war, is now recognised. The Fund's Managing Director, Dominique Strauss-Kahn recently acknowledged: 'history is replete with examples of how economic and financial insecurity stoke social tensions, which in turn can undermine political stability, and even result in war. Getting the economy right and addressing threats to its stability can play an essential role in fostering the conditions for peace.'[24]

In the 1990s the Fund also considered that the issue of poverty was beyond its mandate. Its main concern was ensuring that member countries could finance their needs for goods and services and service their debt, that is, to ensure balance-of-payments sustainability. The belief at the time was that responding to poverty should be left to the World Bank. Ownership of national policies had not yet become a real concern either.

This has clearly changed. The Fund now recognises that the purpose of its support to poor countries is to improve poverty conditions, and that the issue of ownership of national policies is key to achieving this. Following the donors' meeting on Haiti at the end of March 2010, Strauss-Kahn noted that, for reconstruction to work, 'the Haitian authorities need to be in the driver's seat. The IMF experience is that, for such a programme to work there needs to be real ownership by the country.'[25]

Reactivation of the private sector is necessary to fight poverty on a sustainable basis, but it takes time following crises. Safety nets are needed for humanitarian purposes, although they should be phased out as employment opportunities increase so as not to discourage labour supply. Indeed, when food and fuel prices skyrocketed early in 2008, and as the contagion from the global financial crisis hit a few months later, the Fund insisted that countries boost spending on social safety nets as a condition for assistance. For example, to secure an IMF loan of about $8bn at the end of 2008, Pakistan had to agree to treble funding for programmes that included cash handouts and electricity subsidies. In this way, Fund conditionality has acquired a 'human face'.[26]

In another major change for the Fund following the 2008 crises, Strauss-Kahn acknowledged the powerful link between economic policies, poverty and social unrest that could lead to war: 'the threat is not only economic,' he said, adding:

> There is a real risk that millions will be thrown back into poverty. We must ensure that the voices of the poor are heard. We must ensure that Africa is not left out. This is not only about protecting economic growth and household incomes – it is also about containing the threat of civil unrest, perhaps even of war. It is about people and their futures.[27]

In addition to preserving social expenditure, the Fund has also been actively involved in finding ways to protect its membership from contagion from the global financial crisis. In July 2009, the IMF Executive Board approved far-reaching reforms of the concessional lending facilities for low-income countries, under a new Poverty Reduction and Growth Trust (PRGT), designed to be more flexible and more tailored to the different needs of these countries. The three facilities include: an Extended Credit Facility (ECF), to provide medium-term support; a Standby Credit Facility (SCF) to address short-term and precautionary needs; and a Rapid Credit Facility (RCF) to offer emergency support with limited conditionality.[28] The reform is expected to boost concessional resources by $8bn over the next two years – well above the $6bn in two to three years called for by the G20. It also entails exceptional interest relief (i.e., zero-interest payments) until the end of 2011, and permanently higher concessionality (proposed at 0.5% interest rate) until 2014.

Furthermore, in January 2010 the Board approved new eligibility rules for concessional financing. While in the past, eligibility followed the World Bank IDA criteria for entry into and graduation (exit) from the list of countries that are entitled to concessional financing, the Fund has now adopted differential criteria for graduation from the list. Following the IDA criteria for entry, countries become eligible for IMF concessional funding if their annual per-capita income falls below $1,135 (IDA revises this income threshold annually) and they have not had substantial access to international financial markets for an extended period of time. The Fund would be expected to graduate (or stop eligibility for this financing) if countries have: a persistently higher level of income exceeding twice the IDA threshold or capacity to tap the capital markets on a sustainable basis; and if the serious near-term risks of a sharp decline in per-capita income, loss of market access, and/ or debt vulnerabilities diminishes. The Fund updates the eligibility list regularly.

Although scarce concessional resources should be allocated to the most needy members, the Fund believes that premature graduation poses risks and that the country may need to re-enter the list in the future. The new criteria are aimed at reducing such occurrences. Under the new framework, small islands are granted exceptional treatment by having a higher income threshold compared with other small countries, because they face higher vulnerabilities.[29]

Although the main reason for these changes was to allow the low-income countries to weather the aftermath of the global financial crisis, there was an indirect positive impact on countries emerging from conflict, many of which are low-income countries. With the new infrastructure, and even without formal recognition of the special needs of countries in the transition from conflict, the Fund has made concessional financing rapidly available to many of these countries.

In 1995, the Emergency Post-Conflict Assistance (EPCA), became the first facility to address the specific needs of post-conflict countries.[30] At the time, the Fund expanded the scope of its Emergency Assistance Facility for countries recovering from natural disasters, creating two separate facilities, the Emergency Natural Disaster Assistance (ENDA) and EPCA. Since 2001, donors subsidised interest but only for countries with a good track record on economic policymaking that made them eligible for the Poverty Reduction and Growth Facility (PRGF), the facility that preceded the PRGT. This same eligibility test was used for countries applying for debt relief under the Highly-Indebted Poor Countries (HIPC) Initiative of the World Bank and the Fund.

Through the new PRGT framework, low-income countries affected by conflict can have a higher level of access to financing, more concessional terms, enhanced flexibility in programme design, and a more focused, streamlined conditionality than under the EPCA. The PRGT framework will allow the Fund to be more responsive to the immediate needs of low-income countries coming out of emergencies. As an example, the Fund disbursed $114 million to Haiti through its Extended Credit Facility for budgetary support immediately after the January 2010 earthquake. On 21 July 2010, the

Executive Board of the IMF also approved the full cancellation of Haiti's outstanding debt to the Fund of about $270 million.[31]

Although the new infrastructure is an important improvement in the way the Fund supports low-income countries, it is still inadequate for countries in the transition from war in important ways. Three points should be made. Firstly, the new framework improves the EPCA terms for conflict-affected countries that belong to the low-income group. Under the PRGT these countries will be unquestionably better off.

Secondly, the new framework does not contemplate concessional funding for higher-income countries in the immediate transition from war or under special circumstances that may lead to their relapse into conflict. Thus, countries like Bosnia[32] and Iraq, for example, are excluded, despite the fact that they find the terms of EPCA or Stand-By Arrangements (SBAs) particularly harsh.[33]

Thirdly, through the PRGT framework the Fund envisages that countries that have economic and financial vulnerabilities should continue to have access to concessional financing, even if their income is high and their access to capital markets sufficient to graduate. However, the Fund has graduated from the list some conflict-affected countries which are vulnerable to relapse or to increased political turmoil, such as Pakistan, Sri Lanka and Angola. Bosnia and Iraq should have concessional financing on the same grounds, since they have been unable to create functioning economies that could allow them to stand on their own feet and build sustainable peace.[34] The Fund has kept Georgia in the list because of its short-term economic vulnerabilities, such as the lack of jobs for the reintegration of displaced populations (without which renewed conflict is a distinct possibility), rather than the more serious and unresolved political problems.[35]

How to improve BWI support: areas for debate

The experience of reconstruction over the last 20 years reveals how countries in the transition to peace have virtually an even chance of reverting to war or ending up highly aid dependent. On one hand, there is clearly a need for disbursement of aid on concessional terms from the BWI, the regional banks, and other donors as war or chaos ends, when expectations for change and the chances of relapsing into conflict are highest. On the other hand, there is a need to withdraw this aid as soon as possible and create functioning economies in which people can have a visible improvement in living conditions. For this to happen, sustainable job creation is imperative.

The high expectations built up as countries embark in this transition are difficult to satisfy; unrealised expectations are perhaps the main cause of relapse. The BWI could play a more constructive role in ensuring that this does not happen by recognising the special needs and constraints of countries in the transition from war.[36] Working together, these institutions could have a major impact in setting up the bases so that these countries can achieve job-creating, equitable, and sustainable growth.

The macroeconomic framework

Debate on how these institutions could use their expertise, policy advice, technical assistance, and financial resources in the most effective way should focus first on the macroeconomic framework. Because of the characteristics and constraints of countries coming out of war discussed earlier, the framework needs to be as simple and flexible as possible to allow governments to play an active role in reconstruction. The simpler it is, the lower the level of expertise necessary to operate it will be, and the fewer the opportunities for mismanagement and corruption. A flexible framework will also make it easier to integrate the peace and development objectives of post-conflict reconstruction.[37]

With the support of the IMF, complex and inflexible macroeconomic frameworks have been set in countries such as Afghanistan and Iraq in the past. In Afghanistan, for example, the complete independence of the central bank and a no-overdraft rule for budget financing (stipulating that all expenditure be covered by revenue, including grants) proved too restrictive.[38] A more flexible framework and targets in the PRGF programme would have allowed the government in 2007 to engage in deficit financing for subsidising cotton, for example. The government could have used this to establish a level playing field with the production of poppies so that farmers would have been indifferent between the two financially and would have planted cotton, as they had done in the past. This could have had an important security impact at the time when the growing insurgency was strongly financed by drug money. The government did not have the option of using aid for this purpose, because donors were channelling 80% of their aid outside the government budget.[39]

The BWI need to debate the appropriate macroeconomic framework for countries coming out of war. This is particularly timely following the global financial crisis, which showed that central banks, both in the US and Europe, had flexibility and used it to do whatever it took to keep economies from falling into depression, even if their actions diverged from their prime focus on monetary stability. Countries in the transition from war desperately need to have and use such flexibility.

Microeconomic framework

A good macroeconomic framework and management is necessary but not sufficient for the reactivation of investment, trade, and employment. Countries in the transition from war will, however, also need to improve the domestic business climate – all those factors that affect decisions on investment, including its potential return and risks. This is an area in which the World Bank plays the leading role and in which there is a lot of room for improvement, since creating a favourable business climate in the aftermath of war has proved particularly challenging.

In particular, the BWI need to think of ways of strengthening their assistance to governments in creating the right financing mechanisms for new start-up companies as well as the expansion of existing ones; in building up human skills required by agriculture, mining and manufacturing; in creating an appropriate and just framework for domestic and foreign investment; and in building up physical infrastructure.

The current fragmented approach is ineffective. The BWI could assist governments in creating a matrix with the different activities that need to be carried out for effective reconstruction, according to their priorities. The matrix would identify each activity, the organisation that would carry it out, the financing required, the source of the financing, and the target dates for implementation. This could help to promote an integrated approach to reconstruction and ensure that donors do not overlook key government priorities.

Social spending and poverty alleviation
As a result of the global financial crisis, the IMF has placed an increased emphasis on preserving social spending in borrowing countries. Some of these countries were already coping with high food and fuel prices in 2008, before the financial crises hit them. Maintaining spending on health and education in low-income countries required increased flexibility in public expenditure targets in IMF programmes. Of the 19 low-income country programmes initiated in 2008–09, 16 budgeted for higher social spending. As part of the new lending framework for the low-

income countries, the IMF expects that programmes will be able to set explicit targets for safeguarding social spending.[40]

In the past, the negative impact of the Fund's programmes on social spending in poor countries was one of the most oft-repeated criticisms of this institution. The new Fund practice seems to address the problem head on for low-income countries.[41] For countries in the transition from war, however, this creates two problems. Firstly, while low-income countries may be able to reprioritise government spending in the aftermath of the global financial crisis, as the Fund expects them to do, the factors that justify concessionality in countries coming out of war will still be there. Secondly, many conflict-affected countries are not included in the low-income group and the new framework does not apply to them. It is thus important that the Fund examines how best to create a framework for its support of conflict-affected countries on a more permanent and comprehensive basis so that these countries can improve social development.

There is no time when aid is more critical to providing minimum levels of social services and infrastructure than in the aftermath of conflict. The World Bank plays a major role in catalysing resources from donors, administering multi-donor funds, and providing resources from the SPF. One issue to be considered is how the World Bank could become more effective in centralising all information on aid to countries coming out of the transition.[42] Another issue is how mechanisms can be established to ensure that donors deliver on pledges they make at donors' meetings (concerning funds channelled through trust funds under World Bank administration). The case of the Haiti Reconstruction Fund is a good example of the gaps that often exist between pledges and disbursements, which affect reconstruction negatively. $5.3bn was pledged to restore social services and infrastructure at the donors' meeting in March

2010, but six months later the World Bank, as fiscal agent for the fund, had received formal confirmation of only $100m of the $500m that would be channelled through it.[43]

While maintaining best practices in transparency and accountability regarding how money is spent, the trust funds administered by the World Bank could themselves be made less bureaucratic and more efficient, so that money gets to those in need quicker. Slow disbursement of the trust funds in Afghanistan, for example, has been a big problem, particularly since a large portion of its aid continues to be channelled outside the government budget.

Food security

Moving from food aid to food security in the aftermath of war – in countries that often suffered major environmental degradation or required the clearing of landmines as a prerequisite to agricultural production, and which lack credit facilities – has proved challenging. At the same time, given the importance of agriculture in many of these economies in terms of employment, exports and GDP, an integrated rural development programme is key to helping these countries to stand on their own feet.[44]

This is another area in which a broader debate is necessary to discover how best the World Bank can assist countries coming out of war in creating more integrated, rather than fragmented approaches to rural development,[45] and in establishing effective power, water, irrigation and human-development systems that are key to recovering agricultural production, food security and environmental sustainability.

The BWI should also explore ways in which different subsidies could be used most effectively during reconstruction to help wean the country from food aid and to promote food security. These institutions have resisted subsidies in the past, as they have resisted controls on capital movements. Since they have been willing to revise their entrenched position on capital controls, they should perhaps now also debate the issue of subsidies.[46]

Such a review is timely since fertiliser and seed subsidies have worked well in some countries, as recognised even by the Fund.[47] The lack of subsidies, together with reductions in tariffs and other trade restrictions encouraged by the BWI have damned many of these countries to rely on food imports.[48] Subsidies have an impact on the population at large. Reducing them may be a desirable reform, but if it is carried out too drastically or at the wrong time, it may have an adverse political, social and security impact that may jeopardise the transition to peace, as it did in Iraq. To quote scientist Normal Borlaug, who created high-yielding wheat varieties to stave off famine: 'world peace will not be built on empty stomachs or human misery.'[49]

Natural-resource exploitation

Two main issues arise in post-conflict countries with regards to natural resources. The first issue relates to the dilemma that countries in transition from war face in opening up their natural-resources sector to foreign investment. If they open it early on in the transition, their decision could indicate their commitment to an open trade and investment regime, and act as a confidence-building measure to promote investment during reconstruction. However, if they delay until there is improved security and political conditions, and a better legal and regulatory framework, they will see the value of their natural-resource assets increase. The second issue relates to the need to ensure that future generations also enjoy the benefits of such resources. Through the provision of advice and technical assistance to governments making these choices, the BWI have played a key role in this area. There are several issues that the BWI need to address to find ways to support conflict-prone countries more effectively to ensure that the exploitation of natural resources does not become a new source of conflict during reconstruction. These include finding the right framework for the equitable and sustainable exploitation of natural resources; effectively training local people in the skills required by the mining sector;[50] exploring ways to best preserve water supplies and the environment;[51] ensuring that the distribution between present and future generations through the creation of resource funds or other means is just and efficient; finding ways to invest the proceeds from mineral exploitation effectively in infrastructure and other public goods;[52] and proposing ways to add value to mineral production through business development.

Looking at the specific features and uses of resource funds may also provide insights. Chile was able to carry out countercyclical policies during the global financial crisis and avoid a recession because it saved part of the revenues from copper resources. Part of those resources was also used to finance reconstruction after the February 2010 earthquake.

Poor countries affected by conflict have differed in their attitudes towards resource funds. While the BWI promoted putting all proceeds from oil and gas into a fund in Timor Leste and spending only the revenue from that fund into reconstruction, Vietnam resisted an IMF recommendation to save some of its oil windfall in 2006 and 2007. Hanoi argued that it would be better off using the windfall upfront to increase investment and deal with huge gaps in public infrastructure.[53] Thus, it is not just the institutional organisation of resource funds that needs to be examined, but more importantly, the way that the BWI can help the countries to ensure that expenditure from these funds is effective in building up the necessary capacity and infrastructure to create functioning and employment-creating economies.

Conclusion

In the context of the post Cold-War record on conflict resolution, economic reconstruction involves much more than the rebuilding of physical and human infrastructure per se. It requires the adoption of stabilisation and structural reform policies and the design of an appropriate institutional, legal and regulatory framework so as to create market-friendly economies and reactivate broad-based economic growth. This is why the BWI have played such an important role in the reconstruction of countries emerging from war.

Analysis reveals major changes in the way these institutions have supported countries in this transition from war to peace. The World Bank and the IMF have come a long way since they mechanically supported countries emerging from war in the same way and with the same financing mechanisms applied to other countries, a practice that often endangered peace processes. Both institutions – at least at their highest level – have recently recognised the political constraints of economic policymaking and the need to integrate economic and political factors. At the same time, they have both become more open in engaging with a broader audience, including civil society, academics and other stakeholders in debating how best to assist countries coming out of crisis.

The focus of such debate so far has been on how the BWI can best support countries affected by higher food and fuel prices, or by contagion from the global financial crisis. It is now time that the BWI engage in a focused debate on how best to assist countries that are either emerging from conflict and remain likely to relapse into it, or those that have become or are becoming aid dependent. A well-integrated approach between these two institutions could assist countries emerging from war to improve the dismal record they have had in the last 20 years through effective reconstruction. Without this, countries will still fail to move onto a sustainable development path and peace will remain elusive.

Following the recent global financial crisis, the Fund has adopted the practice of creating informal, independent, high-level groups of advisers to discuss the specific regional needs of its membership and how it can support them. Members of these groups include prominent policymakers, private-sector executives, academics and civil-society representatives. The World Bank is already engaged in a process of consultation in relation to their study on conflict and development.

Given all these factors, now seems like the perfect time for the BWI to promote a broad-based debate on how best to design and coordinate their assistance to conflict-affected countries. This could include re-examining the respective roles of national governments and the BWI to best assist countries in reconstruction. In this context, it is necessary to consider the set of policies, practices and instruments that could improve these countries' chances of creating sustainable employment, avoiding aid dependency and moving to normal development in a reasonable timeframe.

As Strauss-Kahn and Zoellick have argued, getting the economy right and addressing threats to its stability can play an essential role in fostering the conditions for peace. It is only by securing development that we can break the cycle of fragility and violence.

CHAPTER FIVE

Aid and Fiscal Capacity Building in Post-Conflict Countries

James K. Boyce

In attempting to support the transition from war to peace, the international community often provides substantial assistance. This aid can play an important role in meeting pressing social needs and building a durable peace, but it would be naïve to assume that positive outcomes are the automatic result of good intentions. An important dimension of the impact of aid in what are optimistically called 'post-conflict settings' is the extent to which it helps build the fiscal basis for a sustainable state – that is, governmental capacities to mobilise domestic revenue, allocate resources through the budget and manage public expenditure.

Sooner or later, however, the flow of aid will diminish and responsibility for ongoing public expenditures must be shouldered by the government. A crucial issue in post-war transitions is, therefore, the building of state capacities to collect taxes and to allocate and manage expenditure. All too often, however,

James K. Boyce is Professor of Economics in the Department of Economics and Political Economy Research Institute, University of Massachusetts, Amherst. This chapter is based on the author's paper, 'Post-Conflict Recovery: Resource Mobilization and Peacebuilding', prepared for the Expert Group Meeting on Post-Conflict Recovery and Economic Insecurity, United Nations Department of Economic and Social Affairs, November 2007.

members of the international community have regarded the building of fiscal capacities as a niche issue than can be left to the international financial institutions to address through technical assistance. This stance of benign neglect can have malign results.

'Dual public sector' or dual control? External support for domestic expenditure

Donors often channel a large share of their resources away from the state, relying upon external agencies and private contractors to carry out the work, a policy rationalised on the grounds that state institutions are incompetent or corrupt. The result is a 'dual public sector': an internal sector that is funded and managed by the government, and an external one funded and managed by the donors. In terms of the sheer amount of money, the latter frequently dwarfs the former.

Whatever its merits, the 'dual public sector' strategy has several adverse consequences: firstly, and most evident, is the failure to tap external assistance to build the state's own fiscal capacities. Secondly, and no less seriously, is the 'crowding-out' effect as professionals are recruited into the external public sector, often for salaries that the government cannot match. Ironically, aid donors then point to a lack of capable government personnel as a rationale for continuing to bypass the state. Thirdly, the fact that the external public sector is managed by numerous agencies, each with its own priorities, poses enormous coordination problems. Last but not least, there are no institutional mechanisms that make donor agencies accountable to the local citizenry. No matter how imperfect the degree of democratic governance, the state arguably has a comparative advantage in this respect.

Donors maintain that they (and the non-governmental organisations and private contractors on whom they often rely) do a more effective job than the government in delivering goods and services. Undoubtedly there are situations in which the short-term advantages make a compelling case for circumventing the state, as when the government is incapable of meeting immediate humanitarian needs. But once we recognise that the long-term aim of aid is – or ought to be – to build state capacities as well as to deliver services in the short run, the argument for the dual public sector loses at least some of its force. Moreover, experience shows that the 'short run' invoked by donors can last a long time. In Cambodia, where more than a decade has elapsed since the United Nations transitional administration handed power to a new government, the donors' focus on delivering results still leads them to 'bypass when possible – and capture when not – the Cambodian civil service,' and that spending on technical assistance remains two to three times greater than the total wages paid to government civil servants.[1]

Concerns about corruption in the internal public sector are often a significant impediment to channelling more external assistance *through* the state. Corruption saps the delivery of public services, deters private investment and fuels popular discontent. But not all corruption is equal, nor is it equally corrosive: in some cases it is driven entirely by individual greed, but in others it provides patronage resources for wider networks. An example of the latter is the use of government revenues and profits from state-sanctioned monopolies to lubricate neopatrimonial governance in the Palestinian Authority.

Donors often adopt an avoidance strategy towards corruption: they seek to avoid aid 'leakages' by bypassing the government and they seek to avoid public discussion of the topic for fear of ruffling political feathers. This strategy is dysfunctional in three respects. Firstly, aid that is routed outside the government is insulated from neither the perception nor the reality of corruption. Indeed, the lack of transparency and accountability mechanisms can fuel public perceptions that externally administered projects are even more prone to corruption than government projects. Secondly, the avoidance strategy fails to harness aid to build state capacity to budget and manage public expenditure effectively. Thirdly, it sends an unmistakable signal to the populace: the government cannot be trusted. This has a negative feedback effect on domestic revenue mobilisation, insofar as the willingness to pay taxes hinges on perceptions that the state will deliver services in return.

An alternative strategy for addressing problems of corruption would have two prongs. The first is to devise transitional assistance programmes for people who have been dependent on patronage networks, recognising that corruption for such 'neopatrimonial' purposes differs from personal corruption. Such assistance would be analogous, in a sense, to job training programmes for workers displaced by the effects of trade liberalisation in industrialised countries, and to the disarmament, demobilisation, and reintegration (DDR) programmes for ex-combatants that are often implemented in post-war countries.

The second prong of an alternative anti-corruption strategy is the use of dual-control systems to build institutions for accountability and transparency alongside public expenditure capacities. The Afghanistan Reconstruction Trust Fund (ARTF), a World Bank-administered account through which donors help to fund government expenditures for salaries and other non-investment items, offers an instructive model for how aid can be rerouted through the government – in effect, helping to internalise external resources[2]. The Afghan government allocates these external resources through its internal budgetary process, reinforcing the budget as the central instrument of policy. When the ministries spend the money – for example, in paying teachers – an external monitoring agent appointed by the World Bank verifies that the accounting standards of the ARTF and government (which are the same) have been met, and releases the funds. In this way the ARTF is like a bank account with a fiduciary screen, similar to the dual-control arrangements established in Liberia under the Governance and Economic Management Assistance Programme (GEMAP).

Channelling aid through the government in this fashion does not imply that the donors abdicate control or responsibility for how their resources are used. Two signatures are required to release funds: one from the government and one from the external monitoring agent. The result is a dual-control system – a set-up analogous to the dual-key system used to prevent an accidental launch of nuclear missiles.

Priming the pump? External support for domestic revenue mobilisation

In many post-war settings, a central task is to raise domestic revenue to provide sustainable funding for new democratic institutions and for expenditures to improve well-being, strengthen public security and ease social tensions. Typically, the amount of government revenue relative to gross domestic product in war-torn societies is far below the average for other countries with similar per capita income.[3] Yet the needs for government expenditure are, if anything, greater. Hence concerted efforts are needed to increase revenues.

Experience has shown that aid can 'crowd out' domestic revenue mobilisation, reducing the incentive for the government to tax its own populace. The international community can support government efforts to mobilise domestic revenue in four ways: (a) by providing technical assistance; (b) by linking some of its aid to progress in domestic revenue performance; (c) by helping to curb taxation by non-state actors (sometimes called warlords); and (d) by reducing tax exemptions on post-war aid.

Technical assistance (TA) is the most common type of support. The IMF, World Bank and bilateral donors have helped to develop revenue capacities, ranging from drafting tax codes to setting up special tax administration units within finance ministries and providing special training and higher pay in an effort to insulate them from corruption.

In some cases, TA providers have shown an impressive ability to cast aside orthodoxies and adapt their policy advice to local realities. For example, despite the aversion of the IFIs to trade taxes, import duties were recognised as the most feasible source of revenue enhancement in Afghanistan, Kosovo and Timor Leste. In the case of Timor Leste, the IMF even supported the introduction of a levy on coffee exports.

The effectiveness of TA could be further strengthened by efforts to adopt technologies and procedures that build on existing capacities, rather than opting for off-the-shelf imported solutions. In Afghanistan, for example, former finance minister Ashraf Ghani, in his 2007 book *Fixing Failed States*, recalls that computerised information systems introduced at the Ministry of Finance were 'unsuitable in terms of complexity and language', prompting subsequent efforts to retool with Persian-language systems from Iran. More attention to training local personnel could also foster capacity building. Emilia Pires and Michael Francino, who served as planning secretary and cabinet member for finance in Timor Leste's transitional government, remark that the concentration on expatriate advisory services in Timor Leste was accompanied by 'some neglect for formal training programs for national staff'.[4] Put another way, the donors in this case appeared to be overlooking the ultimate goal of technical assistance: to make themselves eventually redundant.

Conditionality is a second way that donors can encourage domestic resource mobilisation. On the expenditure side of fiscal policy, it is not unusual for donors to require counterpart funding from the government as a condition for providing aid to specific projects, a strategy intended to ensure domestic 'ownership' and to counteract fungibility (whereby aid merely frees government money for other uses). It would be a straightforward matter to link certain types of aid – notably budget support – to progress in meeting domestic revenue targets. Such a policy is akin to the provision of matching grants by private foundations. In both cases, the aim is to strengthen incentives for aid recipients to seek further resources, counteracting the disincentivising effects of unconditional aid.

Visiting Guatemala in May 1997, a few months after the signing of that country's peace accords, IMF Managing Director Michel Camdessus took a step in this direction when he said that the Fund's only condition for a stand-by agreement would be that the government complied with its peace-accord commitments, including a 50% increase in the revenue-to-GDP ratio.[5] Similarly, the European Union conditioned its budget support for the government of Mozambique in 2002 on increases in domestic revenue.[6] And one of the benchmarks in the Afghanistan Compact signed in London in early 2006, which sets out the framework for international assistance to that country over the next five years, was to increase the revenue from 4.5% of GDP in 2004/05 to 8% in 2010/11.[7] These examples of efforts to link aid to domestic revenue performance remain the exception, however, rather than the rule.[8]

Curbing taxation by non-state actors is a task located on the cusp between public finance and security. When profits from the exploitation of nominally public resources – for example, Cambodia's forests or African minerals – flow into private pockets, this not only deprives the state of revenues but also often finances quasi-autonomous armed groups that threaten the peace. When local warlords levy 'taxes' on trade, sometimes including trade in narcotics, as in Afghanistan, they undermine the state's monopoly not only on revenue collection but also on the legitimate exercise of force. Curtailing such activities may require international assistance. Yet peacekeeping forces, even those with a relatively expansive mandate like the International Security Assistance Force (ISAF) in Afghanistan, typically have not seen this as a part of their job.

Powerful members of the international community may be reluctant to crack down on extra-legal revenue exactions when they regard those involved as political allies. In Afghanistan, for example, efforts to consolidate revenue in the hands of the state and to fight drug trafficking have been complicated – to put it lightly – by the decision of the United States government to enlist anti-Taliban warlords as partners in its 'global war on terror'. Such marriages of convenience, reminiscent of US support to the anti-Soviet mujahadeen in the 1980s, may serve short-term security objectives, but in the long term they undermine the legitimacy and effectiveness of the state – and ultimately security.

Reducing tax exemptions on post-war aid flows could do much to prime the pump of domestic revenue-collection capacity. In the first post-war years, aid often is the single biggest component of the formal-sector economy. Yet today aid flows, and many of the incomes generated by them, are tax-exempt. The incomes of expatriate aid officials and aid workers are often tax-free. The incomes of their local staff, often quite high by local standards, tend to enjoy similar status. Goods imported by the aid agencies, ranging from Toyota land cruisers to cases of Coca-Cola and whiskey, and rents paid by expatriates for office space and housing – again, often exorbitant by local standards – may also be tax-free. So are other services provided to them, such as hotel accommodation and restaurants.

These pervasive exemptions have several adverse consequences. Most obvious are the forgone government revenues. In addition, scarce administrative capacity is devoted to administering different rules for different people. Goods that enter the country as aid may wind up on sale in local markets, undercutting legitimate competitors who pay import duties. Last but not least, the special treatment accorded to expatriates again sends an unmistakable message to the local populace: rich and powerful people do not have to pay taxes. The result can be 'the creation of a culture of tax exemptions', in the words of a recent IMF review of post-conflict experiences.[9] This runs precisely counter to efforts to establish effective and progressive revenue collection systems and undermines the credibility of international agencies when they argue that governments should reduce tax loopholes and tax incentives for local businesses.

Efforts to tax aid bonanzas have met with determined resistance from donors. In Timor Leste, efforts to tax the floating hotels in the Dili harbour that accommodated the post-war influx of foreigners were rebuffed by lawyers at United Nations headquarters in New York, on the dubious grounds that diplomatic 'privileges and immunities' extend to those who provide services to UN personnel. In Afghanistan, the introduction of a tax on rental incomes generated by expatriates in Kabul likewise met resistance; as Ghani remarks: 'the international community's declarations on the importance of enhancing domestic revenue mobilisation have not been matched by willingness to consider new initiatives to tap the revenue possibilities generated by their own presence.'[10] This issue has often pitted the IMF and World Bank, along with national officials, against other donor agencies. In Timor

Leste, Pires and Francino recall 'bitter fights between international officials at the Ministry of Finance and international officials of donor organizations … with the latter winning'.[11] Similarly, non-governmental organisations (NGOs) 'ferociously defended every inch of ground' in resisting taxation of even their local employees: 'Even when UNTAET (the United Nations Transitional Administration in Timor Leste) offered to pay the taxes of international staff working with NGOs provided they were prepared to declare the income they were receiving, the answer was still "No".'[12]

Donor officials argue that paying taxes amounts to budget support. While this is true, its implicit premise – that the government cannot be trusted to use tax revenues well – again sends a negative message to the local populace. Donors also argue that expatriates are already paying taxes in their countries of origin. In cases where this is so, existing tax treaties allow credits for taxes paid elsewhere, thereby avoiding the problem of double taxation. Income-tax payments by expatriate or local aid personnel would not need to come from their own pockets. Those who pay taxes could be given salary 'top-ups' to maintain their after-tax incomes. This is the current practice for US citizens employed by the United Nations, World Bank and IMF.

Initiatives to tap aid inflows for domestic revenue could also take the form of 'payments in lieu of taxes' (PILOTs), a solution that has been adopted in many college towns in the US where municipal governments want tax-exempt institutions of higher education to contribute to the funding of public services such as schools, police and fire protection. PILOTs maintain the legal privileges of the payee, while at the same time opening the door for those donors who are serious about building domestic revenue capacity to act without waiting for across-the-board solutions.

Fiscal policy through a conflict lens

Fiscal policymaking in post-war settings requires careful attention to priorities. Faced with many pressing needs – for spending in areas such as public safety, the demobilisation and reintegration of ex-combatants, health, education, and the rehabilitation of economic infrastructure – how should scarce resources be allocated?

The synthesis report emerging from the World Bank's multi-year research programme on violent conflict observes that the need to consider peacebuilding alongside economic impera-tives 'creates the potential for trade-offs between policies that promote growth and those that promote peace'. For example, a strategy focused exclusively on short-term economic returns might concentrate spending on the capital city and developed regions, leading to 'a trade-off between the growth-maximising geographic distribution of public expenditure and a distribu-tion that might be regarded as fair'. [13] Where such trade-offs exist, the report concludes, 'the government may need to give priority to policies for peacebuilding'.

When public expenditure is viewed through a conflict lens, it is impossible to separate the question of 'what' from that of 'to whom?'. As shown by researchers at the UK-based Institute of Development Studies, grievances rooted in distributional inequalities are often important drivers of conflict, but these inequalities themselves tend to worsen during conflict:

> The already poor often lose the few assets they have, and looting adds to the number of poor. In contrast, warlords and their followers accumulate assets, and so while the early years of peace may see quite rapid growth it can be very narrow in its benefits – unless policies are put in place to restore the productive assets and human capital of the poor.[14]

Two distributional issues are particularly relevant in public expenditure. The first is how to incorporate distributional concerns into spending decisions. The second is how to allocate expenditures across the political landscape so as to bolster incentives for the implementation of accords and the consolidation of peace. Conflict-impact assessments should address both sets of issues. These are analogous to environmental-impact assessments, first introduced in the 1970s, with the difference that here the concern is the social and political environment rather than the natural environment. Conflic-impact assessment aims to incorporate the 'negative externalities' of social tensions and violent conflict. International aid agencies increasingly recognise the need for these assessments as an input into policymaking and project appraisal, and some have begun to put this recognition into practice.[15] Yet efforts to incorporate distributional considerations into expenditure decisions in post-conflict countries are still at an early stage.

Information on vertical equity – the distribution of benefits across the poor-to-rich spectrum – is sometimes collected and sometimes used as an input into policymaking. In many cases, however, even such basic data are not available. The paucity of information is even more severe in the case of horizontal equity (distribution across regions and groups defined on the basis of race, ethnicity, language or religion). In the past decade, researchers have analysed the role of horizontal equity in the genesis of civil wars, and economists have begun to think hard about how to measure it.[16]

Collection of regional data on expenditures in administrative units, such as states, provinces and districts, would seem to be relatively straightforward, both practically (since ministries often allocate their funds across regional units) and politically (since regions can often serve as a proxy for more sensitive categories such as ethnicity). Yet today even such data are remarkably few and far between. Ashraf Ghani and his colleagues at the Institute for State Effectiveness recount their experience in Afghanistan:

> Obtaining the figures on provincial expenditures from line ministries required months of intense discussion and analysis of manual systems of recordings. When the figures were first presented to the Cabinet, it came as a shock that the ten poorest provinces of the country were receiving the smallest amounts of allocation.[17]

Some researchers have suggested that conflict is better understood as being driven by polarisation rather than inequality per se.[18] Polarisation refers to the interaction between alienation (across groups) and identification (within groups). Income polarisation, for example, is more extreme when the gap between rich and poor is wider (resulting in greater alienation between the two), and when income inequalities within the rich and within the poor are lower (resulting in greater identification with others in the same income group).

When economic polarisation (in the distribution of income, wealth, or other attributes such as employment, education, and health) aligns with social polarisation (the distribution of the population into identity groups based on race, ethnicity, language, religion or region), the potential for violent conflict may be multiplied. In a working paper written for the International Peace Academy in New York, Ravi Kanbur explains its effects:

> Polarisation of society into a small number of groups with distinct identities is an incubator of conflict on its own. But add to this the dimension of average income differences between the groups, and a combustible mix is created.[19]

This insight brings us back to the importance of horizontal inequality. The phenomena of between-group alienation and within-group identification have important implications for the role of 'social capital' in the dynamics of peacebuilding. Social capital – trust, norms, and networks that facilitate coordination and cooperation – is often regarded as wholesome and beneficial. But it can also have a dark side, insofar as it enables some groups to cooperate more effectively to the detriment of others. Drawing a distinction between 'bonding' social capital that promotes trust and cooperation within groups and 'bridging' social capital that promotes these between groups, As Robert Putnam acknowledges in his book *Bowling Alone: The Collapse and Revival of American Community*, 'some kinds of bonding capital may discourage the formation of bridging social capital and vice versa'.[20]

During civil wars, group identity can be expressed through violence ('bonding social capital') such as expropriation of property or businesses, pillaging, rape and murder. Meanwhile, bridging social capital is destroyed, with consequences that can be just as serious as losses of physical capital. In the Bosnian war, for example, the destruction of the medieval bridge at Mostar came to symbolise the breakdown of trust between Muslim Bosniaks and Catholic Bosnian Croats. During war-to-peace transitions, therefore, an important aim of public expenditure, and of public policies more generally, is not simply to build generic social capital but rather to build specifically those types of social capital that reduce inter-group alienation.

Cross-group associational ties cannot always be promoted in harmony with other goals of economic policy. One example of this is the potential for trade unions to serve as important arenas for cooperation across ethnic and religious cleavages; hence 'reducing the power of trade unions is an example of a policy that is often put forward in the name of increasing efficiency, but could have the long run result of increasing group tensions.'[21]

A further dimension of the 'who' question in post-war settings relates to balances of power among and within competing political parties and their supporters. This requires attention not only to community-wide characteristics such as living standards and ethnicity, but also to the stances of individual political leaders who often vary in their commitment to peace. Selective allocation of public spending can be one instrument with which to reward those who are committed to peace, penalise spoilers, and encourage the undecided to back peace implementation.

Distributional impacts need to be considered on the revenue side of fiscal policy, too. Inattention to 'who pays?' questions in revenue policy is dysfunctional for three reasons: firstly, because the conventional wisdom that distributional concerns should be addressed on the expenditure side of fiscal policy alone rests on a textbook 'optimal planner' model that does not fit reality; secondly, because even optimal planners would need full information on the distributional impacts of revenue policies to achieve their targets; and finally, because if the public believes that it matters how the tax burden is shared out, then politically it does.

Little has been done, however, to integrate distributional concerns into revenue policies in war-to-peace transitions. The primary revenue goal of post-war government authorities, and of the international agencies that seek to assist them, has been to increase the volume of collections; the secondary goal has been to do so as 'efficiently' as possible. To be sure, increasing the volume of revenue is a central task. And efficiency – if understood in terms of the realities of war-torn societies, as opposed to textbook axioms – is desirable. But neglect of the distributional impacts of taxation can subvert both of these goals.

The starting point for any effort to address this issue must be careful documentation of the distributional incidence of revenue instruments both vertically and horizontally. Collecting the necessary data will be a major task, for today there is a paucity of such information even in 'normal' developing countries, never mind in war-torn societies.[22] This can be contrasted with the situation in industrialised countries, where the distributional impacts of proposed taxes are typically subjected to intense scrutiny by politicians and policymakers alike. Ironically, it is precisely where the need for such analysis is greatest – in societies embarked on the fragile transition from war to peace – that these issues receive the least attention. Technical assistance from the international community could play a valuable role in filling this information gap.

Documentation is only the first step. The second is to incorporate this information into policymaking. In choosing the mix of revenue instruments – the balance between tariffs, value-added taxes and income taxes, for example – their distributional incidence must be considered alongside their revenue potential, administrative feasibility, and efficiency effects. One option that would be likely to receive much more attention is luxury taxation. Taxes on items such as private automobiles and private aircraft would be easy to administer and progressive in terms of distribution, and could raise substantial revenue. Remarkably, these rarely feature in discussions of post-war revenue policies.

Finally, information on the distributional impacts of revenue instruments, and on the ways that government policies are taking these into account, must be disseminated widely to the public, so as to generate trust and facilitate compliance. The importance of this was demonstrated vividly in Guatemala, where the peace accords set explicit targets for increasing government revenue and social expenditure. The first post-war government attempted to increase the tax on owners of large property. This effort was scuttled, however, in the face of protests not only from estate owners but also from indigenous smallholder farmers who thought that the tax would burden them.[23] The lesson is clear: successful revenue policymaking cannot be a purely technocratic preserve; it must be part and parcel of the democratic process.

Thinking about tomorrow, today: Getting serious about fiscal sustainability

External resources that are spent today often have implications for how domestic resources must be spent tomorrow. This is true both for recurrent expenditures, including salaries, and for capital expenditures that will require spending for operation and maintenance in future years. Hence there is an evident need to think about the long-term fiscal implications of current decisions.

In the aftermath of war, attention to pressing short-term needs is perfectly natural and valid. But this does not imply that the future consequences of today's decisions can or should be shunted aside for others to handle later. When building new government institutions and infrastructure, budget constraints must be borne in mind. It would be a mistake to rely on a transitory flush of external funds to create structures that are not fiscally sustainable. The point may seem obvious, but past experience suggests that it is often ignored.

Consider, for example, security spending in Afghanistan, where the Afghan National Army has been built with significant funding from the United States government. According to a World Bank report, security-sector expenditures in the three-year period from 2003/04 to 2005/06 were equivalent to nearly 500% of the Afghan government's revenue, or roughly a third of the country's GDP.[24] 'Total security expenditures will

exceed forecast domestic revenues for some years to come,'
warns the document, describing the situation as 'unaffordable
and fiscally unsustainable'.[25] Even from a security standpoint,
unsustainable expenditures are short-sighted. A well-equipped
army that is not being paid ceases to be a security force; instead
it becomes an insecurity force. A Global Monitoring Report
prepared jointly by the United Nations Development Group
and the World Bank in 2005 draws the clear lesson from such
experiences: 'It is important to ensure that security issues are
treated as an integral part of the national planning and budgetary process, rather than through separate forums which may
lead to a lack of transparency or the taking of decisions which
are fiscally unsustainable or undermine other reconstruction
efforts.'[26]

Capital investments with high operation and maintenance
costs also generate fiscal burdens further down the road. In
Palestine, aid donors have often ignored the development
plans of the Palestinian Authority (PA), 'undercutting any PA
effort to monitor the cumulative long-term costs of donor-
financed investments'.[27] Closely related to this problem is the
bias of many aid-funded projects in favour of excessive reliance on imports. In deciding the extent to which the goods and
services should be imported or procured locally, donors again
face a trade-off between short-run expediency and long-run
capacity building – the capacity in this case being in the private
sector. There are undoubtedly cases where the former trumps
the latter: for example, where local sourcing would require
large investments with long gestation periods. But there are
also cases where local procurement could do more to stimulate
economic recovery, and perhaps save money in the process.[28]

To cite an example of the pervasive bias against local suppliers, during the United Nations Transitional Administration in
Timor Leste, some 250,000 desks and chairs for local schools

were purchased with money from the World Bank-administered Trust Fund for East Timor. At the time, some officials suggested that some of these be procured locally to spur the growth of small and medium woodworking enterprises, but this was rejected on the grounds that local procurement would be too slow.[29]

The interwoven challenges of building an effective state, a robust economy, and a durable peace all require thinking about tomorrow, today. Post-war inflows of external assistance cannot be sustained indefinitely. The success of aid ultimately rests on whether the structures built with it can be sustained without it.

Conclusion

A key statebuilding challenge in post-conflict countries is to build fiscal capacity (the state's ability to raise revenue, allocate resources, and manage expenditure to meet the needs and expectations of the population). These fiscal capacities do not arise by spontaneous generation. They must be developed with deliberation and care.

Well-designed international aid can assist in this vital task, but ill-designed aid can subvert it. When aid bypasses the state and creates a dual public sector – one funded by domestic resources and the other by external resources – a result can be the crowding out of state capacity to allocate resources and manage expenditure. When external resources act as a substitute for domestic resources, rather than serving as a complement to them, a result can be the crowding out of state capacity to raise revenue. When the distributional impacts of expenditure and revenue policies are ignored in favour of a single-minded focus on economic growth and efficiency, a result can be the exacerbation of social tensions that jeopardise the peace. When short-run targets swamp long-run needs, a result can be an unsustainable state and an unsustainable economy.

The obstacles to successful post-war reconstruction and peacebuilding are not only located within the war-torn societies themselves. They are also deeply rooted in the policies and priorities of the international community and donor agencies. Many business-as-usual practices – including the pursuit of commercial objectives, incentive structures that prioritise 'moving the money', and deficits in transparency, accountability and coordination – are ill-matched to the requirements of peacebuilding and state-building.[30] More effective aid for the reconstruction of war-torn societies will require the reconstruction of aid itself.

CHAPTER SIX

Valuable Natural Resources in Conflict-Affected States

Päivi Lujala, Siri Aas Rustad and Philippe Le Billon

Introduction

Revenues from high-value natural resources such as oil, gemstones and timber, or minerals such as coltan, present both opportunities and challenges for countries in transition from war to peace. Resource sectors can greatly assist in post-conflict economic recovery by attracting foreign investments, developing infrastructures, and generating tax revenues and local incomes. Yet resource sectors can also finance leaders or parties who seek to undermine a political settlement for their own interests (known as 'peace spoilers'), negatively affect local populations in resource-exploitation areas, and aggravate perceptions of government incompetence and corruption. Addressing these opportunities and challenges is particularly

Päivi Lujala is a Post-Doctoral Fellow in the Department of Economics, Norwegian University of Technology and Science, and an Associate Researcher at the Centre for the Study of Civil War, Peace Research Institute Oslo. **Siri Aas Rustad** is a PhD student at the Centre for the Study of Civil War, Peace Research Institute Oslo. **Philippe Le Billon** is Associate Professor in the Department of Geography and the Liu Institute for Global Issues, University of British Columbia. This chapter is partially adapted from Siri Aas Rustad, Päivi Lujala and Philippe Le Billon, 'Building or Spoiling the Peace? Management of High-value Natural Resources in Post-Conflict Countries', to be published in Lujala and Rustad, eds, *High-Value Natural Resources and Post-Conflict Peacebuilding* (Earthscan, forthcoming in 2011).

important in the many post-conflict countries that are heavily reliant on resource sectors. In Algeria, Angola, Timor Leste and Sudan, to name a few, resource sectors account for up to 60% of GDP and 90% of government revenue.[1]

The stakes of post-conflict resource management are high given that countries with valuable natural resources are more likely to experience armed conflicts, which furthermore tend to last longer, be more severe and more likely to relapse after peace has been established.[2] In Angola, Liberia, Myanmar, Papua New Guinea, Sierra Leone and many other countries resources have played an important role in motivating or at least financing hostilities. All these issues make management of resources and revenues a primary concern in many resource-rich, post-conflict countries.

Yet it remains possible for countries in transition from war to peace to reap greater benefits from resource sectors to help achieve durable peace, with increased welfare and long-term economic growth. Crucial issues include maximising revenues for post-conflict governments, redrafting contracts that were poorly negotiated by previous authorities, such as a major iron ore-mining contract in Liberia, and better controlling resource exports, such as diamonds in neighbouring Sierra Leone.[3] But there is a delicate balance to be struck: poor contract renegotiation can deter further investments, while a crack-down on 'illegal' exports can greatly undermine informal trans-border economies.

Furthermore, additional tax revenues do not automatically translate into more welfare, growth and peace. For that to happen, revenues need to be spent wisely. Resource-revenue dependence is generally associated with poor economic and political performances, and many countries with poorly managed resource revenues suffer catastrophic outcomes when it comes to the well-being, life expectancy or educational opportunities for their citizens. Such outcomes are disastrous for long-term peacebuilding.

High-value resources and armed civil conflicts

There is good statistical and anecdotal evidence linking valuable natural resources and armed conflicts.[4] Using comprehensive data on all armed civil conflicts in the world, various resource variables such as production and dependence, as well as other relevant aspects such as political regime, economic perform-ance and ethnic composition, researchers have established that the presence of high-value natural resources is related to a heightened risk of conflict onset and to longer and more severe conflicts. Valuable natural-resource sectors can contribute to armed conflicts in several ways.[5] Indirectly, resource sectors can impact negatively on economic performance, the quality of institutions and society in general. Directly, revenue distri-bution inequalities and the negative side effects of resource exploitation – whether real or perceived – can increase conflict risks, while access to revenue can motivate or simply finance belligerents.

The specific characteristics of resources – such as their legal-ity, mode of exploitation, livelihood impacts and divisibility – present different challenges and opportunities for peacemak-ing initiatives. Responding to conflicts involving narcotics, for example, poses a dilemma.[6] Legalising production is rarely an official option for governments and even less so for intervening countries. Yet some governments nevertheless select this option to secure a conflict settlement, support local allies, reduce levels of violence and sustain local livelihoods – not to mention the benefits they derive from narcotics revenues. Foreign forces intervening in the conflict will themselves have to face a similar dilemma, and make choices that influence their relations with local populations and entrepreneurs. In the case of diamonds, governments may have the choice between privileging heavily mechanised international companies in the hope of raising greater revenue and curtailing potential leakages to peace spoilers, or leaving the sector wide open to artisanal mining in the hope of providing employment.[7] In Sudan, agreement over the temporary sharing of oil revenues could postpone the resolution of the oil fields' ownership and thereby help move towards a peace accord between the Sudan People's Liberation Movement and the Sudanese government.

Resource capture

Valuable resources may increase the risk, duration and severity of war by motivating and financing belligerents. Among the most well-known examples of this are 'conflict diamond' revenues, which funded a brutal insurgency in Sierra Leone for most of the 1990s and allowed the main Angolan rebellion to continue fighting for nearly another decade after the end of the Cold War deprived the warring factions of their main sources of backing.[8] There are also numerous examples of secessionist movements occurring in resource-rich areas, such as in the Angolan province of Cabinda, the Niger Delta region of Nigeria or South Sudan. Resource capture is frequently part of the agenda of armed rebellion, whether it is to fund the movement, attract supporters, enrich its leaders, secure allies, or establish future resource control. In turn, the characteristics of resource sectors can affect the strategies, conduct and trajectory of these armed groups.[9]

Unequal revenue distribution and negative side effects

Unequal distribution of natural-resource revenues – real or perceived – may create severe grievances, especially if a region with abundant natural resources is deprived of revenue flows but must bear extraction costs such as environmental degradation and appropriation of land. This is particularly true if the resource-rich region coincides with ethnic, religious or other group cleavages, as for example in the cases of Aceh or South Sudan. In Niger, Tuareg rebel groups have waged a low-intensity conflict against the government in the distant south since the early 1990s, arguing that Niamey gathers uranium revenues without distributing them back to the north. Even in the absence of measurable adverse effects on income level or distribution, discoveries and exploitation of valuable natural resources can increase frustrations – and conflicts – due to rising expectations.

Pollution, loss of land and land rights, and population displacements are common, negative externalities of natural-resource extraction. The large copper mine on Bougainville island in Papua New Guinea brought large revenues for the company, Bougainville Copper Ltd, and the central government, but some islanders perceived mining as environmentally and socially destructive. Frustrated about lack of compensation for environmental damage and unfair revenue sharing, local residents attacked the mine in 1988. The repressive government reaction led to an escalation of the conflict into a decade-long civil war, the closure of the mine and international intervention led by Australia.

Political and economic underperformance

Examples of resource-rich countries with poor political and economic performances abound. Nigeria is an oft-cited example, as are Iraq and the Democratic Republic of the Congo (DRC). The Nigerian government is estimated to have earned $1.6 trillion worth of oil revenues over the past four decades, yet poverty in Nigeria sharply increased during that period as the country experienced recurrent political crises and poor governance.[10] Iraq and the DRC are also highly resource-dependent, but with levels of resource exploitation far below their massive potential. In both cases, heavy reliance on resource wealth not only contributed to poor governance and bad political decisions (the botched nationalisation of the Congolese economy, for example, or the disastrous Iraqi wars against Iran and Kuwait), but these had ripple-effects on investments and market integration. Resource-rich countries do not have a monopoly of underperformance, but resource wealth sustains poor governance and inefficient economies, while resource dependence leaves little opportunity for alternatives to emerge.

Inefficient revenue spending, rent-seeking, commodity-price instability and institutional deterioration are among the main explanations for chronic underperformance. Windfall gains are frequently squandered, thanks to a combination of short-termism, populism and dreams of 'national greatness' resulting in overspending and poor investment decisions. Politicians may use the revenues to secure popular support and thus seek to meet popular requests even if these do not serve the long-term national interest. Alternatively, governments can draw on the easy revenue source to become less accountable to the population and pursue the interests of a small, predatory elite.

The negative impacts on the economy, institutions and society in general generate grievances that can promote unrest and even conflict. Several empirical studies document that a low level of income itself is an important factor in predicting conflict: armed civil conflict is more likely to occur in poor countries than in rich ones. Research also shows that weak institutions and lower state capacity are positively correlated with an increased likelihood of conflict. In most cases war will further erode the economy and governance institutions, causing economic and political havoc and making peace even more difficult to reach.

Increasing government's share of revenues

Managing resource extraction is challenging in most circumstances, but it is particularly so in post-conflict settings. There is a 'rush' as foreign companies and local entrepreneurs compete for access to newly opened resource areas, and domestic authorities and international donors see resource sectors as a means to rapidly increase foreign direct investments and tax revenues. Whether through a lack of competent management, pressure to get extraction under way or simply the lure of high concentrations of valuable minerals, a single poorly negotiated contract for a major mining venture can undermine state revenues for decades. The iron-ore contract in Liberia mentioned above was initially awarded for 25 years. At the same time, unofficial and illegal production and smuggling – by civilians, government officials, soldiers and ex-rebels – may deprive the state of large amounts of revenue. Contract renegotiations and commodity-tracking systems are thus important tools for states to secure greater revenues.

Contracts

Past contracts signed under the duress of conflict by hard-pressed, incompetent or corrupt government officials are often not in the best interest of the post-transition government and population. Sometimes illegitimate governments or rebel groups may even swap present or future extraction rights for security services, as in the case of South African mercenary outfit Executive Outcomes in Sierra Leone's diamond sector. In the immediate aftermath of conflict there is often a shortage of competent management staff. Governance structures are often in a state of flux, with transitional authorities and the legacies of past management regimes blurring the boundaries of legality and 'good' practices, all of which feeds into uncertainty over policy and legislation. The contracts signed *during* the conflict and those agreed consequently by transitional governments often have very favourable terms for the companies. This is also the case for new contracts, which tend to be hastily put together to attract major investments. Such was the case with a rutile mining agreement in Sierra Leone in 2004, which according to reviews resulted in an estimated loss of tax income of about $5 million per year.[11] It is clear that contractual reassessment via renegotiation, outright cancellations, and the careful drafting of new contracts should be part of the peace process in many resource-rich post-conflict countries. Renegotiations of previous conflicts can improve the conditions, as in Liberia, where President Ellen Johnson-Sirleaf was able to revise and sign a significantly improved iron-ore mining contract with a major steel manufacturer in December 2006, replacing the previous contract signed with the transitional government in August 2005.

Unfortunately, contract reappraisal has proven to be a slow and contentious process. In the DRC, the parliamentarian (2004–05) and inter-ministerial (2007) commissions reviewed all mining contracts, but little came out of the reviews as the recommendations were left largely unexecuted. In Liberia *all* timber concessions were cancelled in 2006 following a review of timber-harvesting contracts, and a wide forest-sector reform successfully set stringent conditions for new contracts. The revocation of timber concessions and the reform itself have been deemed successful, even a 'model' case, but critical voices have been raised since the broad reform effectively stopped all large-scale timber harvesting, frustrating companies and those that would like to see more revenues flow to Liberia's strained budget.[12]

The meagre outcomes from such measures can be partly explained by low levels of expertise, insufficient government budgets, outright corruption and lack of support from heads of state and government. Therefore, donors should encourage contractual reassessments by providing technical assistance and budgetary support to contract-review committees, as in the DRC, where the World Bank and the Belgian government provided funds for some of the commissions reassessing the legality of mining contracts. More broadly, donors could contribute by supporting resource-policy reforms that provide greater tax revenues, employment opportunities and government accountability. Donors should also support legislative, judicial and civil-society mechanisms that carry out these reforms. Given that sound and robust institutions are key to reaping the benefits of resource exploitation and avoiding the 'resource curse', external donors could make up for potential revenue losses during review and reform periods.

Commodity-tracking systems

The original objective of commodity-tracking systems is to follow the path taken by commodities from production to consumption in order to curtail rebels' access to resources. It is not war-time smuggling – be it by former rebels, corrupt government officials or civilians who may rely on it for their survival – to continue unabated after the conflict. Commodity tracking schemes play an important role in eradicating and formalising clandestine resource exploitation and trade, with the latter directing more revenues into state coffers. In Sierra Leone, for example, state revenues from rough-diamond exports grew from less than $2m a year in 2000 to $150m by 2009 as clandestine production and smuggling were brought into daylight with a certification system.[13] This shows the potential of commodity-tracking systems to bring in long-sought revenues. Resource companies themselves may have an interest in these tracking systems if only to assuage consumer concerns and distinguish their 'conflict-free' products from those of companies not party to the tracking scheme.[14]

The Kimberley Process Certification Scheme, established in 2003, is the best known and most advanced tracking system to date. First implemented in Sierra Leone, the diamond certification scheme substantially decreased illicit rough-diamonds trading.[15] This has increased the revenues of many diamond-exporting countries, including Sierra Leone as noted above, as a growing proportion of mining activities and exports are officially recorded.

Other relevant commodity-tracking schemes include the European Union's Forest Law Enforcement, Governance and Trade (FLEGT) initiative, which seeks to implement a voluntary timber-licensing system for imports of forest products entering the EU market based on bilateral agreements between the EU and tropical timber-producing countries. The FLEGT is currently negotiating with two African post-conflict countries, Liberia and the Central African Republic. Several commodity-tracking initiatives have been proposed for the extremely resource-rich eastern DRC, which is plagued by violence. These include initiatives by the International Conference on the Great Lakes Region and the governments of Belgium and Germany to create a regional certification scheme for natural resources.[16] An example of industry tracking is the Tin Supply Chain Initiative (iTSCi) of the International Tin Research Industry (ITRI), which seeks to track the tin supply chain from mines in the eastern DRC to exporters.[17]

Management of revenues

Natural-resource revenues are often used to 'buy' peace. This can take the form of revenue sharing, payments and other compensations to ex-rebels in exchange for laying down arms, and providing immediate peace dividends such as clean water, food and other tangible benefits to the population. Revenue allocation can thus play an important part in mobilising resource sectors to build peace in the long term. From a peacebuilding perspective, an optimal allocation maximises both the political objectives of reconciliation as well as the economic objectives of broad development, benefiting society as a whole. Institutional quality is a key driver in this allocation process.

Buying peace through revenue allocation

Natural-resource revenues provide incentives for warring parties to come to the negotiating table, whether for the personal interests of belligerents or as part of a broad political agenda seeking to address past grievances, redistribute entitlements over resource sectors, or redefine the regulatory framework of these sectors. Revenue sharing between state and producing regions is also a salient issue in peace negotiations. An effective agreement on revenue sharing may facilitate the positive conclusion of peace negotiations, as seen in Aceh, Bougainville and South Sudan. Revenue-sharing agreements, however, are no guarantee of durable peace; especially when rebel groups are only given nominal control over resources through a ministerial portfolio rather than a financial stake, as in Angola's 1994 Lusaka Protocol and Sierra Leone's 1999 Lomé Peace Accord.

There are different ways to allocate resource revenues. The most common way is to set up a system through which the local government receives a set proportion of revenues originating from resource exploitation in the region. Oil-producing regions in Nigeria, for example, receive 13% of revenue generated in their territory. Cabinda in Angola receives 10%, Aceh in Indonesia 70%, and South Sudan 50%. Local governments in Sudan have been granted the right to levy property taxes, royalties and excise taxes under the terms of the peace agreement. This right is also enshrined in the post-war Iraqi constitution adopted in 2005.[18] Direct revenue distribution to the population in the form of cash could provide a tangible 'peace dividend' and remove the spur of conflict where dispute over resource distribution has been a root cause of the conflict.[19] Revenues may also be used to compensate groups or regions that have disproportionally suffered prior to the conflict or during it. The 2005 Iraqi constitution, for example, recognises the need to compensate those ethnic and religious groups that suffered systematic abuses under Saddam Hussein's regime.[20]

In practice, setting up a revenue-disbursement system often means balancing between the requests of the producing regions and the needs of the country as a whole – since large transfers to the producing regions may undermine national development in the absence of alternative revenues – as well as between long-term development needs and more immediate needs such as health care, sanitation, and nutrition which are often paramount in the early peacebuilding phase.

Transparency and accountability in resource-revenue management

Although well-drafted contracts may provide the state with more revenues, and revenue sharing may enable a positive conclusion to peace negotiations, long-term settlement is jeopardised by unwise spending decisions. Consider that Nigeria has little to show for the estimated 29 billion barrels of oil pumped from its reserves between 1960 and 2009. The oil rents have fuelled widespread corruption both at the central level and in the oil-producing Delta region, which has experienced chronic unrest. Past attempts to 'pacify' or 'develop' the region have dramatically failed. Nigeria's experience underscores the fact that most high-value resources are non-renewable and therefore irrecoverably lost once exploited; the development benefits to the country from $1tr worth of exports over the last 50 years have been extremely meagre.[21]

Allocation of resource revenues is potentially the most decisive arena in which sustainable peace is built or the future is spoiled when it comes to high-value resources. Transparency and accountability have become key to attempts to foster improved management. Two parallel international initiatives have sought to increase transparency and accountability: the Publish What You Pay (PWYP) campaign founded by London-based NGOs including Global Witness, which focused on mandatory tax-payment disclosure by extractive companies through financial markets, and the UK government-initiated Extractive Industries Transparency Initiative (EITI), which sets norms of fiscal transparency for countries to voluntarily adopt. Both initiatives rest on the idea that an informed public can better hold their governments accountable. Informed and effective public oversight is often difficult to achieve where the government can restrict press freedoms and suppress civil society and political opposition. International supervision, through oversight committees (the Chad–Cameroon oil-pipeline project) or budgetary control (the Governance and Economic Management Assistance Program (GEMAP) in Liberia), can play a limited and temporary role. Such transparency and accountability mechanisms are now being extended to the expenditure side of resource revenues, as well as to the resource contracts.[22]

Conclusion: towards strengthening institutions

Historical and contextual factors are crucial when considering management options for resource sectors in war-torn societies. Central among these are the role played by resources in driving the conflict, the quality of governance institutions, the expectations and living conditions of local populations, and the characteristics of resource sectors. Unsurprisingly, badly governed countries with poor populations living in areas with easily 'lootable' resources are among the most challenging contexts, as suggested by the conflicts in Liberia or the eastern provinces of the DRC. Management priorities should also be set according to what the sectors can deliver in terms of peacebuilding: the priorities of small-scale logging companies providing building materials and local jobs should differ from those of large-scale mining projects generating important tax revenues. More generally, the legitimacy and implementation capacity of authorities should be taken into account when deciding the speed and depth of reforms. Liberia has implemented drastic reforms (in its logging industry, for instance), but to such a degree that some consider the changes a de facto embargo closing down the sector. Post-conflict interim governments made up of former belligerents should see their capacity to award long-term contracts curtailed; at the same time, international trusteeships could provide an opportunity to promote better norms of governance. Reforms conducted under UN's Transitional Administration in East Timor (UNTAET) in Timor Leste's oil sector, including renegotiation of oil rights with Australia and prudent macroeconomic management, have frequently been lauded.[23] Post-conflict election campaigns should also provide an opportunity to debate resource policy options and commit politicians to implement reforms once elected.

Setting up commodity-tracking systems, auditing and renegotiating contracts, agreeing on revenue-sharing formulas, and investing revenues efficiently and towards a goal of maximum long-term development depend to a large extent on the quality and capacity of governance. If resource revenues are swallowed by corruption (as in Nigeria, where even the 13% that is transferred back to the Niger Delta states disappears before reaching the population), or used to increase military power to repress the population, as in Myanmar, even large revenues will have no positive effect on development.

Sound, robust institutions, at both the national and local levels, provide the backbone of resource-revenue management and peacebuilding, and therefore institution-building should be of high priority in the immediate post-conflict period even when it is a long-term project with few immediately visible results. Sometimes it may be necessary to postpone the application of the principles of 'good governance' to end hostilities in the short run, as institution-building efforts may destabilise the peace negotiations. Institution-building is a challenging process in any society, and especially so in post-conflict society; planning for the process should start before the conflict is officially over.

The most relevant resource-management institutions are those providing the legal framework to establish property rights as well as to negotiate and enforce contracts, including for taxation purposes. These need to be rebuilt and freed from corruption and opportunities for fraud. An important step in managing this is establishing legal provisions. Domestic laws regarding high-value resources generally define the principles and objectives of the resource base and revenue management. In order to avoid revenue capture by narrow interest groups and to reduce risks of armed conflict, these laws should be based on principles of transparency, accountability, representation and equity.

Liberia provides an example of sector-specific institution-building. The post-conflict forest-sector reform in Liberia explicitly addressed the issue of good institutional and financial management in the Forest Development Authority that manages Liberian forests. Evaluations conducted during the reformation of the authority uncovered clear evidence of corruption and large-scale financial mismanagement.[24] In addition, it was established that the authority's staff was too large and that many of the workers did not have the required qualifications. Through training, restructuring and resizing its workforce, and implementing new financial management systems under the auspices of the GEMAP, the authority has been able to constrain fraud and corruption and improve efficiency.[25]

Valuable natural resources are a major asset for post-conflict recovery, but equally they present many challenges to peacebuilding. Resource sectors are prone to mismanagement, while the risks of resources funding peace spoilers and frustrating populations with high expectations for a 'peace dividend' are high. Natural-resource management should, therefore, be a priority for peacebuilding initiatives in resource-dependent countries, with a clear focus on building up the capacity of domestic institutions to collect and allocate resource revenues more effectively.

CHAPTER SEVEN

Foreign Direct Investors in Conflict Zones

Andreea Mihalache-O'keef and Tatiana Vashchilko

In the past three decades, investors have shown increased interest in the opportunities afforded by regions with unexploited resource and market potential. Although the majority of foreign direct investment (FDI) continues to flow between developed countries, investments in the developing world have risen at a steady pace. FDI is now the largest source of external finance for developing countries. In 2006, for instance, inward stock of FDI to developing countries amounted to about a third of their GDP, compared to just 10% in 1980. After 2003, FDI to developing countries grew steadily (at an average annual rate of approximately 20%) until late 2008, when the economic downturn in major export markets affected developing economies and the risk premiums of their sovereign and corporate debt increased considerably.[1]

Developing countries clearly rely on FDI as a major source of capital, which is an integral part of economic and political development processes. Firms also play active political roles in

Andreea Mihalache-O'keef is Senior Research Assistant at the Niehaus Center for Globalization and Governance, Princeton University; **Tatiana Vashchilko** is Visiting Assistant Professor of Political Science in the Department of Political Science, University of Rochester.

their home and host countries, using their financial power as political leverage.[2] FDI can thus shape the initiation, intensity and resolution of conflict both directly, through contributions to lobbyists, politicians or interest groups, and indirectly, through its effects on development and welfare.[3] Furthermore, different types of capital have different consequences, some beneficial to the host and some detrimental.[4] The success of conflict-prevention and management efforts might therefore increase with the ability to predict how much and what types of FDI a host at risk of increasing political violence can expect.

'Political violence' is defined here in the context of the risk-insurance industry as declared or undeclared war, hostile actions by national or international forces, civil war, insurrection, and civil strife, including politically motivated terrorism and sabotage. This generally implies the presence of armed conflict, internal or international. But can countries marred by political violence really attract foreign direct investors? Conventional wisdom answers, resoundingly: 'No.' Conflict increases non-commercial risks, such as regulatory risks, industrial espionage, security threats and disruption of operations. When selecting a location for a foreign affiliate,[5] investors are buyers of the investment environment produced by host states. Countries are suppliers in this market, competing for consumers (that is, foreign direct investors). Many developing countries actually market themselves to foreign investors, tourists and trading partners through Investment Promotion Agencies (IPAs) and other outreach initiatives. The product they sell is an investment environment more advantageous than any other. Recent or ongoing episodes of conflict damage this product and sully the reputation of its provider. Furthermore, the advantages firms seek when they internationalise are present in most developing countries. Since the market for FDI hosts is a buyers' market, it is highly unlikely that any rational investor would select a damaged good when the full-functioning alternative comes at a bargain-basement price.

It is certainly tempting to take this conventional wisdom at face value and forget all about foreign direct investment in countries with armed conflict. But a closer look reveals that countries plagued by political violence continue to receive FDI inflows. Even more surprisingly, these flows are not confined to mining operations, which are tied to specific locations because of the presence of natural resources.[6] For instance, a Hyatt Regency hotel opened in Kabul in 2003, at a time when Afghanistan faced civil conflict.[7] In 1998, when civil conflict in Angola took a toll of more than 1,000 human lives following two years of equally deadly conflict, AMT invested in a battery-manufacturing facility in this very country.[8] In Colombia, the Kimberly-Clark Corporation has been producing paper goods since 1991, despite ongoing civil conflict.[9] In Iraq, the Motorola Credit Corporation has been operating a cellular network since 2004,[10] a year when the conflict between insurgents and coalition security forces caused more than 1,000 deaths (more than 10,700 deaths were attributed directly and indirectly to the presence of coalition troops in the country that year, according to the Iraq Body Count website).[11] The Overseas Private Investment Corporation (OPIC), a US government agency that provides support and political-risk insurance for US firms investing abroad, records that at least some investors stay on and rebuild in environments with high political violence risk, such as Colombia, Haiti, Liberia, Rwanda and Sierra Leone.

To shed some light on the puzzle of foreign direct investments in war-torn countries it is necessary to examine how political violence affects foreign direct investors and what happens to such investments during and after episodes of conflict.

Table 1. Impacts of political violence on the operations of foreign direct investors as recorded in political-violence insurance claims submitted to OPIC

Threat type	Illustrative anecdotes
Direct destruction of assets	*Cross-fire* Nicaragua, 1979: American Standard lost more than $500,000 in inventory, equipment and buildings when its facilities, located strategically on the highway between Managua and the airport, were occupied as a defensive position, first by government troops and then by the Sandinistas. The insurgents and the National Guard took turns directing artillery bombardment and small-arms fire at American Standard's facilities (OPIC, American Standard 1979, pp. 6–7). *Looting and vandalism* The 1979 revolution in Nicaragua created food shortages. General Mills' plant in this country, producing wheat flour and animal feeds, lost a significant share of its grain inventories due to 'vandalism and looting by either the military forces or the civilian population or both' (OPIC, General Mills 1979, pp. 6–8).
Indirect destruction of assets	*Transportation delays* Haiti, 1994: The Charles Hoyt tannery watched $420,000 worth of hides and skins rot after uncertain political conditions caused delays in the delivery of necessary chemicals to the plant (OPIC, Charles Hoyt 1995). *Disrupted goods markets* Charles Hoyt's predicament worsened when the tannery's licence to import chemicals from and export processed skins to the US was revoked, as the US joined the UN embargo against Haiti (OPIC, Charles Hoyt 1995).
Increases in costs to firms	*Operating costs* West Papua, Indonesia, 1977: During an upsurge of separatist fighting, Freeport Minerals' copper mine became the target of dissident action. As the Indonesian government dispatched military units to protect it, the corporation incurred expenses 'totalling $17,024, related to the support of [government] military personnel engaged in security operations in the vicinity of its facilities' (OPIC, Freeport 1979, p. 12).
Increases in policy uncertainty	*'Good' changes* Dominican Republic, 1967: To avert an economic crisis following the 1965 coup against the Reid government, the US government provided incentives and guarantees for Chase Manhattan Bank and First National Bank to open branches in Santo Domingo (OPIC, Chase Manhattan Bank 1967; OPIC, First National Bank 1967). *'Bad' changes* In 1965, Western Hemisphere Enterprises, Inc., owners of an automobile-leasing operation in the Dominican Republic, submitted an expropriatory action claim in conjunction with its war claim. The company's 'politically powerful Dominican' partner used its connections in the post-coup environment 'to harass West. Hem. Officers and employees and to obtain physical control of the company's assets, books, and records' (OPIC, Western Hemisphere 1965, p. 2).

Consequences of political violence for foreign investors

To explain and predict FDI responses to political violence, we must first understand why and how political violence is important to foreign investors. OPIC's public records provide a window onto the lives of some multinationals with foreign affiliates in countries affected by conflict. OPIC was established in 1971 with the mission to help US businesses invest overseas, foster economic development in new and emerging markets, complement the private sector in managing risks associated with foreign direct investment, and support US foreign policy.[12] Towards these goals, OPIC provides political-risk insurance against currency inconvertibility (whereby the value of investments plummets due to hyperinflation or cannot be repatriated due to exchange restrictions), the expropriation of assets (such as technology, buildings, land, or revenue) by the state or another group, and political violence against US multinationals. Political violence coverage compensates for damage to tangible assets and for business income lost due to damage to tangible assets, or caused by violence undertaken for political purposes (such as declared or undeclared war, hostile actions by national or international forces, civil war, revolution, insurrection and civil strife, including politically motivated terrorism and sabotage). Two-hundred and seventy-nine claims have been settled by OPIC and its predecessor, the US Agency for International Development (USAID) since 1961[13]. Of these, 44 were for political violence.[14] Useful for our purposes, investors who make claims on their OPIC insurance provide detailed lists of the losses suffered, accompanied by reports of how the losses were incurred.

These accounts point to four broad types of impacts of political violence on the operations of foreign direct investors (as seen in Table 1). Most importantly, political violence directly destroys assets. At a minimum, civil war devalues assets, lowering their expected returns.[15] In many cases, however, political violence causes direct damages. Firms can be caught in the crossfire between the combatants; they can be directly targeted by the insurgents; or their assets can be lost for lack of law enforcement. Political violence can also indirectly destroy assets by disrupting labour and goods markets and causing transportation delays. In extreme cases, fear of death prompts abandonment of land and displacement of the population.[16] Firms lose access to crucial inputs or markets as conflict slows down production in upstream industries (which produce their inputs) or downstream industries (which consume their output). During conflict, more stringent security measures increase operating costs.[17] In some cases, costs increase because of guerrilla or paramilitary taxes, extortion, and kidnapping of employees for self-financing and rent-seeking purposes.[18] Safety from violence is not cost-free even in those cases where the host government provides protection. Transport costs also increase, due to the destruction of infrastructure and to the strategic value of fuel and vehicles by those engaged in combat. Finally, political violence increases policy uncertainty – after all, effecting policy change is the impetus for conflicts. Some policy changes can favour foreign investors, while others can harm them: claims for expropriated assets accompanied several political-violence claims to OPIC.

FDI patterns in countries affected by civil conflict

In 2004, the United Nations Conference on Trade and Development (UNCTAD) counted 'about 64,000 transnational corporations (TNCs) engaged in international production, with about 866,000 affiliates located abroad'.[19] Approximately a quarter of the TNCs and more than half of the foreign affiliates worldwide are located in developing countries.[20] Several of these affiliates operate in countries with high probabilities of conflict, or even recent or ongoing political violence. Overall levels of FDI fluctuate through episodes of political violence and in the aftermath of conflicts, but generally remain above zero. A reverse flow or negative FDI occurs when divestments are greater than investment flows for a given country and year, because 'at least one of the three components of FDI [equity capital, reinvested earnings and intra-company loans]

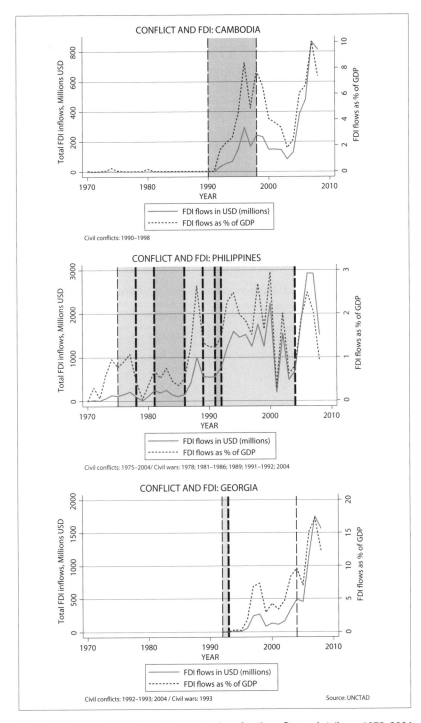

Figure 1. Patterns of FDI flows during episodes of civil conflict and civil war, 1975–2004

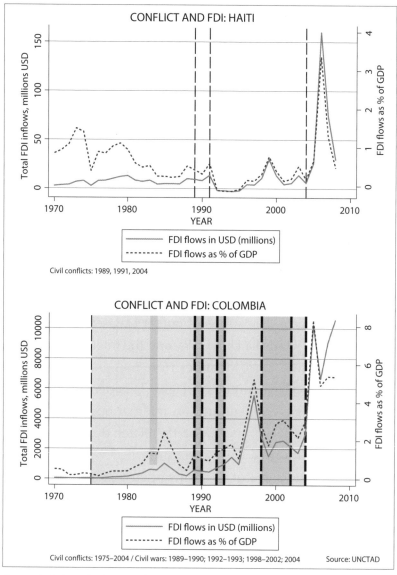

Figure 2. A closer look at FDI flows during episodes of civil conflict and civil war

is negative and not offset by positive amounts in the remaining components', according to UNCTAD analysis. On average, flows of FDI during episodes of conflict do not differ significantly from peacetime inflows. In fact, countries like Algeria, Cambodia, Ethiopia, the Philippines, Sri Lanka and Sudan register substantial increases in inward FDI despite political violence. For other countries, like Egypt, Georgia and Pakistan, FDI inflows are positive and relatively small while conflict is continues, but increase rapidly within a brief period after peace is re-established.

Haiti, for instance, continued to receive FDI inflows throughout episodes of political violence over the past 20 years (Figure 2). In 1989, an attempted coup against President Prosper Avril was accompanied by street fighting that disrupted productive activities across all economic sectors. The 1991 coup against President Jean-Bertrand Aristide also caused street violence, to which international organisations responded with trade embargoes lasting until 1996. In 2004, Aristide resigned amid public protest and violent clashes between government forces and armed rebels. The Armed Conflict Dataset, an analytical tool created by Uppsala University and the International Peace Research Institute, Oslo, identifies 1989, 1991 and 2004 as years of low-level internal conflict in Haiti. This denotes a conflict involving the government and an internal opposition group that causes between 25 and 999 battle-related deaths in a year.[21] Claims on political-violence insurance filed with OPIC indicate that at least some of the firms operating in Haiti during these episodes suffered losses due to the fighting. Yet, despite the exacerbated risk for investors, net FDI flows in Haiti rarely fell below zero.[22] In 1989, Haiti received $9.3 million in FDI, amounting to 0.4% of GDP, followed by $8m (0.3% of GDP) in 1990; these inflows are not significantly lower than in previous years.[23] In 2004, multinational corporations invested $5.9m (0.2% of GDP) in their Haitian affiliates.[24]

Colombia is another interesting case. Unlike Haiti, which has experienced brief and isolated episodes of violence in its recent history, Colombia has faced constant civil conflict since FARC (the Revolutionary Armed Forces of Colombia) was established in 1964 as a military wing of the Colombian Communist Party. Civil conflict in Colombia has repeatedly escalated to war, causing more than 1,000 deaths per year.[25] Nonetheless, during the past three decades, FDI flows to this country remained consistently positive and have, in fact, been on the rise. Total FDI flows in Colombia increased from $37m (or 0.2% of GDP) in 1975 to over $10 billion (or 8.3% of GDP) in 2005.[26] Since 1990, 35 investment projects grossing over $2bn and spanning all three economic sectors (primary, manufacturing and services) have been insured through the Multilateral Investment Guarantee Agency (MIGA, part of the World Bank Group) and OPIC.[27] As discussed below, some explanations for the observed resilience of FDI to conflict do exist.

Investors' diverse responses to political violence

The first explanation for the unexpected FDI flows to countries affected by civil conflict focuses on the demand side of FDI: the investing firms. Different investment projects face different levels of risks from the asset-obliterating effects of conflict; furthermore, not all projects can be relocated equally easily, regardless of the risks they face in the host country. On the supply side of FDI – the host countries that sell the investment environment – it should be noted that governments cannot credibly commit themselves to protecting firms from the material destruction associated with political violence. Governments can, however, take steps towards lowering the policy uncertainty associated with conflict. International law, specifically bilateral investment treaties (BITs), provides just the tool governments need to allay foreign investor concerns regarding future policies. Through BITs, government promises to foreign investors are sanctioned and monitored in the international arena, thus increasing the costs of reneging on commitments and increasing government credibility.[28]

Demand-side explanation: investor diversity

Every firm involved in FDI transfers a combination of physical assets (such as plant or equipment) and non-physical assets (technology, managerial know-how, marketing techniques and so on) to the host country, in order to establish a presence and operate there. The nature of the firm's investment dictates the mix of assets it owns in its host. A bank opening a new branch in a foreign country, for instance, invests a smaller share of its capital in physical assets than does a diamond producer opening a mine. The type of capital involved in a firm's foreign operation influences its susceptibility to destruction, either direct or indirect. Relative to knowledge capital and liquidities, physical assets can be more easily targeted and harmed during conflict.

The characteristics of inputs (labour and capital), as well as their relative intensities in the production process, vary widely across investments; so too do the characteristics of outputs. OPIC, for instance, assigns higher risk profiles to 'projects whose inputs and outputs are perishable'.[29] Furthermore, different types of inputs and outputs have different transportation needs. As a result, only some investors suffer when conflict renders roads and waterways unsafe, increases fuel prices, or damages infrastructure.

Finally, the host-country advantages sought by firms when investing abroad also matter for their vulnerability to political violence. These advantages differ by investment profile. Resource-seeking firms look for access to natural resources. Efficiency-seeking firms respond to factors that minimise their production costs, such as favourable government policies, an appropriately trained, low-cost labour pool, or good infrastructure. Market access appeals to market-seeking firms. Natural resources, unlike markets, inexpensive labour and investor-friendly policies, are globally scarce and geographically concentrated, limiting the relocation options of resource-seeking firms. While asset type and input/output characteristics affect firms' incentives to relocate when faced with political violence, the host-country advantages sought influence firms' ability to relocate. For, just as the different advantages sought by foreign investors have different geographic distributions globally and at the state level, so too do conflicts within countries. When the fighting is contained within a small and well-defined region, the risk to investors of operating elsewhere in the country is relatively low. In contrast, the presence of militarised violence within a country generates higher risks to investors relative to countries entirely at peace. Firstly, conflicts can spread easily. Secondly, host-government resources expended in the conflict are necessarily lost to production-enhancing activities (law enforcement, infrastructure development, human capital growth and so on). While the threats posed by political violence to investors are lesser in countries where conflict is concentrated, these threats are non-existent in countries at peace.[30]

Despite some degree of intra-sectoral differences, firms tend to share similar characteristics, and therefore the same vulnerability to conflict, within rather than across economic sectors. Primary-sector firms, with high intensity of physical assets and physical inputs and outputs, are likely to perceive political violence as threatening and to have strong incentives to relocate. However, their resource-seeking nature limits their ability to exchange hosts. Consequently, conflict ought to have no effect on primary-sector FDI. At the opposite end of the spectrum, service-sector firms, with relatively low physical capital and mostly non-physical inputs and outputs, perceive a relatively low threat from political violence. Their market-seeking nature allows them to relocate easily to violence-free hosts, but they have little incentive to do so. It is therefore unlikely there would be significant changes in FDI flows to the service sector as a result of conflict. Production in the manufacturing sector is typically characterised by a relatively high share of physical assets, potentially perishable inputs and outputs, and relatively high transportation costs. Overall, manufacturing investors tend to perceive a moderate to high threat from conflict. Their efficiency- or market-seeking nature translates into a large number of potential hosts. As a result, manufacturing FDI, with both incentives and ability to relocate, is prone to decrease during episodes of political violence.

A 2006 survey of executives[31] suggests a pattern similar to that described here: fewer investors in the services industries than in the primary sector perceive conflict as threatening.[32] Furthermore, sectoral FDI data show that manufacturing investors are more responsive to political violence than their primary and tertiary counterparts. In years with conflict, the share of manufacturing FDI in host-country GDP tends to decrease, but primary- and service-sector FDI remains unchanged.[33] In both years of peace and years of conflict, primary-sector FDI flows represent, on average, 1.4% of GDP, while service-sector FDI flows average 1.9% of GDP. Average manufacturing FDI flows are lower in years of conflict (1.1% of GDP) than during episodes of peace (1.5% of GDP).

This is the demand-side explanation for why FDI does not decrease dramatically in response to conflict: not all investors want or are able to leave. An investment decision, however, is the result of bargaining between prospective investors and prospective host countries. Government concessions or incentives for foreign investors matter to this decision as much as investor motivations.

Supply-side explanation: BITs as credible commitments by governments

Put in the simplest terms, governments 'supply' the environment for investments. Host states have a large range of incentives for foreign investors (by reducing or eliminating capital controls, for example, or by establishing special economic zones, reducing entry barriers for multinationals, or signing international investment agreements). However, not all these incentives attract FDI effectively. The 'dynamic inconsistency problem' (which arises when the future course of action formulated at the time of the investment ceases to be the optimal alternative for either the host government or the investor, and is not undertaken[34]) casts doubt on the credibility of government promises. Foreign investors are aware of the governments' incentives to expropriate or otherwise damage their operations once the investment has been made, in response to changing international and domestic circumstances. In this situation, only those governments who credibly guarantee *ex ante* not to infringe upon foreign investors' rights or property, despite changes in their incentives, can hope to attract FDI. This is especially true in the context of civil conflict, when policy, social and economic volatility peak, exacerbating the host state's lack of credibility.

Governments can commit themselves to treat foreign investments differently through either domestic or international law. Domestic law lacks credibility from the foreign investor's perspective because, at any point, a host country can 'change its domestic laws to suit its own purposes'.[35] International customary law[36] also lacks credibility, since 'the mechanisms for the enforcement of a contract between a state and a private firm are at best extremely weak and at worst altogether non-existent'.[37] Only international investment law providing 'a binding and credible contractual mechanism secured by the host' can truly protect foreign investments.[38] BITs meet these requirements.

BITs constitute legal arrangements between two countries with unique domestic political orders and unique bilateral politico-economic relations. Generally, BITs make provisions for various issues involving foreign investors, including compensation terms and the dispute-settlement mechanism in cases of civil conflicts, expropriation and the treatment of FDI. Because they specify rules for foreign-investor treatment and are adjudicated mostly in international rather than host-state courts, they are major contributors to the decline in non-commercial risks. Most home countries conclude [BITs] mainly to make the regulatory framework for FDI in host countries more transparent, stable, predictable and secure, thus reducing obstacles for future investment flows.[39] Currently, BITs represent almost half of the 5,600 international investment agreements in force.[40]

BITs affect FDI inflows to developing countries through three channels. Firstly, they serve as commitment devices.[41] Secondly, they provide costly signals (promises that, if broken, create large reputation costs to governments) that the host will treat investors well.[42] Finally, by imposing restrictions on host countries' sovereignty, BITs increase the bargaining power of multinational corporations relative to hosts.[43] Certainly, BITs differ in the scope of their terms, providing varying levels of protection to foreign investors across home and host countries. However, the presence of even one BIT can stimulate FDI inflows, credibly committing a host government to protect foreign investors' assets under any politico-economic circumstances, As such, they basically compensate for policy uncertainty associated with, among other things, civil conflict.

A cursory examination of general patterns of FDI, civil unrest and BIT ratification reveals some interesting relationships. Countries experiencing political violence often sign and enforce BITs. In fact, a country's history of civil conflict appears to correlate positively with the number of treaties entered into. In our sample, countries with a recent history of violence are bound by, on average, 15.5 BITs, while the average for countries with peaceful histories is only 13.7.[44] Furthermore, among countries with civil conflict experience, those that enter into more BITs tend to receive more FDI.[45] Still, the socio-political impact of any policy ought to be assessed prior to implementation: abuses of human rights and outright exploitation of workers are too high a price to pay in exchange for sustaining FDI inflows.

There is a clear relationship between conflict, BITs and FDI in several countries. For instance, during the 1975–2004 civil conflict in the Philippines, higher inflows tended to coincide with the country's ratification of additional BITs. The sharp increase in FDI to the Philippines after 2004 can be attributed, at least in part, to the additional international legal protection conferred on foreign investors by the 25 BITs enforced throughout the conflict. Colombia is another interesting case: the signing and ratification of its first BIT, with Peru in 2004, were paralleled by unprecedenced increases in FDI flows, despite the ongoing civil conflict. Peru's history of conflict, BITs and FDI tells a similar story. This preliminary evidence points to the effectiveness of international commitments (BITs in particular) as marketing tools for countries competing in the global market for FDI.

Lessons learned?

Despite the obvious risks, FDI continues to flow to countries affected by civil unrest. On the one hand, differences among investment projects lead to variations in both the threats perceived by individual investors and their ability to relocate to alternative hosts. As a result, only manufacturing investments decrease in the context of political violence. Manufacturing projects are vulnerable to violence because they involve a relatively large share of physical assets and inputs. However, they have many relocation options, which allow them to avoid conflict-torn countries. FDI flows in the primary and service sectors do not differ significantly in years of conflict relative to years of peace. The resources sought by primary-sector investors are location specific, making relocation difficult. Service-sector firms (such as communications, finance or banking firms) lack a strong incentive to relocate because they use predominantly non-physical assets that are relatively invulnerable to the threats of destruction posed by conflict.

On the other hand, some governments employ more effective marketing strategies, increasing the credibility of their *ex ante* commitments to investors through bilateral investment treaties (BITs). BITs alleviate investor concerns with non-commercial risks and increase their confidence that the host government will not treat them unfairly after they make their investment. BITs reduce the risk that host states will engage in predatory behaviour (including the expropriation of assets, technology theft, regulatory changes or tax increases) towards the investors within their borders, although such behaviour might benefit the governments in the short run. Host states that commit to investors through BITs tend to receive relatively high levels of FDI during and after periods of conflict. Although the discussion here has focused on militarised conflict, the reasoning (and therefore conclusions) could be extended to non-conflict (criminal) violence. Now, what are the policy lessons to be learned from all this?

The fact that not all types of FDI decrease during episodes of conflict, for reasons solely linked to the foreign investment projects, provides the first lesson: there is no need for over-arching FDI incentives. Narrow policies targeting firms in the industries most likely to divest because of conflict can be both effective and cost-saving, whether we think of costs as tax revenue or domestic political goodwill. Since FDI flows in the primary and services sectors are unresponsive to conflict for reasons inherent in the firms' activities, governments need not offer these firms any incentives in order to offset the costs of conflict. They will continue with their activities anyway. Instead, governments ought to focus their attention on manufacturing firms, which tend to avoid conflict. As discussed, manufacturing firms respond to efficiency and market advantages, which governments can enhance through pro-market policies, targeted tax breaks or relaxed labour or environmental regulation. If such policies offset the high expected costs associated with conflict, manufacturing firms may continue their activities despite political violence. This is particularly important, as research shows that transfers of production capital in the manufacturing industries are more important for development than either primary- or service-sector FDI.[46]

A further lesson applies to the credibility of policies relevant to FDI. Incentive policies or promises of protection for foreign investors do not count for much, unless governments back them through commitments under international law. BITs appear to be effective tools for attracting significant flows of FDI, especially for countries whose reputations have been tarnished by civil conflicts. Through such treaties, government promises to foreign investors are sanctioned and monitored in the international arena. As a result, governments pay high costs (both financial and reputational) for reneging on their commitments to investors, the prospect of which, in turn, increases their credibility. By reducing non-commercial risks, BITs offset the expected costs of conflict and reduce the likelihood that more investors will avoid conflict locations.

Finally, the patterns of investment identified here also present a potential solution for speeding up or consolidating peace. Those investors trapped in the host country (primary-sector companies) or forced to leave because of conflict (manufacturing firms) have a strong preference for peace and might take actions to ensure that violence is avoided.[47] When conflict is imminent or ongoing, primary- and manufacturing-sector investors can become powerful allies for host states or third parties interested in establishing and sustaining peace. Beyond their wilful actions, foreign investors can also indirectly affect conflict and peace processes through their presence and economic impacts. Most importantly, they create alternative employment opportunities for actual and potential rebels. Additionally, certain types of FDI (such as manufacturing or knowledge-intensive tertiary investments) increase wages for workers, thus increasing the opportunity cost of fighting. Furthermore, technology and know-how transfers that parallel FDI penetration can increase overall welfare in the host country. The presence and activities of foreign investors, particularly in the manufacturing and services industries, can also consolidate institutions rendering the host-country political environment less volatile. More jobs, higher incomes and stronger institutions reduce the probability that conflict will start and can ensure that peace is consolidated in the aftermath of violence. Thus, foreign investors have the potential to influence the dynamics of conflict and peace both directly and indirectly. Nonetheless, it is always true that the *raison d'être* of any corporation is profit maximisation, so while their input may sometimes be helpful, corporations ought not to be given carte blanche for participating in politics.

CHAPTER EIGHT

War Transitions and Armed Groups

Jennifer Hazen

Introduction

Insecurity is often a problem in post-conflict countries where there are numerous challenges to re-establishing the state, stability and security, and where evolving and newly emerging forms of insecurity threaten progress.[1] This is particularly true in settings where a security vacuum follows the end of the conflict (when the controlling regime, both state and rebel, gives way) and the resulting state apparatus is unable to provide security effectively. Violence, including a range of criminal and other unlawful activities, often remains at high levels after the end of intrastate conflicts. This violence can be war-related, but often it is not.

A key question is: who perpetrates this violence? Sometimes it is the former combatants, involving those unhappy with dispensations or the termination of the war. However, despite the ease with which government officials and communities point the blame at ex-combatants, there are often no statistics to support such accusations. It is easy to point the finger at the

Jennifer Hazen is a Postdoctoral Fellow at the University of Texas at Austin.

vague label and make 'ex-combatant' synonymous with 'criminal'. This may in part account for the focus of governments,
donor agencies and the United Nations on this particular category of people in post-conflict societies. But doing so denies
the growing evidence that many post-conflict situations,
where the lack of law-and-order and weak governance structures prevail, offer numerous opportunities for violent and
criminal activities that are not directly related to the past war.
Understanding post-conflict violence requires more than a
focus on ex-combatants.

Conflict-armed groups can continue to pose a challenge
after wars end, but in fewer cases than might be expected.
Many convert into political parties or simply fade away after
elections. The challenges they pose to the state and to law
and order vary. In some instances, the peace process breaks
down and the same rebel groups return to conflict.[2] In some
cases, new groups emerge or former rebel groups reform later
under new names and once again challenge the state.[3] In other
cases, the threat is not an armed group trying to overthrow
the government, but rather an armed group that arises in the
security-poor but opportunity-rich post-conflict environment.
These groups include gangs, organised crime, and drug cartels,
all of which pose challenges to law and order, and may raise
the risk of violence, but none of which directly aims to overthrow the state.

Ex-combatants are not the only type of armed group that
poses a threat in post-conflict settings. Armed groups can
emerge through conflict transformation processes in which
former combatants can join or create new types of armed
groups. Disarmament, demobilisation and reintegration (DDR)
programmes can be one way to address this concern, but such
programmes rarely track ex-combatants once they have finished
their short-term reintegration training programmes – making it

difficult to determine whether they are involved in armed-group activities. Armed groups can also strengthen or emerge through the transformation of their environments *during* conflicts due to the absence of the state, the lack of security and the economic opportunities available in conflict settings. Non-conflict groups, such as gangs and those involved in organised crime, are likely to try to maintain their activities in post-conflict settings, and will be difficult for weak states to address. Armed groups can also emerge in the security vacuum and in response to the evolution of economic opportunities, resulting in the rise of vigilante and criminal gangs. There is a clear need to look beyond the stereotype of ex-combatants as 'the bad guys'. Focusing attention on this group alone, when evidence suggests a wide range of actors is involved in post-conflict violence, ignores the realities on the ground and the broader panorama of violence that threatens stability and security.

Emerging from war: Post-conflict settings

Post-conflict states are often viewed as weak or fragile where the ability of the government to provide governance and security is limited or compromised. These states 'struggle to maintain a monopoly on the use of force, control borders and territory, ensure public order, and provide safety from crime ... [and] fail to meet the basic needs of their populations by making even minimal investments in health, education and other social services'.[4] Post-conflict states are also seen as potential incubators of crime that harbour opportunities for the emergence, growth and proliferation of criminal actors, armed groups and violence.[5] Such actors pose local challenges to law and order and to the state's monopoly on the use of force, can replace state security mechanisms in some areas, and present serious threats when they are capable of spreading security problems (for example, drugs, arms and violence) transnationally.[6]

The focus of peacebuilding on preventing a return to war has necessarily included a focus on ex-combatants, who are seen as the primary threat to the peace process. DDR programmes are quite common in post-conflict settings, despite the fact that many peace agreements do not contain specific conditions for disarming and disbanding conflict groups and reintegrating ex-combatants into civilian life.[7] DDR programmes face a number of challenges.[8] There are risks to the peace process that stem from: the failure of combatants to enter the programmes or to turn in their weapons; the exclusion of armed groups not part of the peace process; the failure to break chains of command and ensure the dispersal of combatants; the inability of reintegration programmes to provide sufficient training or for the economy to absorb those who are trained; and the poor stockpile management of weapons. Such lapses can leave guns in circulation, thousands of unemployed ex-combatants, and small groups of combatants under the leadership of their former commanders. This situation does not necessarily ensure a return to war, but it does provide the basis for organised violence in the post-conflict period.

It is widely asserted that, after the initial ceasefire, levels of violence increase in post-conflict settings.[9] This includes various types of violence: political, state, economic and criminal, and community.[10] However, measuring its rate and recording any increases in the initial post-conflict period is far from straightforward. Data is often poor in conflict periods, leaving little to compare the post-conflict period against. Criminal violence that may be obvious in a post-conflict period may have been less obvious or simply considered war-related during the conflict, leading to inaccurate reports of rises in criminal activities in the post-conflict period, when it is merely the continuation of past practices. Mechanisms to measure violence often improve as the post-conflict period progresses. But it can be difficult to determine if the rate is increasing or if data collection is improving. Citizens are often afraid to report incidents to the police after civil wars, but this can improve over time as the police demonstrate a willingness to uphold law and order, leading to more reporting, but not necessarily a higher rate of perpetration. Non-conflict violence is a problem in some post-conflict countries, but it is by no means clear that violence always escalates after war, nor is it easy to generalise about who is responsible for that violence.

Post-conflict settings are extremely difficult to manage. Although they may not be the safe havens for transnational terrorists and international organised crime that some believe them to be,[11] these conditions do present incentives and opportunities for a range of armed groups to emerge, persist or evolve. Yet it remains an open question of whether armed groups take advantage of what are often fortuitous circumstances in post-conflict contexts. An initial assessment of several post-conflict situations suggests that sometimes they do, and sometimes they do not; and when they do, different types of groups emerge depending on the circumstances.[12]

Pathways to organised violence after war

The following begins the process of developing a typology of pathways for the transformation and emergence of armed groups in post-conflict settings (see appendix 2) through the review of 12 cases of terminated intrastate conflicts.[13] Five pathways stand out as the most common. The pathways described here emphasise three elements: understanding what happens to conflict-armed groups, identifying post-conflict armed groups and identifying the threats these groups pose.[14]

Pathway 1 – Termination of conflict groups at the end of the intrastate conflict: What happens to conflict-armed groups at the end of an intrastate conflict depends on the way in which the war ends. In victories by the government, the rebel group is defeated and presumed defunct. In victories by the rebel group, the group takes power and the government military largely disbands. In negotiated settlements, the main parties to the conflict must agree to terms for managing the conversion of two (or more) warring factions into one state military. In many cases, rebel groups (and sometimes government forces) are offered opportunities to disarm and demobilise and return to society, with the intent of disbanding the conflict-armed group, as happened with the Revolutionary United Front (RUF) in Sierra Leone, and rebel groups LURD (Liberians United for Reconciliation and Democracy) and MODEL (Movement for Democracy in Liberia). In a number of cases conflict-armed groups transform into political parties and compete in the political arena through legitimate democratic means. Examples include the Farabundo Marti National Liberation Front (FMLN) in El Salvador, RENAMO or National Resistance Movement in Mozambique, and the National Union for the Total Independence of Angola (UNITA).[15] In these situations conflict-armed groups largely give up their means to return to conflict and pursue their goals via political processes. Whether disbanded or converted into political parties, the conflict armed groups no longer pose a pressing security concern for post-conflict efforts.

Pathway 2 – Continuation of conflict groups despite a formal peace process: Some conflict-armed groups persist as residual groups despite a formal peace process. This situation refers not to a breach of an agreed peace, but to those cases where not all of the armed groups who are party to a conflict are also parties to the peace agreement. Examples include the Salafist Group for Preaching and Combat (GPSC) in Algeria, the National Forces of Liberation (FNL) in Burundi, and the western militias in Cote d'Ivoire. In some cases, there is no formal peace process because rebel groups are weakened to the point of posing minimal threat to the government, such as *Sendero Luminoso* (the Shining Path) in Peru.

These residual conflict-armed groups can continue to pose challenges to the state when they remain intent on over-throwing it. They may not always be large enough to depose the government, but continued clashes affect the capacity to implement any peace agreements, to provide security to the population, and to move forward with recovery efforts. Failure to address these groups allows them to regroup and rearm and, ultimately, can enable a renewal of the conflict. In all cases these groups remain perpetrators of violence outside the control of the state and therefore a threat to law and order and to individual security.

Pathway 3 – Transformation from conflict-armed group to another form of armed group: After war a conflict-armed group may transform into another type of armed group. In Nicaragua ex-combatants disarmed and demobilised following the end of the 1980s civil war, but then banded together in gangs as a way of regaining their lost social status and providing a form of commu-nity security. By the early twenty-first centruty ex-combatants had aged out of the gangs. Many had married, started families or taken jobs, and the gangs once again took on a new form. This incarnation was more violent and criminal in its activity, and less related to community protection.[16] In Colombia, demo-bilised pro-government paramilitary groups transformed into organised criminal gangs.[17] In Algeria, the residual GSPC, which never participated in the peace process following the civil war, transformed into a transnational terrorist organisation, al-Qaeda in the Islamic Maghreb (AQIM). In Sierra Leone, politicians remobilised ex-combatants into security squads, effectively groups of political thugs, for the 2007 elections.[18]

The nature of the threat posed by the transformed group largely depends on the type of group that emerges. Localised gangs threaten public security, but often remain minimal threats to the state. Terrorist organisations can threaten the state, and pose broader regional or even international threats. AQIM transformed from a local problem into a transnational threat; although operating locally, AQIM claims links to al-Qaeda's global jihad. Organised criminal groups rarely threaten the state directly. Instead, their illegal activities pose a challenge to law and order. Organised criminal activities are driven by economic profit, which can be threatened by high levels of violence, thus organised crime groups would prefer non-interference from the state rather than antagonistic engagement.[19] The mobilisation of political thugs for electoral gains is common in many countries, not just post-conflict countries. Their use can weaken the democratic system, exchanging political power for military power, and establish a precedent for violence as a means of achieving political goals. Such practices can also provide a basis for the emergence of anti-state armed groups, as happened in the Niger Delta following the 2003 elections.[20]

Pathway 4 – Transformation of previously existing non-conflict group into strengthened armed group: During and after conflict, previously existing non-conflict groups have transformed into groups that are stronger, and often more violent. In El Salvador, common street gangs evolved into today's *maras*, a type of gang that is much more organised, violent, and powerful than those existing before or during the war. A number of factors contributed to this change: the influx of ex-combatants into the gangs, the return of refugees from the United States, the deportation of arrested Salvadoran gang members from Los Angeles, the economic and political situation in El Salvador, and the heavy-handed response of the government to gangs. In Tajikistan, organised crime blossomed in the aftermath of civil war. Bolstered by militias left over from the conflict, and the opportunities in the post-conflict economy, the mafia emerged a much stronger political and economic power.[21]

The emergence of gangs in post-conflict settings is common, but in many cases they are small and localised in their activities. The threat that gangs pose is often portrayed in two ways: a threat to the state itself or a threat to law and order. In most cases, it is the latter. Gangs are rarely intent on overthrowing the state or seeking political power. Instead they are more concerned with issues of respect, solidarity, family and turf. While gangs do defend their territories with violence, few reach the level of organisation and power at which they pose a direct threat to the state. Gangs rarely fit the insurgency model. Instead they pose problems of law and order, violence and crime. Gangs can, however, be a destabilising force in post-conflict settings. When they involve former combatants they can reinforce the maintenance of former conflict groups and those chains of command. They can provide an organising force for violence and crime against other groups, communities or individuals.

Pathway 5 – Emergence of new non-conflict armed groups: After war, in unstable and often insecure contexts, new armed groups can emerge in response to the post-conflict setting. This includes limited economic opportunities that make criminal activities more attractive options for earning money, and the lack of law and order and effective policing to counter incentives for violence and crime. Sometimes the groups are violent and criminal in nature. Localised gangs appear quite common in post-conflict settings. In other cases groups emerge in response to insecurity. For example, Liberia witnessed the growth of vigilante groups in the years following the 2003 peace accord. These vigilantes provided a community response to the rising trend of house break-ins and other crimes.[22] Post-conflict settings often provide the conditions conducive for the formation of gangs and other armed groups. While such groups do not necessarily emerge in the initial post-conflict period, they may do so in the years following the end of a conflict if conditions fail to improve.

Vigilante groups can provide a source of security to communities. Although they commit acts of violence, they may be seen as protectors rather than predators by the people who enjoy their protection. However, they ultimately act outside of and undermine any rule of law that may exist, highlighting the inability of the police to provide protection. Vigilante groups also threaten other groups, commit acts of violence in the name of protection, and challenge the re-establishment of law and order. As discussed above, most gangs present a localised law and order problem. The emergence of new armed groups suggests a weakness of governance, law and order, and security in the post-conflict environment.

Managing armed groups

In addressing post-conflict armed groups there are two important considerations. Firstly, it is important to tackle them early and inclusively. This can entail including disarmament and other measures in peace processes, as well as extending such measures to parties not included in the formal peace agreement. Ignoring violence and crime because of either a lack of capacity or a lack of concern can lead to further problems down the road, because post-conflict conditions often provide economic incentives and security reasons for armed groups to expand. Secondly, it is important to know which kind of armed group is operating and the conditions under which it operates. There are important differences among armed groups – gangs, cartels, rebel groups, organised crime etc. – they have different aims, operating strategies, and organisational structures. They also have different relationships to the state, the economy, and the communities in which they operate.[23] It is important to tailor responses to the circumstances and the group, rather than implementing broad sweeping measures for all armed groups.

The most common state response to armed groups is to view them as a criminal problem, and therefore to deploy the police, or to view them as a threat to the state, in which case the military is often engaged. This leads to an over-emphasis on a criminal justice approach of heavy-handed policing tactics in many countries. In most places, military-style tactics have not worked well, such as the major crackdown *mano dura* (*Operation Hard Hand*) in El Salvador in 2003, involving troops and police.[24] Although these tactics may initially reduce gang violence, they do not appear to have a sustainable impact on reducing gang presence. Instead, heavy-handed tactics can increase violence and gang cohesion and improve their capacity to expand and proliferate.[25] Despite not demonstrating long-term effectiveness, these tactics remain the most commonly used. A number of factors contribute to a preference for quick results: political pressure to address high levels of crime, political concerns to avoid appearing weak and ineffective, and widespread views that armed groups are merely criminals without any political or social agendas. Although criminal justice measures are undoubtedly warranted in many cases, they are also insufficient on their own to address problems of armed groups.

In addition to security measures, actions taken to address the factors that drive the creation and perpetuation of armed groups can help treat the causes and not merely the symptoms of armed groups. Numerous options exist. Alternative suppression strategies that are not coercive, include using community policing, community mediators, and non-custodial sentencing. Measures that aim to curb a group's development include reducing access to funding, recruitment and weapons. Strategies may also target the motivations that help armed groups form and recruit, such as: job training, recreational services, and reintegration and transition services. Preventive strategies focus on behaviours and risk factors that are commonly associated with armed group membership; information campaigns, education programmes, life skills training, substance abuse treatment, and youth mentoring schemes aim to prevent youth from joining armed groups. Negotiations also offer a means of managing armed groups and their activities.[26]

The various options available are too numerous to cover in detail here. Those presented aim to suggest the broad scope of interventions that are possible (suppressive to preventive) and the range of approaches that can be taken (at the individual, group, or community levels). They are raised to highlight the need to think more broadly about options for managing armed groups and for preventing their emergence. The tendency to use DDR as the primary means of managing armed groups in post-conflict contexts is insufficient. Other measures will be needed to address the various types of armed groups that can emerge, and the factors that drive and support them in post-conflict contexts.

Conclusion

Armed groups continue to pose challenges in post-conflict settings. Yet these groups are not always the same groups that fought during the conflict. The transformation of previously existing armed groups and the emergence of new groups suggest the need to broaden post-conflict efforts to disarm groups and deter group violence. How post-conflict armed groups evolve and emerge gives some indication of their intent, whether that be community protection, state power or economic gain, and, therefore, suggests possibilities for managing the risks these groups pose and the levels of violence they perpetrate. While research has explored different types of violence that take place in post-conflict settings, there has been no systematic assessment of post-conflict armed groups. Addressing high crime rates, threats to law and order, and insecurity in the population will require a better understanding of how armed groups evolve, emerge and operate after conflict.

Appendix I: Cases reviewed

Country	War dates [a]	Rebel conflict armed groups	Armed groups in post-conflict period [d]
Algeria	1992–2002	GIA MIA/AIS GSPC	 AQIM
Angola	1975–2002	UNITA	Gangs [e]
Burundi	1993–2005	CNDD-FDD FNL	Paliphehutu-FNL [g]
El Salvador	1980–1992	FMLN	Gangs Maras
Guatemala	1960–1996	URNG	Gangs Organised crime
Liberia	1989–2003[b] 1989–1997	NPFL ULIMO J ULIMO K	LURD MODEL
	1999–2003	LURD MODEL	Vigilante groups
Mozambique	1977–1992	RENAMO	Gangs Organised crime [f]
Nicaragua	1979–1990	Contras	Gangs
Peru	1980–2000	*Sendero Luminoso* (Shining Path) Tupac Amaru (MRTA)	Shining Path continues at low level
Rwanda	1990–1994	RPF Interahamwe	ex-Far Interahamwe
Sierra Leone	1991–2002[c]	RUF AFRC	Political thugs (2007 elections)
Tajikistan	1992–1997	UTO	Organised crime Militias

[a] These dates are not definitive. In most cases the start dates are not disputed. The termination dates are more difficult to establish and tend to be years in which peace agreements were concluded with the major parties.

[b] The Liberia war has been presented in two ways: one war lasting 1989–2003; or two wars during 1989–1996 and 1999–2003. This author uses the two-war scenario, seeing the second war as an example of former rebel groups reforming as new groups and fighting a new war.

[c] Although many databases list 1999 (Lome peace agreement) or 2001 (ceasefire) as the end date, 2002 is used here because the government of Sierra Leone officially declared the war over in January 2002 and the population widely recognises this as the end of the war.

[d] The post-conflict period is here viewed as five years after end date

[e] In 2009 there were reports of gangs mushrooming in Angola, but these groups do not reportedly have ties to the past war.

[f] By the mid-2000s Mozambique was experiencing large rises in crime linked to organised crime syndicates, unrelated to the war.

[g] In 2008 the Paliphehutu-FNL agreed to negotiations and signed a peace agreement late that year.

Appendix 2: Pathways after war

Pathway	Process	Examples
Termination of *conflict* armed groups	Conflict armed group dissolves after war	RUF in Sierra Leone
	Conflict armed group becomes political party	RENAMO in Mozambique UNITA in Angola
Continuation of *conflict* armed groups	Residual conflict armed groups who are not defeated but are no longer considered a threat	*Sendero Luminoso* (Shining Path) in Peru
	Residual conflict armed groups who are not party to peace process	AQIM in Algeria ex-Far and Interahamwe in Rwanda FNL in Burundi Militias in Cote d'Ivoire
Transformation of *conflict* armed groups	Conflict armed group transforms into a non-conflict armed group	GSPC into AQIM in Algeria, AUC into criminal gangs in Colombia Ex-combatants in Nicaragua into gangs
Transformation of *non-conflict* armed groups	Non-conflict armed groups become stronger and transform in post-conflict setting	Gangs into maras in El Salvador Organised crime in Tajikistan
Emergence of *non-conflict* armed groups	New armed groups emerge in post-conflict setting	Vigilantes in Liberia Localised gangs

CHAPTER NINE

State Failure and Ungoverned Space

Ken Menkhaus

Failed states pose security threats – to citizens of those failed states, to neighbouring states, and to the international system. On this general point few have disagreed since failed states first became an item of global concern in the aftermath of the Cold War. But the nature, scope and severity of the threats posed by state failure remain the subject of debate and confusion.

Threat assessments of failed states have changed since 1990, reflecting shifts in broader security concerns of the time. In the 1990s, failed states were viewed as the most dramatic symptom of what Robert Kaplan famously called 'The coming anarchy' – the unravelling of weak states in the face of multiple internal and external pressures.[1] While their most immediate impact came in the form of horrific humanitarian disasters, crises such as those that afflicted Liberia, Somalia, Congo, Afghanistan and Haiti quickly demonstrated their capacity for destabilising regional spillover. The significance of the threats generated by these crises was the subject of contentious debate throughout the 1990s. Some observers argued for a wider definition

Ken Menkhaus is Professor of political science at Davidson College, North Carolina.

of national security to account for the instability produced by failed states, while others insisted that state collapse in remote areas was mainly a humanitarian problem to be left to relief agencies, not the military, and that at any rate nation-building was a fool's errand.[2]

Advocates for 'fixing failed states' generally won out. Within a remarkably short time, an entirely new architecture of international intervention, including UN Chapter VII peacekeeping (heavily armed peace operations designed to enforce a peace where none exists), grew in importance and frequency; the focus of international aid swung dramatically towards much more politically intrusive programmes of state-building and peace-building, reflecting a new consensus that state failure and bad governance were key constraints on development and security. Post-conflict transitional governments became a new and rapidly growing type of political system; evolving norms to justify intervention in failed states, most notably in the form of the Responsibility to Protect doctrine[3], were articulated; and in a few instances (Timor Leste and Kosovo in 1999) the UN's old role in trusteeship was revived, with the UN assuming temporary control of sovereign functions of the state. Most, but not all, of this new interventionism was done with a UN Security Council mandate, and justified as a response to a 'threat to international peace and security'. In the process, the problem of state failure was at least partially securitised.

Since the September 2001 terrorist attacks on the United States, failed states have earned top billing as threats to international peace and security. Now they are viewed primarily as 'ungoverned space' which transitional criminal and terrorists can exploit. Territory beyond the reach of effective law and order is understood to be a natural safe haven for al-Qaeda and other terrorist groups, making failed states a weak link in the global war on terror. Failed states and bad governance are also seen as a contributing cause of underdevelopment, crime, radicalisation, and insurgency, all of which create favourable conditions for terrorist recruitment and operation. President George W. Bush's introduction to the US National Security Strategy of 2002 summed up the new consensus when he noted that: 'America is now threatened less by conquering states than we are by failing ones.' Almost a decade later, US Secretary of Defense Robert Gates reiterated that position. 'Dealing with such fractured or failing states', he observed, is 'the main security challenge of our time.'[4]

Despite the prominent place failed states have assumed in global security, few international security problems since the end of the Cold War have been so misunderstood as state failure. And few international aid programmes have met with such consistent frustration as state-building. These two failings are not entirely unrelated, as flawed diagnosis almost always produces bad prescription. What, then, do we think we know about state failure, ungoverned space and the threats they pose? And which nuggets of our conventional wisdom on failed states in fact deserve a rethink?

Defining, measuring, and predicting state failure

for years, the terms 'failed state' and 'fragile state' were tossed about with little attempt to define and refine them.[5] As a result, countries with dramatically different circumstances – ranging from Somalia to Pakistan – were lumped together in a single, unhelpful category. This also led to analysts talking past, rather than with, one another when referring to weak, failed, fragile, and post-conflict states. Analytic confusion over the syndrome of state failure also complicated efforts to design and measure the effectiveness of capacity-building programmes in failed states.

Research has made progress over the past decade. Scores of studies have produced useful schemes for breaking the syndrome of state failure down into discrete items; others devised systems of measurement of each of these characteristics of state failure; and some have proposed useful typologies of failed and fragile states. Empirical studies have also sought to identify the structural and precipitating causes of state failure, while efforts to monitor, predict, and prevent state failure (and more broadly armed conflict) have led to the rise of 'early warning systems' such as the work of the International Crisis Group.[6]

The result is an abundance of much richer information and analysis on failed states. The State Failure Task Force (since 2001 known as the Political Instability Task Force, or PITF), was established in 1994 to assess and explain the vulnerability of states to instability and failure.[7] It has been followed by a number of other projects to measure, compare and rank aspects of state failure, vulnerability and performance, including the World Bank's Governance Matters Project;[8] the Fund for Peace Failed States Index[9]; the Brookings Institution's Index of State Weakness;[10] and the Mo Ibrahim Index of African Governance.[11] Many other projects are attempting to define and measure specific aspects of poor governance, such as Transparency International's Corruption Perceptions Index.[12] One recent survey estimates the number of these types of governance performance indices as being 'in the hundreds'.[13]

What has been the cumulative result of this flurry of research? Firstly, the search for the most parsimonious set of governance indicators that matter most in measuring fragility remains a work in progress, though recent research has honed in on a few particularly salient factors. For the moment, most monitoring projects err on the side of comprehensiveness of indicators, producing lengthy lists of variables that can make it difficult for policymakers to identify priority issues. There is broad consensus on the general syndrome of state fragility and failure, if not on the specifics of how to measure and weigh each factor. These include weak capacity to provide public security, rule of law and basic social services; low levels of democracy and civil liberties; de-legitimisation and criminalisation of the state; rising factionalism; poor, socially uneven and declining economic performance; inability to manage political conflict; extensive interference by external actors; and, in some but not all cases, outbreaks of armed insurgencies.

Secondly, the same set of countries – mainly concentrated in sub-Saharan Africa – tends to appear at the bottom of every ranking related to fragility, poor governance and conflict vulnerability, regardless of methodologies and measurements.

Thirdly, although the same countries tend to be flagged as fragile or failed states in every monitoring system, they vary considerably across specific indicators. Some fragile states, like Zimbabwe, possess devastatingly poor scores across most indicators, and yet manage to avoid armed conflict; others, like Chad and Iraq, enjoy a stronger overall economic performance profile and yet score very poorly in almost every other indicator.

Finally, state fragility is ubiquitous. The Fund for Peace's Failed States Index 2009 lists 131 of 177 states as either critical, in danger or borderline for state failure.[14] Only a handful of states in the global south – such as Chile, Argentina, Oman, Uruguay and Mauritius – rank as 'stable' on the index. Even when more restrictive definitions are employed, leading monitoring projects typically identify between 40 and 60 failed states.[15] This reminds us that state fragility is not an exceptional circumstance. Nor it is new.

This research is not without its critics.[16] One concern is that deterioration of fragile states – either into state failure or armed conflict, or both – remains very difficult to predict. Many states are vulnerable, but only some actually slip into serious levels of failure. A seminal study in 2005 suggested that 'highly factionalized partial democracies' are most susceptible, but concedes that precipitating causes are highly situational and context-specific.[17] 'All stable nations resemble one another; each unstable nation is unstable in its own way,' the study's authors conclude.[18] A second concern is that the main findings of this body of research – that many, if not most, states are at risk – may well be true, but this provides no means of ordering priorities for policy makers and diplomats. The findings are to some extent overwhelming, given the enormity of the problem and the limited resources available to respond. In sum, these tools need to be supplemented with a means of classifying fragile states according to the degree of strategic, political or humanitarian impact they would have were they to fail.

The political economy of state failure

policies designed to address failed and fragile states generally operate on the assumption that the problem of state failure is low capacity. Were the leaders of a failed state given adequate means, this reasoning goes, they would naturally put those resources to use to strengthen their state. Leaders who fail to strengthen the capacity of their government are thus irrational, venal or both. The view that state failure is a matter of low capacity, lends itself to 'off-the-shelf' technical solutions that, not coincidentally, are ideally suited for conventional foreign aid programmes. More funding, better trained civil servants, a more professional and better-equipped police force, and a healthy dose of democratisation (where not politically inconvenient) have been the main elements of state-building strategies.

Yet two decades of research on the dynamics of weak and failed states suggests that in some circumstances state failure is viewed by local elites as a desired outcome, not a problem to be solved. This reflects a political strategy of survivalism and an economic strategy of personal enrichment that has its own rationale. Intentionally cultivating and perpetuating state failure follows much the same logic as war economies, in which armed conflict is perpetuated for group and personal gain.

There are a variety of ways that local interests can be advanced by state failure. Rulers have long been known to intentionally de-institutionalise their governments as part of a strategy of political survivalism and personal rule. As political scientist Will Reno has argued, leaders whose principal preoccupation is regime survival can view a well-functioning ministry as a potential power base for a rival, and hence go to considerable lengths to undermine and weaken governmental departments and branches.[19] The judiciary is often singled out in this regard, giving the leader free rein to conflate state coffers with personal finances, thereby improving his ability to use government resources freely as part of patronage politics. Where governments have become deeply complicit in criminal activities – West Africa's narco-states come to mind – perpetuation of state failure is essential for the criminal enterprise to operate. Likewise, where deeply embedded corruption in government is the norm, complicit leaders must ensure that key law enforcement and judicial departments cannot function as intended.

Even in instances where government officials are fully committed to strengthening state capacity, spoilers can effectively perpetuate state failure. Spoilers come in many forms, ranging from situational to 'total' depending on the nature of their interests.[20] Total spoilers are typically warlords or war criminals who have no interest in the revival of effective rule of law, for fear of eventual arrest. Situational spoilers are not opposed to state revival per se, but are unhappy with their allocation of power and resources and have the means of exercising veto power over political developments with which they disagree. The ubiquity of small arms and powerful, violent non-state actors in most post-conflict settings creates favourable conditions for veto coalitions (an affiliation of groups that block attempts at progress) to form with ease.

Risk management is a key factor in the formation of situational spoilers, a fact which sometimes goes underappreciated in policymaking circles.[21] Populations living in zones of protracted state failure and armed conflict must navigate very dangerous environments to survive and secure livelihoods. Not surprisingly, groups, households, and companies tend to be risk-averse, preferring sub-optimal but relatively predictable settings to new political dispensations that offer potentially greater security and economic opportunities but also greater risks. This has enormous implications for state-building in failed states. Businesspeople and others who have adapted to a context of state failure can be very reluctant to embrace efforts to reintroduce state authority into their lives and in the process create new uncertainties and risks. This is especially true when their previous experience of the state was negative – when the government was predatory and oppressive. Research in zones of protracted state collapse such as Somalia suggests that risk aversion is a powerful factor in the reluctance of some business and civic interests to throw their full support behind state-rebuilding efforts, even though the potential pay-off would be large.[22] Fear that the state may be captured by a rival ethnic group, nationalise their business or impose heavy taxes without providing security and services all conspire to reinforce this reluctance. Preference for the sub-optimal but predictable is hardly irrational in the high-risk setting of failed states.

'Hinterland' state failure has a somewhat different logic. Many large, poor states in the developing world essentially enjoy government services in core areas (the capital and economically important rural areas) while expansive hinterlands go almost entirely ungoverned. The Central African Republic, Chad, the Democratic Republic of the Congo, Kenya and Somalia are among the many examples of this phenomenon. In these instances, responsibility for day-to-day governance typically falls on the shoulders of local communities. In some cases peripheral zones come under the control of criminal or insurgency elements. Because peripheries are often in border areas, this increases problems of cross-border smuggling and spill-over of violence. In some cases states are simply too weak to project authority into their remote peripheries, but this is often the result of a careful political and financial calculation. Jeff Herbst, an eminent scholar of African politics, persuasively argues that it is economically rational for state authorities, which enjoy juridical sovereignty over territory within their borders regardless of whether they 'earn' it, to avoid the high cost of projecting the state into thinly populated, expansive, uneconomic regions in their peripheries.[23] Only when those burning peripheries create security problems or political embarrassment to the government – or when economic assets like oil are discovered – does this calculation change and the government begin to extend authority in its peripheries.

State failure can also be cultivated by neighbouring states seeking to produce weak, satellite states in their sphere of influence. This type of regional intervention is often portrayed as proxy wars and is an important factor in protracted armed conflict in some countries, but there are instances where regional hegemons are only interested in fostering state weakness, not outright warfare, in a neighbouring state.

The most important analytic contribution made by this research is its emphasis on understanding the *interests* of key actors in state failure. This is critical for several reasons.

Firstly, this helps to move us away from crude labelling of local players as total spoilers when they may not deserve the title. Interests of local actors are nuanced and complex; taking those interests seriously forces analysts to confront the mixed motives that define the calculations of all parties to the crisis. Secondly, interests are dynamic, not fixed, and can and do change over time. This is critical if we are to develop theories of change related to state failure. Successful bandits, pirates, warlords and mafia bosses accumulate wealth, and evidence from early modern Europe to contemporary Somalia reminds us that under the right circumstances the interests of spoilers can shift as they gain a new appreciation for the virtues of a certain level of public order. In Somalia, some war entrepreneurs who made small fortunes out of the civil war in 1991–92 began diversifying into quasi-legitimate business and fixed investments – plantations, real estate, remittance and telecommunications companies. This shift 'from warlord to landlord' was pivotal for the rise of a business community in Somalia, which helped support rather than undermine local systems of law and order.

This trajectory does not occur everywhere, of course. In Liberia in 1997, Charles Taylor won the presidency and continued to engage in warlord behaviour. Some ministers in the government of Afghanistan actively undermine the state in order to continue to profit from illegal economic activities (mainly drug production and export). But the fact that in some cases interests shift to support systems of governance is reason for hope that a condition of state failure is not necessarily a trap. The relevant analytic question is: under what conditions are local interests likely to gravitate towards support of governance?

Here, a critical distinction must be made between an interest in governance and an interest in a revived and strong central government. The two are often wrongly conflated, when outsiders assume that state-building and improved rule of law are synonymous. Research in zones of failed states such as Afghanistan, the DRC and Somalia suggests that local communities and business interests have a strong interest in supporting local systems of law and order but often view a revived state with apprehension. Local systems of governance that provide roads, a reduced threat of crime and attack, and other public goods bring immediate and tangible benefits; these are positive-sum outcomes, and are low risk. State-building, by contrast, is viewed as risky and potentially zero-sum. A stronger state can be used by rivals at your expense, can appropriate property or business, and can tax without providing services. Not surprisingly, some local communities and business interests simultaneously support local governance systems while blocking state-building efforts.

Governance without government

Zones of state failure are conventionally viewed as anarchic. This perspective is routinely reinforced in the media – images of criminal lawlessness, warlords and more recently, pirates make a compelling if sensationalist backdrop for stories on global security threats, refugee crises or international relief interventions. The assumption of anarchy has also found its way into policy formulations at the highest level, as witnessed in the US counter-terrorism strategy's emphasis on the threat posed by 'ungoverned space'.

It is certainly the case that the broad stretches of real estate where tens of millions of people live beyond the effective reach of the state are dangerous and insecure places to live. But it is a serious misreading to label these areas as anarchic. In reality, communities are not passive victims in the face of state failure or collapse. They actively forge systems of security, law, deterrence of crime, conflict management and mutual support. Researchers in dozens of failed states, from Afghanistan and Yemen to Sudan and Somalia, have documented the rise of informal systems of governance where the state has ceased to function.[24]

This 'governance with a small g' varies enormously in composition and effectiveness. Most versions of it are hybrid in nature, drawing on a variety of different actors – tribal elders, women's groups, local protection forces, business-people, clerics, civil society groups and others – to cobble together routinised patterns of law and order in their locale. Most tend to draw heavily on customary law, administered by customary authorities, but must not be seen as a simple retreat to tribal authority. Customary authorities almost always partner with other local actors to manage these difficult new problems. Most are fragile and vulnerable to powerful spoilers. Some are strained beyond their capacity by new and unfamiliar challenges related to state collapse, displacement and armed conflict. While some of these local governance systems develop into formal polities – regional states or municipalities – most remain informal and fluid, and as such they tend to be invisible to most external observers. They can emerge as very crude and rudimentary arrangements, such as armed neighbourhood watch groups, or develop into surprisingly sophisticated mechanisms of governance covering roles such as regulating private-sector fees for electricity and managing piped water systems. They tend to enjoy legitimacy in the eyes of the local community. Some of the most remarkable of these local polities, such as the self-governed city of Butembo in North Kivu, DRC, keep the peace and provide effective administration and basic services to hundreds of thousands of residents.[25]

Even so, it is a mistake to romanticise local governance systems. Most apply customary or religious laws that are illiberal and extra-constitutional, treat different social groups (especially women) unequally before the law, and are weak on due process. Some fall under the control of venal or predatory local elites and constitute little more than warlord fiefdoms.

These local systems of governance have expanded wherever the state has failed, but they are not new. Throughout the developing world, informal justice and conflict management systems, typically in the form of customary law and tribal or religious authorities, have always been the primary source of law and order for local communities, even when the formal state functioned in their area.

The argument that zones of state failure are not necessarily 'ungoverned' has been largely won in academia and increasingly in policymaking circles. But what are the implications for state-building projects? Are these local 'emerging orders' potentially significant, and if so, how?

There are several schools of thought on this question. The first answer is simply 'no'. Informal governance and security arrangements, according to this argument, reflect short-term coping mechanisms that will evaporate as soon as the central government is strengthened. Most state-building programmes operate on this assumption, and as a result devote little attention to mapping and understanding informal governance. Since local governance systems are seen to be of little consequence, this approach is not unduly concerned about adhering to a 'do no harm' principle as it promotes state revival.

A second school of thought argues that informal systems of governance are actively harmful. To the extent that local communities have successfully adapted to state failure, their incentives to support a revived state are reduced. Moreover, stakeholders in the informal governance systems will feel threatened by and will resist state-building. From this vantage point, informal governance arrangements are a dangerous source of potential spoilers to state-building, while they enshrine illiberal and tribal forms of rule of law. They are, from this perspective, a step backward.

A third school of thought sees informal polities as both significant and positive, a key part of a transitional process from failed to effective state. Informal governance is often the only form of governance local communities have, this argument goes, so they must not be inadvertently undermined by formal state-building projects. State-building is a long and slow process that can require years or even decades, during which informal governance systems can perform vital functions and prevent local populations from suffering years of lawlessness. As formal state authorities gradually strengthen and gain legitimacy, they will overlap with and then replace the informal polities.

A variation on this theme is the strategy of formal incorporation of tribal and other authorities into the state structure. This has been done in a number of places, such as south Sudan (where local government and judiciary consists of traditional *Boma* courts), Somaliland (where the upper house of parliament consists of the *guurti* or assembly of top clan elders) and Botswana (where customary courts have long co-existed with and played a key role in the formal judiciary). In contrast to Sudan and Somaliland, Botswana was not a locus of conflict.

Finally, some observers propose that the mosaic of local polities that emerge in zones of state failure may serve as building blocks for a new and more organic form of state authority. Weak state authorities will not replace informal systems of governance, this argument goes, but will have to enter into negotiated relationships with them. This is known as a mediated state model and has a long pedigree as a state-building strategy, stretching back to early modern Europe.[26] It differs from policies of indirect rule in that the negotiated arrangement with local informal authorities is not a matter of choice (to govern on the cheap) but rather the only option the state has if it wishes to claim any authority at all in its hinterlands. This is an unavoidably messy, contentious, constantly nego-tiated and renegotiated set of relationships between a weak central government and robust local authorities, but it is in fact a common if unspoken practice in most weak states today.

These different models of state-building that seek to incor-porate rather than supplant informal systems of governance can be driven by three distinct logics: convenience, efficiency or necessity. The convenience logic produces a policy of 'indi-rect rule' in which the state authority wants to minimise the burden it must bear to govern uninteresting parts of a terri-tory, and hence turns to (or invents) local authorities. The efficiency logic produces a sub-contracting policy, in which the state judges that other non-state actors – private firms, local non-profit organisations, or informal authorities – are better positioned to deliver key services at lower cost than is the state. The state contracts out these governance duties to these more efficient actors. Many governments around the world, rich and poor, draw heavily on this model. Finally, the necessity logic produces a mediated state, in which a weak state simply has no other option than to negotiate with existing local authorities if it wants to project even indirect authority in a territory.

State failure as a wicked problem

when a weak government is willing but not able to govern, conventional capacity-building and state-building measures are well-placed to help. This is, to borrow from systems theory, a 'tame problem'. But what to do when a government is both unable and unwilling to address its own failure? In this situa-tion, state failure becomes a 'wicked problem'. State failure is an essential condition within which political and economic elites profit. These elites are more than happy to accept external state-building assistance, but are committed only to state-building as a lucrative project, not an actual objective. Capacity-building projects to train and professionalise the civil service, police and military are destined to fail when the top political elite does not want them to succeed. Continuing to throw more funding at these weak states not only does not work, it arguably reinforces the very problem the international community is trying to solve, by rewarding the bad behaviour that is at the root of state failure in the first place. In this way, state-building in countries where the leadership intentionally undermines its own government capacity runs the risk of moral hazard.

This frustrating predicament is immediately familiar to policymakers working on Afghanistan, Iraq, Somalia and Yemen, to name but a few. The typical reaction is to call for replacement of the venal leaders in question, and in some cases – Somalia, for instance – this has taken place several times. But the dynamic often remains unchanged. Once an entire political economy develops around conditions of state failure, resistance to state revival can become structural and much more difficult to overcome. In this situation, external actors often partner with local authorities, including the many informal systems of governance described above, as an alternative to the state.

Ungoverned space and security threats

All of this concern over failed states is a reflection of the perceived security threats that ungoverned spaces pose to the wider world. US national-security strategy posits that ungoverned space is a threat because it provides transnational criminal and terrorist organisations a physical base from which to operate beyond the reach of the law. But is this in fact an accurate threat assessment?

The answer lies in part in how we define 'ungoverned'. A study by the Combating Terrorism Center at West Point concluded that, at least in the Horn of Africa, zones of complete state collapse (i.e. Somalia) were as difficult and non-permissive an environment for al-Qaeda as for international relief agencies. Declassified documents captured from al-Qaeda and made publicly available as part of the Harmony Project out of West Point provided compelling evidence that al-Qaeda's first forays into Somali-inhabited areas of the Horn of Africa in the early 1990s were unsuccessful.[27] East Africa al-Qaeda (EAAQ) operatives found Somalia to be too insecure, too wracked by clan divisions and too great a logistical challenge. As the only foreigners, they were easily exposed and found it difficult to keep their movements and activities secret. By contrast, the EAAQ cell found an ideal site in neighbouring Kenya, a weak but functional state with corrupt police and a non-existent system for tracking the hundreds of thousands of foreign missionaries, tourists, aid workers, and businesspeople coming and going to the country. It was in Kenya, not Somalia, where the EAAQ cell based its operations, rented houses and light aircraft, set up businesses and charity fronts, and planned and executed several major terrorist attacks, including the 1998 bombing of the US embassies in Nairobi and Dar es Salaam.

This finding suggests that terrorist groups prefer weak and corrupted states to zones of complete state collapse, for many of the same reasons that other types of organisations prefer them. If the finding is not unique to East Africa, it challenges the notion of ungoverned space as a principal site of terrorist activity, and underscores the importance of distinguishing between different types and degrees of state failure when assessing their potential threat to global security.

Policy implications

Getting the diagnosis of state failure right is critical for effective policy response, but has often been elusive. State-building policies generally reflect a belief that the problem is low capacity and the solution is an infusion of external cash, training and technical assistance. But conventional state-building policies will not work when local interests are served by continued state failure – when leaders preside over criminal economies, are committed to de-institutionalising the government in the name of political survivalism and personal rule, or calculate that the short-term benefits of state-building assistance outweigh the long-term benefits of a strengthened state.

When state failure is a problem for the external community but an opportunity for local elites, policy options are very limited, especially in countries where conditions are attractive for al-Qaeda or other terrorist groups. This has prompted some external states to seek to engage sub-national polities and actors as partners in development, local governance and security. A growing body of research confirms that zones of state failure are not in fact 'ungoverned', but feature a wide array of informal governance and security arrangements. These local governance systems are often quite effective in providing local communities with basic security and order, but are not always suited to partnering with outside actors on security and development agendas. Where appropriate, local political orders can and should be provided with carefully targeted support, but must not be compromised or overwhelmed by foreigners.

CHAPTER TEN

Crime, Corruption and Violent Economies

James Cockayne

Today's wars – business by other means?

In nineteenth-century Europe, Carl von Clausewitz likened war to the continuation of politics by other means. Today, in a globalised economy, war can be increasingly difficult to distinguish from business by other means. Access to global markets has made it easier for a range of violent entrepreneurs to sell goods and services, and in turn raise money, men and arms.[1]

Violence is no longer monopolised: instead, it is competed over and colluded in, providing a fast track to profit. State rulers, warlords and violent entrepreneurs now use external illicit finance – often based on the sale of resources they control, including minerals and drugs – to facilitate *internal* war-making: they use violence to extract revenues and profit from their own population. Political–criminal and military–criminal networks cloak themselves in the veil of sovereignty to loot state resources and carve up national and global markets. Indeed, in a globalised economy, organisations embedded in

James Cockayne is a Senior Fellow and Director of the New York office, Center on Global Counterterrorism Cooperation

systemic violence enjoy a specific comparative advantage: the availability of violence as a factor of production, distribution and competition. Politics and ideology are invoked to sustain popular support amid – or even for – violence. But frequently, the profit motive becomes dominant, with armed groups devolving into criminal organisations, often embedded within political organisations.

The implications of this convergence of crime, conflict and corruption are profound – not only for our understanding of how and why wars start and endure, but also how they end. Political deals may no longer provide a comprehensive solution to large-scale violence, since economic motives – often hidden or downright criminal – may also be major factors in determining conflict-termination outcomes. Indeed, apparently opposed belligerents may in fact be benefiting from the violence, and engaged in illicit joint ventures. As we have seen in Afghanistan, the Balkans, the Democratic Republic of the Congo (DRC), Guatemala and arguably Somalia, conflict actors may stand to profit more from ongoing violence than they do from peace. Since, in many cases, the economic value of these transactions derives from the sale of these goods and services into global markets, political stability may depend as much on effective regulation of cross-border financial and trade flows, development of new markets, due diligence by private economic actors and effective international law-enforcement cooperation as it does on more traditional tools of conflict termination such as territorially focused military and diplomatic intervention.

The financing strategies of armed groups in the post-Cold War era have driven a convergence of crime, corruption and conflict, which in turn presents challenges for those engaged in efforts to end war and consolidate peace. Peacebuilders must, therefore, differentiate between violent groups based on whether they adopt a predatory, parasitic or symbiotic fundraising strategy, before considering which tools and incentives may be available to wean such organisations away from violence, and the spoils it brings.

Turning blood into treasure: financing violence in a global economy

The costs of funding armed groups vary hugely, depending on the scale and ambition of the bureaucracy involved – and their need to control territory. Since the end of the Cold War diminished superpower patronage and closed traditional channels of funding, armed groups have increasingly been forced to develop their own autonomous revenue streams – either through developing new sources of state or private patronage, or by developing new commercial fundraising strategies. The result has been a convergence of business, crime, conflict and corruption.

Improvements in global transportation, communications and financial transfers reduced barriers to market entry and operating costs for commercial entrepreneurs around the world – including those who wished to offer violence as a service, or used it for illicit activity. Armed groups and governing regimes stood to take advantage of these opportunities. In some cases – such as Slobodan Milosevic's Serbia, parts of Russia in the mid-1990s or more recently in the case of the alliances between military forces and drug traffickers in Guinea-Bissau – this has led to a direct 'political–criminal nexus'.[2] In Afghanistan, the relationship is more indirect and is predicated on collusion, corruption and the extraction of criminal rent.

As the work of the economist and historian R.T. Naylor makes clear, the financial strategies of armed groups differ significantly depending on the types of violence in which they seek to engage. Symbolic violence (sporadic, spectacular attacks against symbols of existing authority and hierarchy) by guerrillas and terrorists requires comparatively little expenditure – so revenue-raising strategies may be limited simply to small numbers of donations, or infrequent predatory actions such as bank or credit card theft and kidnapping. But if an organisation seeks larger, ongoing involvement in the political or economic governance of a territory – whether for formal rule, or to assert an informal racket – it may engage in more sustained military operations. This means that the organisation acquires increasing non-operational organisational costs – social-security costs such as healthcare, care of militants' dependents, social outreach and assistance, and education. The provision of 'rough justice' or dispute-resolution mechanisms features significantly, from the Islamic Courts Union of Somalia to the resolution of disputes by criminal dons in the Italian mafia, Russian 'roofs' and leaders of Haitian and Central American gangs. In some cases these groups also provide access to credit and agricultural finance – a key mechanism of control exploited by groups from the Revolutionary Armed Forces of Colombia (FARC) to the Afghan Taliban. Fundraising activity consequently moves from being sporadic and predatory to persistent and parasitic.[3]

Finally, if a group controls territory and a population, it will incur protection costs – including costs of coercion and control (policing, intelligence, propaganda), payroll, and infrastructure maintenance (even if minimal). This moves its revenue-raising strategy towards a more extraction and taxation-based 'symbiosis' approach (e.g., Hizbullah, Hamas and the Liberation Tigers of Tamil Eelam or LTTE).[4] Once at this level, revenues can be very substantial: in the 1990s, FARC's revenues were thought to be about $1 million *per day*.[5]

To date, of these three financing strategies – predation, parasitism and symbiosis – most attention has been paid to predation. Analysts have explored whether conflict onset and duration correlate to the availability of lootable resources, to the volume:value ratio of those resources, or to barriers to market access and how predatory violence relates to competition between multiple potential providers of protection and criminal services.[6] Less attention has been paid to the role that parasitic and symbiotic strategies play, or to how international responses might influence organisations to shift from one strategy to another, or adopt multiple strategies. Yet understanding these patterns is becoming increasingly crucial to the success of efforts to end war and consolidate peace, given the observed convergence of organised crime, transnational terrorism and insurgency.[7]

Predation

Where government capabilities are weak and the state monopoly on the use of force is already shaky or absent, the risks of using violence to acquire capital – a strategy of primitive capital accumulation – are low. It is unsurprising, then, that there is a long history of armed groups using bank robberies, resource theft, and kidnapping – all of which are basic forms of predation – to finance both start-up and ongoing costs. Armed groups as diverse as the LTTE, Jewish nationalist Irgun Zvai Leumi, the Baader Meinhof urban guerrilla gang in Germany and Tehrik-e-Taliban in Pakistan have all used bank robberies at crucial points. In the 1970s, Italian Communist terrorists mounted a joint heist with the Ndrangheta criminal network on a Club Med resort, while the Palestinian Liberation Organisation (PLO) cooperated with the Corsican mafia to rob a bank in Beirut. Today, militant groups have graduated to robbing jewellery stores (to finance the Bali bombings), ATMs and cash-distribution centres,[8] serious cheque fraud (with one North African terrorist group raising £550,000 in 12 months in the UK), credit-card fraud, and internet-based money-laundering.[9]

Other valuable commodities may also become predators' targets. FARC raised perhaps 6% of its revenues from cattle theft.[10] Stolen and looted wildlife is a major source of revenue for some armed and extremist groups, as have been stolen oil, looted diamonds and other minerals. And because state control is weak at sea, maritime theft and fraud has also been a popular fundraising strategy for armed groups – long before the Somali pirates arrived.[11] Well-organised violent groups also have a history of taking advantage of cross-border differences in state regulation and capabilities, through smuggling of cigarettes – a key source of funds for the National Congress for the Defence of the People (CNDP) in the eastern DRC,[14] Hizbullah, the IRA (with an arrest in the US as recently as March 2009),[12] the Kurdistan Workers' Party (PKK), and more recently the Taliban[13] This form of tax-dodging is essentially a form of revenue theft from governments.

Because it relies on overt violence, predation can be hard to distinguish from politically or ideologically motivated military activity. In cases such as Bosnia and Iraq, sectarian and ethnic organisations have undertaken ethnic-cleansing operations clearing territory for military, political *and economic* reasons.[15] Clearing a valley or suburb served, in each case, an important military and political objective. But it also served an important economic objective, allowing the cleansing force to pillage those areas, take control of black markets and trafficking routes (in drugs, cars, sex and guns in Bosnia; and oil in Iraq), and profit from control of housing stock (which rulers lease or dole out to populations under their control). And the context of armed conflict allows the use of violence to commoditise goods and services that would normally be unavailable – such as forced labour, sexual servitude and illegally extracted or plundered resources.[16] Similar patterns can be observed elsewhere, for example in Kosovo, Colombia, Myanmar, Tajikistan, and Afghanistan.

Parasitism

Parasitism is in some ways a lower-risk strategy than predation, because it relies less on overt violence and more on the
shadow or threat of violence. The most common form of parasitism is extortion – closely related, of course, to bribery and
other forms of corruption, including protection rackets. These
involve violent groups extracting a tax from others controlling a productive asset or providing a service, in return for the
withholding of violence against that asset or its controller, or
the disruption of the market for the service.

These rackets develop around a range of different valuable goods and services. Historical examples include mines,
oil production, cattle ranches, wheat, tea production, labour
services, commercial trucking and even drug smuggling.
Shakedowns of diasporas and key businessmen also loom
large in the financing strategies of established armed groups.
Some such rackets are very sophisticated: FARC, the LTTE and
the PLO all used detailed population censuses as the basis of
their taxation strategies, and used the imposition of taxes as a
claim to legitimate governance.

Kidnapping is a closely related, perennial favourite in
financing violent organisations. It provided almost the entire
operating budget of the Italian Red Brigades, and allowed the
El Salvador Farabundo Martí National Liberation Front guerrillas to shift from symbolic violence to sustained insurgency.[17] In
Colombia, rebel groups run highly centralised, computerised
administration of these schemes, often using stolen credit-
card information to identify potential targets and estimate the
ransom prices they will attract. Kidnapping has also been a key
technique of al-Qaeda in Iraq and the Sahel, and the Taliban in
Pakistan.

In extreme cases, competition between different armed
groups for control of these rackets and criminal markets can

become very violent. Competition for control of mines has been central to understanding conflict dynamics in eastern DRC; similarly, control of the racket around a cement factory (a particularly lucrative asset in the context of repetitive episodes of post-civil war reconstruction) became a central concern at one point during the Lebanese civil war. And of course in Mexico, more than 22,700 people have been killed since 2007 as a result of competition between different narcotrafficking organisations for control of certain drug-trafficking related markets and rackets, with 2,600 killed in Ciudad Juárez in 2009 alone. Yet such violent competition may take place entirely outside the framework of any formal peace agreement.

Symbiosis
Eventually, organised violent groups may use the sustained background threat of violence to embed themselves in routine business activities. There is a long tradition of armed groups investing in licit economic activity: IRA investment in bars and gaming rooms, LTTE investment in Hindu temple management and phone-card businesses and extensive licit-sector investment by Colombian armed groups. The PLO is thought to have been making as much as $1 billion per year from investments, including in a variety of stockmarkets, by the early 1980s.[18] Sometimes the investment is not in legitimate business, but organised crime: violent groups that have passed along this trajectory from political violence to organised crime include the *Cosa Nostra*, IRA and arguably the Kosovo Liberation Army. It is particularly associated with drug production and trafficking: examples of belligerent groups transforming into narcotics organisations include ethnic armed groups in Myanmar, and other factions in the broader Golden Triangle opium-producing region in Southeast Asia, numerous insurgent, political and paramilitary groups in Latin America (especially

in Bolivia, Colombia, Ecuador, Guatemala, Peru and more recently Mexico), state and non-state groups in Afghanistan, Pakistan and Central Asia, armed factions and criminal gangs in Southeastern and Eastern Europe, and more recently state security forces and non-state militias in West Africa and the Sahel.

In some crucial cases, this economic symbiosis becomes politically institutionalised. Historical examples abound of states using criminal and paramilitary organisations to defend the political *status quo*, through access to illicit finance and illicit, violent political activity – Vietnam in the 1950s, Serbia under Milosevic, Iraq under Saddam Hussein, Haiti in the early 1990s, contemporary Guatemala. It is an increasingly prevalent form of 'mediated' rule:[19] state-ruling elites and security forces acquiesce in the operation of terrorist, extremist, paramilitary and violent organised criminal groups on their territory – in return for clandestine political, military and financial pay-offs from the illicit trades those groups conduct – in a kind of clandestine state sponsorship. This pattern can be seen in southern Afghanistan, the Federally Administered Tribal Areas of Pakistan, border areas of Myanmar, some slums (*favelas*) in Brazil, Haitian *bidonvilles*, and some weakly governed states in West Africa. As Vanda Felbab-Brown has convincingly argued, belligerents who support illicit economies gain both freedom of action (from patrons) and political capital; those who suppress illicit economies typically lose political capital.[20]

In fact, in many cases, this form of mediated rule seems to institutionalise violence. Both rebels and rulers may perceive greater political and financial pay-offs from continued violence than from peace. This can give rise to a kind of rebels–crime–rulers chain, with crime forming the hidden link between the nominally opposed enemies – the rulers and the rebels. Examples of this kind of clandestine collaboration can be found in numerous recent conflicts: Afghanistan, Bosnia, Central Asia, Myanmar and now, arguably, West Africa.[21] In some of these cases, rulers simply abandon any pretence of controlling parts of their territory, ceding control and the provision of social services and protection to populations in those areas to rebel groups. The institutionalised presence of armed criminal groups on a state's territory can thus create a win-win situation: governing elites can plausibly deny their control over these spaces even as they collect a clandestine 'protection' fee from the criminal groups, a 'criminal rent'; while the armed, criminal groups are left relatively free to conduct their profit-making activities – whose formal criminalisation serves to allow them to charge a higher price for their services, because of the nominal risks involved. The result is a system that profits from apparent conflict and instability, while in fact functioning on a basis of hidden collusion. Both sides enjoy high profits: only the local population, unprotected by the state and vulnerable to coercion, corruption and violent, criminal rule, suffers – greatly.

Implications for peace efforts

The convergence of crime, conflict and corruption greatly complicates international efforts to end war and consolidate peace. It makes the dynamics of the shadow economy – rather than formal politics or the military balance as traditionally understood – increasingly influential on political stability and conflict outcomes. It gives ruling elites and military actors easy access to relatively unfettered finance for their own personal enrichment or for political or organisational expenditures – making them more responsive to external financial factors than domestic constituencies. This may make it hard to broker peace deals, and make them stick – not least because international peacemakers and peacekeepers rarely have the tools to identify or map – let alone control – these shadowy financial dynamics.

This means that what we might call 'political geography' – national borders, and the shape and relations between major political groups within a country – may, perhaps unexpectedly, take a back seat to what we might call 'economic geography'. A peace agreed between rebels and rulers at the national level will not necessarily endure at the local level, since local violent entrepreneurs may have stronger incentives to defect from a peace deal using connections to foreign markets and finance, than to abide by deals imposed by distant 'national' leaders. Groups in rural hinterlands near borders, in particular, may have stronger ties through cross-border trafficking to transnational networks than to leaders in urban centres: consider the difficulties capitals have had imposing discipline over borderland subordinates in countries such as the DRC, Myanmar and Pakistan. The result of national peace deals may in fact be group splintering and even violent competition for control of illicit markets – leading to increased, not reduced, violence.

Clandestine connections between state elements and illicit markets may reduce discipline within state security institutions, raising the risk of coups. Control of the state and the privileges of sovereignty – including control of security institutions – becomes the ultimate prize for which criminal syndicates compete, sometimes violently, since it guarantees access to monopolistic profits from criminal rents.[22] In West Africa, for example, a spate of recent coups is considered by many to be a result of competition between different groups within these states to control revenues derived from the burgeoning Latin America–West Africa–Europe drug trade.[23] Similar claims have been made about recent ethnic violence in Kyrgyzstan.[24]

The involvement of state and non-state belligerents in internationally criminalised activity traps decision-makers between two contending policy regimes – peace and justice. The 'peace' camp tends to be pragmatic, focusing on engagement with groups that control social access, provide public goods and services, and enjoy military power as a necessary evil – even if they have violated international norms by, for example, engaging in drug trafficking. Proponents of this approach tend to emphasise humanitarian and developmental objectives. The 'justice' camp, in contrast, insists more on the ostracism of such norm-violators from the international system, through sanctions, law enforcement and, if necessary, military action. At present, different parts of the international system – and even different national agencies – pursue each of these objectives, rarely in coordination. That can lead – as we see, for example, in relation to Hamas and Hizbullah – to policy fragmentation and even incoherence.

Unravelling violent economies: elements of an integrated strategy

Perhaps the central insight from this analysis of violent groups' predatory, parasitic and symbiotic strategies is that the comparative advantage such groups enjoy in the global economy is essentially structural: it comes from low-risk access to violence in conflict-affected situations, combined with access to global markets, into which to deploy that violence as a factor for production. It is not simply that armed groups look to crime to fund themselves for political purposes; now, increasingly, we see them looking to *conflict* as the perfect operating environment. And indeed, the limited spatial analysis that has been conducted – in Afghanistan and Colombia – bears out this hypothesis: the conduct of hostilities in a particular location normalises violence and wipes away regular economic activity, leaving little to grow there but crime, forcing the economy back towards predation and primitive capital accumulation.

Efforts to remove or control this comparative advantage, therefore, must change this opportunity structure, by increasing normative and social obstacles to the use of violence, by better enforcing norms against that violence or by providing participants in these organisations better life prospects down some other path.

Grappling with the legitimacy of violent organisations

Organised crime and corruption are central to the social experience in violent and insecure communities – especially those affected by wholesale armed conflict. What is labelled 'organised crime' may at times manifest a deeper politico-economic system that satisfies the survival, dispute-resolution and other basic needs and interests of extensive constituencies straddling the state–society boundary.[25] In many conflict-affected and weak states, the lines between legality and illegality, and between legitimacy and illegitimacy, do not run along parallel tracks. State-backed laws may lack popular legitimacy, and state officials – or outside peacemakers – may risk *losing* local legitimacy by enforcing the law. Alternatively, state officials may engage in activities – such as corruption and bribery – that are illegal but entirely normalised or legitimate in the local context. A similar disconnect can emerge between international norms and local legitimacy.

Peacemakers and peacebuilders may in the short term consequently have legitimate reasons to tolerate activities that might be, internationally, considered criminal: witness the blind eye being turned by the International Security Assistance Force to poppy production in parts of southern Afghanistan in which it is currently conducting military operations. Other examples, such as the role played by illegal arms and food smuggling in Bosnia in the 1990s point to the constructive role that organised crime can play in shifting a military balance against a violent, dominant belligerent, or even in providing vital social services in conflict zones.[26]

So far, the international community's peacemaking and peacebuilding strategies have largely overlooked this intermediate institutional level of violent and criminal organisations – to their detriment. In particular, as we have learnt in the Balkans, Russia and even in parts of Latin America and Africa, the rush to integrate conflict and post-conflict economies into global financial and trading systems simply rewarded those with existing market power in those economies – even though that market power had been won at the barrel of a gun.[27] Little was done to vet or control efforts by violent entrepreneurs to use post-conflict privatisation programmes and elections as opportunities to launder their looted assets and their coerced legitimacy.[28] The danger of such an approach is that it may simply lead to the embedding of violent organisations at the heart of state power, using licit companies and political parties as fronts, sowing the seeds for future volatility – all without addressing the underlying structural opportunities that may spur a return to violence in the future.

The dangers of rewarding violent organisations through political deal-making are clear: witness the recidivist violence of the Revolutionary United Front in Sierra Leone, even after it was brought into the government; or the ongoing drug-related violence in Guatemala, long after an internationally monitored peace settlement. As those cases show, peace processes that fail to grapple with the underlying economic incentives violent groups enjoy can in fact become unwitting allies of organised crime, by further undermining already weak social and state institutions, creating opportunities for violent entrepreneurs.

The challenge, then, is to change these violent actors' perceptions of their future pay-offs from engagement with the legitimate political economy, making it more attractive than the prevailing, violent, often illicit, norm. Yet we must realise that violent groups and their members are not simply isolated individuals engaging in cold cost-benefit analyses, but providers and consumers of social meaning, embedded in larger social structures. What 'crime' and 'corruption' mean to these actors may be heavily mediated by other social variables, since criminal and kleptocratic groups often colonise and corrupt the informal institutions such as tribe, clan, kinship and political parties that mediate between state and society in such countries.[29] It may, as a result, be necessary to work with these mediating institutions – even as we try to transform them, wooing them away from violence.

The aim must be to offer a range of positive incentives for transformation to these intermediate institutions, harnessing the legitimacy they enjoy, as well as the social access and services they afford, and incorporating them into state-building strategies, even as the violent and discriminatory aspects of their influence are eliminated. As Professor Will Reno, a noted authority on West African governance and conflict, writes, 'networks that enjoy measures of popular legitimacy may present opportunities for post-conflict state-builders'.[30] The difficult reality is therefore that criminal groups may, in some cases, be short-term allies for peace, even though they may be its long-term enemy.

Our decision-making and operational institutions related to international peace efforts are currently poorly equipped for such an effort. On the contrary, at present, international peace efforts at times risk unwittingly playing into the hands of violent, criminal elements in the conflict-termination and post-conflict process, strengthening their legitimacy. The change in wage structures produced by the arrival of large numbers of foreign peacekeepers, peacebuilders and other international actors can recalibrate economic power within communities, in some cases fuelling a rise of consumerism that makes organised crime more attractive as a 'fast-track option' to material success. Peace operations personnel may supply – wittingly or not – goods for black markets (such as skimmed fuel, misappropriated food aid or corruptly provided service contracts). They can provide transport mechanisms (through access to fuel, vehicles, road improvements, increased mobility and permission to travel). And they can provide demand for black-market goods such as fuel, gold, diamonds, DVDs, smuggled cigarettes and, notoriously, sexual services.[31] In extreme cases, peace-operations personnel may also be targeted by criminal networks for corruption and become directly involved in organised crime.[32]

What tools would peace efforts require to tackle these problems? As explained above, they are the tools that would allow a structural and normative transformation of the political economy, removing the comparative advantage that violent, criminal entrepreneurs and organisations enjoy. This could involve increasing normative and social obstacles to the use of violence by strengthening non-violent mediating institutions – for example, through the use of anti-corruption campaigns and commissions, or working with traditional (religious, tribal or other) authority figures, or through long-term engagement with post-conflict political parties. It might involve better enforcement of norms against violence – for example through improved policing, judicial and prosecutorial capabilities, or strengthened independent electoral oversight bodies. And it will probably involve creating better prospects through economic development. Yet all of this must begin with strengthened analytical capacity.

Strengthening analytical capacity

Perhaps the most fundamental challenge is in identifying when armed and illicit groups will be an enemy and when they will be an ally to peace. We should not be romantic about organised crime: it is an inherently coercive, often authoritarian, force. Its victims are frequently the weakest and most vulnerable, including women and children. Even as it serves to bind some segments of society to the state, it may exclude others: as Reno sums it up – 'protection and predation are two sides of the same coin'.[33] Consequently, this must be determined on a case-by-case basis – with careful analysis of the predatory, parasitic or symbiotic strategy that the group seems likely to adopt.

For policymakers, this means, first and foremost a need to equip peacemakers, peacekeepers and peacebuilders with the tools to map and understand organised crime and related forms of non-state armed violence. Some national institutions are moving in this direction: for example, the US military is increasingly using its intelligence resources in Afghanistan to analyse networks of graft, crime and corruption, recognising that tackling those networks is central to breaking the hold of the Taliban over southern Afghanistan.[34] But analogous attention at the international level to crime–conflict connections is less frequent. The UN Security Council has recently called for the UN Secretary-General to mainstream drug trafficking and other transnational threats as factors of analysis into the UN's conflict analysis, peacekeeping, peacebuilding and mission-planning work.[35] But there seems to be little activity within the UN Secretariat to make good on this invitation, perhaps in part because officials are not sure where to start.

The international community often, in fact, has significant information at its disposal about the financial networks underpinning conflict constellations, as numerous UN sanctions group reports on eastern DRC – and more recently investigations into the financial networks underpinning Somali piracy – make clear.[36] But that information is frequently locked within bureaucratic silos, trapped in national agencies or UN institutions that have not been integrated into international conflict assessment, mediation and post-conflict planning processes. Strengthening this integration – for example, by including crime-analysis experts from the UN Office on Drugs and Crime, the UN's Police Division, or INTERPOL in integrated mission-planning processes, or on international mediation teams – is an obvious place to start in strengthening international processes.[37] At the field level, operational intelligence arrangements (such as the UN's Joint Mission Analysis Cells) should also be strengthened through access to criminal-analysis experts and member states' national criminal intelligence systems. Frequently, however, effective analysis will also require developing new human intelligence on the ground. This may require a shift in operational concepts, planning and force postures, to incorporate greater reliance on civilian, police and financial intelligence-gathering capacities.

Strengthening norms and their enforcement

Analytical capacity is crucial for identifying the clandestine economic and financial dynamics that shape contemporary conflict arrangements. To be effective, however, it must be complemented by tools that raise the normative and material costs of continued involvement in such activities, altering the incentive structures that give rise to them in the first place. This involves two elements: enforcement, and normative transformation.

Strengthened enforcement will frequently require long-term engagement by the international community to foster local and national policing, judicial and prosecutorial capabilities, and independent electoral oversight. Although attention to police-building has been growing in recent years, the international community is still at the early stages of configuring its decision-making processes and resources to allow for the long-term engagement that is needed to build resilient, effective and responsible police, judicial, prosecutorial and electoral capacity in war-torn countries. And there is little institutionalised capability, to date, for long-term international partnering with these institutions to break the hold of criminal organisations in post-conflict contexts – though the International Commission Against Impunity in Guatemala provides an extremely valuable precedent.[38]

Improved enforcement will frequently also require better joining up of efforts to build national and even regional resilience through improved financial governance, law enforcement, air traffic, border and customs controls, cross-border industry regulation, pricing and security arrangements. Normative transformation will involve not only anti-corruption campaigns and commissions and asset-recovery initiatives, but also potentially increased efforts by peacemakers and peacebuilders to work with traditional authority figures to strengthen resistance to criminal violence, or sustained engagement by international actors to foster civic dialogue and political parties. A number of lessons can be learned about how to combine these elements, from recent experiences with efforts to transform violent economies in countries such as Bosnia and Liberia. In those places, success appears to have been greatest when a 'decapitation' strategy targeting the leaders of criminal networks for international prosecution was married to strong economic incentives for their cohorts and the general population to abandon the illicit economy, together with robust capacity-building efforts targeting local political parties, courts and security institutions.[39]

Adjusting the geography of peace efforts

The current, single-country mandate of most peace efforts simply does not square with the transnational geography of the crime and corruption that sustains these violent economies. The networks and transactions that sustain such violence are often highly regionalised, diaspora-based, and flows through channels in international banking, telecommunications, weapons and commodity sales systems. Steps should therefore be taken to ensure that mediators, peace operations and post-conflict reconstruction efforts are connected up to existing mechanisms for obtaining information about what is going on in such channels, such as UN sanctions panels, INTERPOL National Central Bureaux and criminal investigation mechanisms, as well relevant national criminal-and financial intelligence systems.[40]

This may, likewise, require rethinking how and where peace-operations personnel ought to be deployed: it may be equally fruitful, for example, to send a civic-affairs officer to a diaspora community in a third country as it is to locate them 'in-country' where a conflict has recently terminated. Regionalised, multi-country peace packages may also be needed in some cases – not only to avoid the cross-border price and regulatory distortions that may come with national-level peace efforts, and may actually encourage illicit market growth, but to create the networks of trust and support that may be needed to resist corrupting pressures at the national level.

Regional organisations – both intergovernmental and trans-governmental, such as regional police chiefs' organisations –could take on a greater role in international capability-building programming in international peace consolidation efforts. And regional institutions – such as the judiciary supported by outside actors – may become increasingly important as a cost-effective and resilient form of regional justice 'insurance'. The recent creation of regional piracy courts in Kenya and the Seychelles provides an example of how coordinated international action can foster such outcomes, as do current efforts to regionalise the International Commission against Impunity in Guatemala, and efforts by the UN Security Council's Counter-

Terrorism Committee Executive Directorate to foster the development of effective counter-terrorism law-enforcement networks in East Africa and South Asia. Such efforts will require significantly improved donor coordination if they are to be effective on a larger scale.

Strengthening alternative development and livelihoods

Ultimately, however, a life of violent crime may simply remain the most attractive option for young men who see themselves at a comparative disadvantage in the global economy to which they believe they have little to offer other than a willingness to take risks and a low estimation of the value of their own lives. Until the international community provides such young men with realistic alternative life prospects, that brutal calculus may remain, providing the fuel for engineers of violence, crime and conflict in many places around the world.

Both macroeconomic and microeconomic development strategies are clearly crucial in developing alternatives to illicit economic activity. Micro-incentives – changing individual fighters' cost–benefit calculations – are important. Disarmament, demobilisation and reintegration (DDR) programming is clearly, therefore, crucial – though few DDR programmes account for the lure of criminal activity for fighters exiting war. And in fact, as the situation in southern Afghanistan's opiate-dominated economy seems to suggest, in the absence of radical institutional reform, it may be unrealistic to expect a fighter to escape the criminalised system in which he must survive. A Taliban fighter in southern Afghanistan currently has few realistic means of earning a livelihood outside the criminal economy.

Structural reform is clearly, therefore, also crucial to any effort to wean an economy away from violence and crime, and towards peaceful, legitimate economic activity. Primary among these reforms must be those that provide populations access to income divorced from violence: the provision of specialist skills in something other than violence; improved access to licit markets, for example through infrastructural reform (roads, irrigation) and regulatory reform (marketing arrangements, adjustments to cross-border taxation and customs arrangements); and the provision of effective, non-violent dispute resolution options. Further examination is needed of how post-conflict engagement with illicit markets can be tailored better to address all the structural drivers that push communities into violent economies: access to markets, pricing, infrastructure, skills, credit, and integration into global markets.

But because conflict-affected political economies are highly localised, reform at the national, provincial or municipal level may not be sufficient (though it may be necessary). Instead, those seeking to end war and the consolidation of peace may need to work with the institutions, organisations and networks that mediate between the micro- (including individuals, households and communities) and macro-levels: warlords, tribal authorities, religious authorities, political bosses – and perhaps even those we label as criminal dons and kingpins. All the lessons we have learnt about community-driven development (CDD) strategies will be needed in thinking about how to woo communities away from illicit markets and violent economies. The development community has limited experience in this, though there are interesting lessons from Latin America and the National Solidarity Programme in Afghanistan, as well as the UN's Office on Drugs and Crime and the Organisation for Economic Cooperation and Development's (OECD) Development Assistance Committee (in particular, its Armed Violence Reduction agenda). There has been too little attention to urban alternative development strategies, leaving poor, often dislocated communities in countries such as Mexico particularly vulnerable to becoming trapped in violent economies run by gangs and fuelled by global illicit market revenues, particularly from drugs and human trafficking. With urbanisation predicted to increase in developing states in coming years, this is a pressing problem.

But it is also crucial to note that violent economies are often sustained largely by *private* economic transactions – in the extractive sector, in private illicit markets for sex, drugs or trafficked commodities. So, effective preventive action may also need to place more emphasis on effective risk management within the private economic sphere, embedding conflict-sensitive practices in international private economic activity.

The importance of enlisting the private sector in efforts to consolidate peace becomes clear when we consider the recent history of peace efforts in the African Great Lakes region. Over a decade of conflict in the eastern DRC has been driven at least in part by competition over that region's resources by states and their brutal predatory proxy militias.[41] The UN Security Council has imposed numerous bans on trading in arms and restricted access to certain resources in various parts of these conflict zones, but UN forces on the ground have struggled to enforce these limits, with illicit resource extraction and trafficking in the region deeply integrated into international trading and manufacturing networks, with some commentators even suggesting most mobile phones around the world risk incorporating illicit minerals from the region. The result is a highly predatory political economy, especially in the eastern DRC, with human-rights abuses – especially forced labour and sexual violence – becoming a tool in the pursuit of control, extraction and trading of mineral resources – all sustained by revenues generated by export to foreign markets.[42]

To date, the international community has sought to deal with this war economy primarily by extending the reach of the DRC state into the areas in question, in particular through assistance provided by the United Nations Organisation Mission in the Democratic Republic of the Congo (MONUC). Yet in the process MONUC has become increasingly ensnared in the dynamics of corruption and human-rights abuse that weave through the extraction networks and ethnic militias that mediate Kinshasa's rule in the region, failing to implement effective controls on the ground.

A better approach might require home states to impose obligations on importing companies to engage in due diligence to ensure that the resources they are importing have been extracted in a manner that complies with human-rights norms. This might be married to a certification scheme. And this is, indeed, the direction that the international community is now beginning to head in, with the United Nations Security Council, in Resolution 1896 (7 December 2009) calling for an examination of how to have companies and states to discharge these 'due diligence' obligations while business is conducted in the region, and regional security conferences considering the possibility of a certification scheme.

Such a 'due diligence' oriented approach might be expanded to other peace efforts. But systematising such an approach will probably first require clarification of the norms governing participation in such economies. Without additional work to clarify the norm that is being violated by specific forms of inter-action with actors in such violent economies (such as financing, purchase of their goods and services, or other forms of support), there will not be adequate political and social support for the adjustments required to do business as usual. Still, the outlines of a set of clear, enforceable, interlocking norms clarifying acceptable and unacceptable forms of participation in violent economies – with associated implementation machinery – may already be visible. Some activists and commentators are calling for the extension of the anti-money laundering system built up around drug and terrorist financing offences to include the enforcement of other existing predicate offences, such as other forms of transnational crime, corruption and violations of international humanitarian law.[43] There are some precedents: the US has used domestic counter-terrorist financing norms as a basis for the attempted extradition of Viktor Bout, a notorious arms trafficker from Thailand (by charging him with providing 'material support' to FARC), and for the settlement of a case against the company Chiquita for protection-racket payments to a proscribed group in Colombia. And there is extensive implementation machinery already in place in the global financial sector. Extending this system might arguably be feasible through simply issuing Interpretative Notes in the Financial Action Task Force, which governs how many states and private-sector actors interpret their due diligence and reporting obligations in this area.[44] And the UN Human Rights Council has also created the post of Special Representative on business and human rights, held by Professor John Ruggie for the last six years, which seems likely to provide detailed operational guidance to companies on human rights due diligence in conflict contexts in the course of 2010.[45]

Exclusion or compromise? Integrating strategy
Effective strategy to woo a population away from a political economy based on violence requires combining all these measures: brakes on private economic activity that fuels violence, the decapitation of the architects and leaders of a violent political economy, and economic and normative transformation. There are signs that it can be achieved: in Liberia, for example, the Governance and Economic Management Assistance Programme has worked in combination with anti-corruption programming, international prosecution of Charles Taylor and

others on war-crimes charges, international sanctions and DDR programming in a way that seems to be slowly drawing that country towards a sustainable path to peace.[46]

But Liberia is an exceptional case for many reasons – not least because of the strategic unity that key international actors (the US, EU, UN, World Bank, International Monetary Fund and other African states) have demonstrated since at least 2004. None of these actors had a financial, military or other reason to tolerate ongoing violence. The same cannot be said in other conflict zones around the world. And strategic disunity has, in some cases, also been born out of less cynical motivations. Indeed, perhaps the thorniest challenge posed by crime and corruption to efforts to end war and consolidate peace is whether there should be any room at all for 'criminals' in a peace process. If they have violated the law, why should they not simply be punished, excluded and ostracised?

We should be cautious about applying labels such as 'crime' and 'corruption' to behaviour during war. Calling violent disorder 'crime' suggests that there has been a violation of an international norm. And crimes are typically met with coercive responses to correct the deviation and hold the responsible actor accountable. By contrast, labelling disorder as 'conflict' suggests the existence of two or more adversarial actors, and possible impartiality about the need to restore the normative status quo through coercive action. Rather, peace and stability may be the only objectives of a response.[47] Labelling a phenomenon as 'crime' implies the need for a punitive response, excluding criminals from legitimate social interactions. Political processes may – in contrast – require overlooking earlier 'transgressions' (or involvement in conflict) in favour of inclusive social interactions. It is hard to know – even on a case-by-case basis – which approach – the penal or the political – is more likely to be an effective peace-consolidation strategy.

What we can say is that criminalisation is a dangerously rigid instrument: once an actor has been labelled a 'criminal', it can be difficult to resile from such a characterisation, limiting bargaining options. There is a danger that a binary analysis that seems to pit conflict against peace, and criminal non-state actors against legal state actors – will obscure the more complex, messy reality of contested legality and legitimacy in war and post-conflict contexts.

The danger is that the 'organised crime' label may in fact obscure the complex interpenetration of the legitimate and the illegitimate, the state and the criminal network, that is part of the lived experience of many populations in weak states and conflict-affected areas. Labelling a phenomenon as 'organised crime' risks overlooking the associated opportunities to turn peace spoilers into peace partners. If used imprudently, it may in fact turn potential allies into determined enemies. A first step, therefore, is to be aware of its power to ostracise and stigmatise, and to use it cautiously within a broader strategy designed to woo actors towards legitimate and legal activity.

Yet the existing international policy architecture offers little 'wriggle room', for how we deal with 'criminals', 'terrorists' and proscribed groups. There is no clear process that can be pursued to allow the temporary suspension or modification of global prohibition regimes such as those outlawing the trade in opiates, for example, to allow political negotiation with leaders who are also involved in the drug trade. It is unclear under what circumstances the international community would tolerate attempts to negotiate with internationally listed 'terrorist' groups; indeed, in many countries, national-implementing legislation designed to make such interaction more difficult prevents public and private actors from engaging in outreach to these groups. Exactly such concerns underlie the recent decision of the US Supreme Court in the case of *Holder v. Humanitarian Law Project*, which upheld a federal statute criminalising the training of proscribed terrorist groups even in human rights law.[48]

These concerns have immediate relevance for how we go about ending war and consolidating peace – for example in Afghanistan. We risk trapping decision-makers between incompatible characterisations of violent economic actors in that country as both potential partners for peace, and necessary targets for law enforcement. If we rigidly and immediately enforce the law in Afghanistan – laws against drug production and trafficking, against terrorism and against human-rights abuse and violations of humanitarian law – we may alienate necessary partners for peace and undermine the only real development opportunities many communities enjoy. We risk encouraging military and law-enforcement solutions to violent economies even as no realistic alternative is in place.[49] A more holistic strategy, which provides a phasing-in of alternative development while gradually reducing violence, is needed. Yet even on such a strategically important case as Afghanistan, there are few mechanisms in place for integrating strategy at the global level – for example by making narcotics listings by the International Narcotics Control Board or terrorist listings by the al Qaeda/Taliban Committee of the United Nations Security Council subject to spatially and/or temporally-limited suspension, to allow developmental or political strategies to work unimpeded by the imperatives of law enforcement. Instead, the letter of the law goes unenforced, creating a risk of apparent hypocrisy and regulatory dissonance. Further thought is urgently needed on how a more coherent policy could be developed, for example by creating mechanisms for allowing strictly controlled strategic exceptions to those global prohibition regimes.

Conclusion

As we consider our readiness to respond to the strategic changes that are being wrought by the convergence of conflict, crime and corruption, there are some reasons for optimism. Attention to these issues is clearly growing, as the recent UN Security Council Presidential Statements make clear.

But there are also reasons for serious concern. Conflicts are, increasingly, the product of illicit structural opportunities in the global economy. Yet our existing systems of regulation at the international level separate out into unconnected compartments the tools for dealing with security, trade, finance, development assistance and crime control. We deal with violent political crises like wildfires popping up in isolated countries, neglecting the underlying structures and networks that connect and produce these localised conflagrations. And our conflict-management systems are built by, of and for states; we struggle to identify, let alone manage, the webs of influence, affiliation and even debt that stretch across national borders and around the world through private trading and financial systems.

All of this leaves violent and criminal entrepreneurs at a distinct advantage in their competition with law-enforcement agencies and peace makers for the support and control of populations and territory. The danger is that vulnerable populations, particularly those burdened with unresponsive and irresponsible state rulers, will be relegated to a system of perpetual war, targeted by gangs, warlords, traffickers, predators, parasites and symbiotes for the cheap labour and 'throwaway' lives they offer. Ultimately, however, it may be those of us who are not trapped in such corners of the world who – wittingly or unwittingly – provide the demand for this cheap labour, cheap resources (in our mobile phones, in the diamond rings on our fingers, in our wooden tables, in cheap oil) and these cheap thrills (counterfeit DVDs, smuggled cigarettes, illegal drugs, trafficked sex). The convergence of crime, corruption and conflict is, in that sense, very much a problem of collective action and collective security.

Conclusion

Achim Wennmann

The ending of wars and the consolidation of peace are transition processes that require a constant effort to deliver security, welfare and representation. In the early 1990s, these processes involved relatively ad-hoc responses by the international community, and the countries in which these took place were compared to a patient 'on the operating table with the left and right sides of his body separated by a curtain and unrelated surgery being performed on each side'.[1] While peace processes, peacebuilding and economic recovery are still characterised by many different types of actors, there is a growing realisation that the establishment of a lasting peace requires a coherent, coordinated and complementary approach.

Standing in the way of such comprehensive approaches is the persistence of long-held beliefs and the reluctance to leave intellectual silos, the latter of which breeds a disinclination to question institutional practice and mandates. These impediments have made it harder to form partnerships between

Achim Wennmann is a Researcher at the Centre on Conflict, Development and Peacebuilding (CCDP) of the Graduate Institute of International and Development Studies in Geneva, Switzerland.

institutions and sectors necessary to assist and drive the transition out of war. By stepping back, it may be possible to identify new opportunities to end war and consolidate peace, and to better understand the underlying transformative processes in which these are embedded.

Overall, the book highlights three general principles that could guide efforts to support a country that has turned its back on violence.[2] The first is that conflict resolution and development in the aftermath of war is inherently a locally defined – yet internationally embedded – transformation process. This process has its own complexities, risks and limitations and is, therefore, resistant to blueprint solutions. Rather, a solid understanding of each specific context should be the starting point for any external assistance. While recognising the self-interested nature of many activities, in recent years international practice has continuously emphasised the importance of local ownership of change, and the alignment of donors behind nationally defined transition strategies.[3]

A second general principle is that the effectiveness of external assistance for peace processes and economic recovery can be measured by its ability to support local conflict-management capacities, and make them self-sustainable over time. It is only when societies can deal with their divisions and disputes by themselves that one may be able to speak of a lasting peace. This is particularly important for the resolution of economic disputes, such as those over land, property or natural resources. Constructing the frameworks for dispute resolution can, therefore, free up productive opportunities and investments, and consolidate economic recovery.

A third general principle is that the expectation of local populations in peace and economic recovery – and of mediators and donors in peacemaking and development – must be carefully managed so that it does not exceed local realities, international constellations, and the local and international commitment to assist change. In as much as peacemaking is about ending a conflict, it is also about delineating what comes next. In this context, economic dimensions are critical because the process of leaving behind the pain and suffering inflicted by war can be accelerated if people invest their time and energy into productive activities. Opportunities to take a job, build a house or cultivate the land are personal proof that a war is over, and something new has begun.

These economic issues are often subsumed in the vision-based politics of transition contexts. This kind of politics is rooted in the desire to make life better for people, although it must acknowledge the difficulties of achieving its goals in the face of common post-conflict challenges, such as increasing criminal violence, devastation and trauma, unexploded ordinance, persisting trade barriers, or low prices for agricultural products. In order to build safeguards against the problem of rising expectations – and deep disappointments – vision-based politics must be discussed among all stakeholders in a responsible manner. This means that vision-building must be consensual, the vision should be as broadly owned as possible, and there should be no major gap between the vision and the capacities of local or international stakeholders to deliver change.[4]

Economic perspectives can contribute to such forward-looking strategies by placing business, economic and development expertise and experience in the service of conflict resolution and peacebuilding. The following distils a set of concluding observations that could help policymakers plan for and mitigate the external and internal pressures that threaten peace settlements.

Economies are a crucial component to increase the quality and longevity of peace. Rapid economic revival is important to buy confidence in the peace process; the implementation of peace accords must be backed up by sufficient financing for specific commitments; and there must be economic institutions that sustain economic recovery over the long term.[5] Private-sector growth and development, investments, natural-resource exploitation, macroeconomic governance, the availability of jobs and social safety nets are at the heart of ensuring development yields. Overall, economics can act as a source of moderation and a stimulus for cooperation. The challenge is to reward work that promotes economic expansion, thereby increasing the size of the cake from which all of society can benefit.

The private sector deserves greater attention in peacemaking and economic recovery. Conflict and fragile countries can be recipients of significant levels of foreign direct investment (FDI) even if an armed conflict is ongoing or escalating, and especially if they are rich in natural resources. A central element for engaging the private sector in peace is the degree to which individual companies or sectors have a joint appreciation of the costs of the conflict to their business, and the potential benefits to be derived from peace. However, when mobilising the private sector for peace it is important to recognise how diverse this set of actors can be: it can range from a one-person business or multinational company, spanning various economic sectors and levels of local or transnational partnerships. Engaging the business community also requires a good understanding of the patrimonial networks that often blur the distinction between the public and private sphere. In these contexts, business leaders may fulfil various functions including mandates in politics, while politicians – or their families – can control parts of an economy.

There is a need for new partnership to address the challenge of conflict economies. Conflict economies have long become central aspects of armed conflicts and, therefore, a key concern for peacemakers and peacebuilders alike. Partnerships between local stakeholders, the development community, and local and international business could create concrete economic alternatives to conflict economies. In these contexts, the economy can be crucial to strengthen the pacts that drive transition processes, but practitioners may have to experiment with new policy tools. These may include channelling a greater part of external assistance through business if it has a reputation for 'getting things done', or recognising the legitimacy and stabilising potential of powerful authority figures who control the levers of security, justice, and welfare at the sub-national level.

New emerging economies are an opportunity for consolidating peace. Investors from emerging economies such as Brazil, China and India represent a new capital stream into countries that have long remained at the margins of commercial interests. In Africa, they have clearly changed the way of doing business, by contributing to the construction of infrastructure and public buildings, and investing in natural-resource ventures. While quality issues, employment standards, reciprocal market access and other issues remain contentious, peacemakers must recognise that the composition of external stakeholders in fragile and conflict countries has changed, and that there is a new set of interests to consider.[6]

Improving the domestic resource base and taxation systems is crucial for a viable economic recovery and the consolidation of peace. Building efficient and just taxation systems has been found to be critical to post-conflict recovery and statebuilding. Historically, these have formed the foundations of strong state–society relations. While a balance has to be found between taxation and the enabling of private enterprise, the development of a locally earned state income is widely held as a cornerstone for sustainable peacebuidling. More attention may need to be given to the questions of how natural-resource ventures can strengthen taxation systems, and whether international development investments should be taxed in support of statebuilding.

Natural resources are an opportunity – not an obstacle – for peace. Politicians and researchers have tended to view natural resources as a problem, in as much as they enable armed conflicts and shape their dynamics. However, this ignores opportunities for ending conflict and consolidating economic recovery. Natural resources can be integrated into a vision-based policy that offers belligerents a different outcome if they agree to stop fighting and engage in a peace process. In addition, the income from natural resources can be used to pay for state-building and public investments that support peacebuilding and private entrepreneurship, hence emphasising the importance of institution building to safeguard the transformation of natural-resource wealth into lasting development benefits.

A sustainable economic recovery should be placed into an overarching policy framework of peacebuilding and state-building. Making peacebuilding and state-building an explicit goal for conflict-affected and fragile states facilitates the management of war-to-peace transitions.[7] On the one hand, it structures a forward-looking political process involving domestic stakeholders; on the other, it directs the international assistance necessary to support a domestic consensus for change. Economic recovery is part of these broader transition processes and it often involves addressing crucial political economy challenges such as monopolised control of economic opportunities, patronage networks or corruption. In these circumstances it is critical to recognise the many manifestations peace can have, and adopt what best fits the local context. The same is true for the state, which does not always comply with the prevailing Western model of statehood. Neither peacebuilding nor state-building are blue-print solutions for instability and armed violence. This is especially true in contexts where a large percentage of the population associates human-rights abuses, corruption and incompetence with 'the state'. Peacebuilding and state-building should remain open to existing and traditional governance mechanisms, and be rooted in a locally owned political process.

Placing economics at the heart of conflict resolution and peacebuilding certainly does not imply that it is a magic solution for armed violence, instability and injustice. The chapters have illustrated that economics on its own has little practical value unless it is related to the broader political, social or military processes taking place within a conflict-affected or fragile state. Thus, for conflict resolution to achieve its maximum impact, it is important to understand how economic issues and instruments translate into political value for the main stakeholders, and strengthen the glue of transitional pacts that drive change.

GLOSSARY

AFRICOM	United States African Command
AQIM	al-Qaeda in the Islamic Maghreb
ARTF	Afghanistan Reconstruction Trust Fund
AUSAID	Australian Government Overseas Aid Programme
BITs	bilateral investment treaties
BWI	Bretton Woods Institutions
CDD	community-driven development strategies
CNDD/FDD	National Council / Forces for the Defence of Democracy, Burundi
CNDP	National Congress for the Defence of the People (eastern DRC)
CSR	Office for the Coordinator of Stabilization and Reconstruction (US)
DfID	UK Department for International Development
DDR	disarmament, demobilisation and reintegration programmes
DRC	The Democratic Republic of the Congo
ECF	Extended Credit Facility, IMF
EITI	Extractive Industries Transparency Initiative
ENDA	Emergency Natural Disaster Assistance, IMF
EPCA	Emergency Post-Conflict Assistance, IMF
FARC	Revolutionary Armed Forces of Colombia
FCO	UK Foreign and Commonwealth Office

FDI	Foreign Direct Investment
FLEGT	EU Forest Law Enforcement Governance and Trade
FMNL	Farabundo Marti National Liberation Front, El Salvador
FNL	National Forces of Liberation, Burundi
GEMAP	*Governance and Economic Management Assistance Programme (Liberia)*
GIA	Armed Islamic Group of Algeria
GNI	Gross National Income
GPSC	Salafist Group for Preaching and Combat, Algeria
HIPC	Highly-Indebted Poor Countries initiative of the BWI
IBRD	International Bank for Reconstruction and Development
ICISS	International Commission on Intervention and State Sovereignty
ICRC	International Committee of the Red Cross
IDA	International Development Association
IFI	International financial institutions
IMF	International Monetary Fund
IPAs	Investment Promotion Agencies
ISAF	International Security Assistance Force in Afghanistan
LTTE	Liberation Tigers of Tamil Eelam (Tamil Tigers)
LURD	Liberians United for Reconciliation and Democracy
MDGs	Millennium Development Goals
MIA/AIS	Islamic Armed Movement /Islamic Salvation Army, Algeria
MIGA	Multilateral Investment Guarantees Agency
MINUSTAH	UN Stabilisation Mission in Haiti
MODEL	Movement for Democracy in Liberia
MONUC	UN Organisation Mission in the Democratic Republic of the Congo
MSF	Médecins Sans Frontières
NATO	North Atlantic Treaty Organisation
NPFL	The *National Patriotic Front of Liberia*
OECD	Organisation for Economic Cooperation and Development
OPIC	Overseas Private Investment Corporation

PA	Palestinian Authority
PCNA	Post Conflict Needs Assessment
PILOTs	payments in lieu of taxes
PKK	Kurdistan Workers' Party
PLO	Palestinian Liberation Organisation
PRGF	Poverty Reduction and Growth Facility, IMF
PRGT	Poverty Reduction and Growth Trust, IMF
PRSP	Poverty Reduction Strategy Papers
PRTs	Provincial Reconstruction Teams (in Afghanistan)
PWYP	'publish what you pay' initiative
RCF	Rapid Credit Facility, IMF
RENAMO	National Resistance Movement in Mozambique
RUF	Revolutionary United Front, Sierra Leone
SBA	Stand-By Arrangements
SCF	Standby Credit Facility, IMF
SPF	State and Peace-Building Fund
SPLM/A	Sudan People's Liberation Movement/ Army
START	Stabilization and Reconstruction Task Force (Canada)
TA	Technical Assistance
TNCs	transnational corporations
ULIMO-K	The United Liberation Movement of Liberia for Democracy, Kroma faction
ULIMO-J	The United Liberation Movement of Liberia for Democracy, Johnson Faction
UNDP	United Nations Development Programme
UNCTAD	United Nations Conference for Trade and Development
UNITA	National Union for the Total Independence of Angola
UNTAET	United Nations Transitional Administration in East Timor
URNG	Guatemalan National Revolutionary Unity
USAID	United States Agency for International Development
UTO	United Tajik Opposition, Tajikistan

NOTES

Introduction

1 Ken Menkhaus, 'State Failure and Ungoverned Space', p. 181.

2 David Keen, *The Economic Functions of Violence in Civil Wars*, Adelphi Paper 320 (Oxford: OUP/IISS, 1998), p. 32.

3 James K. Boyce, 'Aid and Fiscal Capacity in Post-Conflict Countries', p. 101.

4 James Cockayne, 'Crime and Corruption', p. 209.

5 Achim Wennmann, 'Peace Processes, Business and New Economic Futures', p. 17.

6 Menkhaus, 'State Failure and Ungoverned Space', p. 173.

7 *Ibid.*, p. 176.

8 *Ibid.*, p. 179.

9 Cockayne, 'Crime and Corruption', p. 190 and 191.

10 Boyce, 'Aid and Fiscal Capacity-Building in 'Post-Conflict' Countries', p. 119.

11 Päivi Lujala, Siri Aas Rustad and Pilippe Le Billon, 'Natural Resources and Conflict', p. 135.

Chapter One

1 This chapter is based on A. Wennmann, *The Political Economy of Peacemaking*, (London: Routledge, forthcoming 2011), and draws from a broader project on economic issues and instruments in peace processes supported by the Swiss Federal Department of Foreign Affairs.

2 M. Ahtisaari, 'Lessons of Aceh Peace Talks', *Asia Europe Journal*, vol. 6 no. 1, 2008, p. 11.

3 D.A. Baldwin, *Economic Statecraft* (Princeton, MA: Princeton University Press, 1985), p. 9.

4 M. Berdal and D.M. Malone (eds), *Greed and Grievance: Economic Agendas in Civil Wars* (Boulder, CO: Lynne Rienner, 2000) p. 2.

5 A. Wennmann, *Wealth Sharing Beyond 2011: Economic Issues in Sudan's North-South Peace Process* (Genevea: CCDP Working Paper 1, 2009), p. 8.

6 R. MacGinty, *No War, No Peace: The Rejuvenation of Stalled Peace Processes and Peace Accords* (Houndmills: Palgrave Macmillan, 2006), pp. 152–153; D. Sriskandarajah, 'The Return of Peace in Sri Lanka: The Development Cart Before the Conflict Resolution Horse?' *Journal of Peacebuilding and Development*, vol. 1 no. 2, 2003, pp. 21–35.

7 P. Rimple, 'Economic Development: The Latest Recipe for South Ossetian Peace', *Eurasianet*, 20 February 2007, available at http://www.eurasianet.org/departments/insight/articles/eav022007.shtml.

8 A. Vines, 'Angola: Forty Years of War', in P. Batchelor and K. Klingma (eds) *Demilitarization and Peacebuilding in Southern Africa – Volume II* (Aldershot: Ashgate, 2004) pp. 74–104.

9 A. Wennmann, *Economic Issues in Peace Processes: Socio-Economic Inequality and Peace in Nepal* (Geneva: CCDP Working Paper 2, 2009), p. 5.

10 F. Grignon, 'Economic Agendas in the Congolese Peace Process', in M. Nest (ed.), *The Democratic Republic of Congo: Economic Dimensions of War and Peace* (Boulder, CO: Lynne Rienner, 2006) pp. 62–98.

11 A. Wennmann and J. Krause, *Managing the Economic Dimensions of Peace Processes: Resource Wealth, Autonomy, and Peace in Aceh* (Geneva: CCDP Working Paper 3, 2009), available at http://graduateinstitute.ch/webdav/site/ccdp/shared/6305/CCDP-Working-Paper-3-Aceh.pdf.

12 C.L. Siriam, *Peace as Governance: Power Sharing, Armed Groups, and Contemporary Peace Negotiations* (Houndmills: Palgrave Macmillan, 2008) pp. 25, 182.

13 Sudan Ministry of Finance, 'Template for Publication of Sudan Oil Sector Data 2007', (2008); Global Witness, *Fuelling Mistrust: The Need for Transparency in Sudan's Oil Industry* (London: 2009); 'Oil Revenue in Sudan Slashed by 60% in 2009: GoSS', *Sudan Tribune*, 2 March, 2010.

14 Wennmann, *Economic Issues in Peace Processes*, p. 18.

15 J. Frieden, 'International Development and Conflict Transformation', in Federal Department of Foreign Affairs, *Swiss Peace Policy: Nepal* (Bern: Federal Department of Foreign Affairs, 2006), pp. 73–74.

16 United Nations Department of Political Affairs, 'Conflict Prevention in Partnership with UNDP', *Politically Speaking*, Spring, 2009, p. 16.

17 J. Goodhand, *Violent Conflict, Poverty and Chronic Poverty* (Manchester: University of Manchester, 2001) pp. 30–31; D. Sweetman, *Business, Conflict Resolution and Peacebuilding* (London: Routledge, 2009) p. 11.

18 J. Bray, 'Attracting Reputable Companies to Risky Environments: Petroleum and Mining Companies', in I. Bannon and P. Collier (eds), *Natural Resources and Violent Conflict: Options and Actions* (Washington DC: World Bank, 2009), pp. 287–352.

19 J. Nelson, *The Business of Peace: The Private Sector as a Partner in Conflict Prevention and Resolution* (London and New York: The Prince of Wales Business Leaders' Forum, International Alert, Council on Economic Priorities, 2001), pp. 73–140.

20 C. Charney, 'Civil Society, Political Violence, and Democratic Transitions: Business and the Peace Process in South Africa, 1990–1994', *Comparative Studies in Society and History* vol. 41 no. 1, 1999, pp. 182–206.

21 G. Ben-Porat, 'Between Power and Hegemony: Business Communities

in Peace Processes', *Review of International Studies,* vol. 1 no. 2, 2005: pp. 325–348.

22 Portland Trust, 'The Role of Economics in Paecebuilding: Our lessons Learned', unpublished paper, June 2010.

23 A. Vines, 'The Business of Peace: "Tiny" Rowland, Financial Incentives, and the Mozambican Settlement', in J. Armon, D. Hendrickson and A. Vines (eds), *The Mozambican Peace Process in Perspective* (London: Conciliation Resources, 1998).

24 C. Batruch, 'Oil and Conflict: Lundin Petroleum's Experience in Sudan', in J.K. Alyson Bailes and I. Frommelt (eds), *Business and Security: Public-Private Sector Relationships in a New Security Environment* (Oxford: Oxford University Press, 2004), pp. 148–160.

25 S. Tripathi and C. Gündüz, *A Role for the Private Sector in Peace Processes? Examples and Implications for Third-party Mediation* (Geneva: Centre for Humanitarian Dialogue, 2008), p. 24.

26 A. Rettberg, *Business-Led Peacebuilding in Colombia: Fad or Future of Country in Crisis?* (Crisis States Programme Working Paper 58 (phase 1), London: London School of Economics, 2004), p. 1, available at http://www.crisisstates.com/download/projectnotes/rettberg.pdf.

27 See J. Brauer and J.T. Marlin, *Defining Peace Industries and Calculating the Potential Size of a Peace Gross World Product by Country and by Economic Sector* (Sydney: Institute for Economics and Peace, 2009), available at http://www.economicsandpeace.org/UserFiles/File/DefiningPeaceIndustrieAndCalculatingAPeaceWGP.pdf.

28 C. Ksoll, R. Macchiavello and A. Morjaria, *Guns and Roses: The Impact of the Kenyan Post-Election Violence on Flower Exporting Firms* Working Paper 6 (Centre for African Economies, 2009), p. 1, available at http://www.csae.ox.ac.uk/workingpapers/pdfs/2009-06text.pdf.

29 'Kenya Post-Election Violence Costs Country Loss in Tourisms Income', *Ghana Business News,* 16 May 2009.

30 C.M. Blanchard, *Iraq: Oil and Gas Legislation, Revenue Sharing, and U.S. Policy* (Washington DC: Congressional Research Service, 2009), p. 6.

31 S. Raine, *China's African Challenge* (London: Routledge for the IISS, 2009) pp. 105–129.

32 D. Large, *China's Role in the Mediation and Resolution of Conflict in Africa* (Geneva: Centre for Humanitarian Dialogue, 2008) p. 38.

33 A. Wennmann, *Wealth Sharing Beyond 2011,* p. 18.

Chapter Two

1 A range of fragility indices is used to monitor and measure 'fragility'. A number of these are neatly summarised in A. Wennmann, 'Grasping the Strengths of Fragile States: Aid Effectiveness between Top-down and Bottom-up Statebuilding', *CCDP Working Paper 6* (Geneva: CCDP, 2010), available at http://graduateinstitute.ch/webdav/site/ccdp/shared/6305/Broch_6_BD.pdf.

2 See A. Ghani and C. Lockhart, *Fixing Failed States: A Framework for Rebuilding*

a Fractured World (Oxford: Oxford University Press, 2008).

3 See, for example, the country and thematic reports prepared by the OECD at http://www.oecd.org/docum ent/5/0,3343,en_21571361_42277499_42 283205_1_1_1_1,00.html.

4 See P. Collier, V.L. Elliott, H. Hegre, A. Hoeffler, M. Reynal-Querol, and S. Sambani, *Breaking the Conflict Trap* (Oxford: Oxford University Press, 2003).

5 From Robert Zoellick's keynote address to the 2008 IISS Global Strategic Review, available at http://www.iiss.org/conferences/global-strategic-review/global-strategic-review-2008/keynote-address/.

6 See R. Muggah, T. Sisk and S. Lakhani, *Post-conflict Governance: A Strategic Framework* (Geneva: UNDP/BCPR, 2010 forthcoming).

7 See *Human Security Report 2009: The Shrinking Costs of War* (Oxford: Oxford University Press, 2010).

8 See R. Muggah (ed.), *Security and Post-Conflict Reconstruction: Dealing with Fighters in the Aftermath of War* (New York: Routledge, 2009).

9 Meanwhile, World Bank President Robert Zoellick told an IISS conference in 2008 that 'when states are breaking down or overcome by conflict, they pose waves of danger'. For the full text see http://web.worldbank.org/WBSITE/EXTERNAL/NEWS/0,,conten tMDK:21898896~pagePK:34370~piPK:42770~theSitePK:4607,00.html.

10 UK Stabilisation Unit, *UK Concepts of Stabilisation* (London: Stabilisation Unit, 2007): http://www.stabilisationunit. gov.uk/resources/factsheets/ Stabilisation%20Unit%20UK%20 Concept%20of%20Stabilisation%20 Factsheet.doc, Accessed 20 April 2010.

The G7+ comprises Afghanistan, Burundi, Central African Republic, Chad, Cote d'Ivoire, the Democratic Republic of the Congo, Haiti, Liberia, Nepal, Solomon Islands, Sierra Leone, South Sudan and Timor Leste.

11 See US State Department, *2009 in Review* (Washington DC: CRS, 2010): at http://www.crs.state.gov/. Accessed 20 April 2010.

12 See Canada. *START: Organisational Structure* (Ottawa: DFAIT, 2008): www. international.gc.ca/START-GTSR. Accessed 20 April 2010.

13 See, for example, the Colombian government's Presidential Directive 01 of 2009.

14 See, for example, R. Muggah and I. Carvalho, 'Brazil's "Southern Effect" in Fragile Countries' (Paris: OECD-PDG, 2009): available at http://www.opendemocracy.co.uk/robert-muggah-lona-szab%C3%B3-de-carvalho/brazils-southern-effect-in-fragile-countries.

15 See Zoellick, 2008.

16 See C. Cramer, *Civil War Is Not a Stupid Thing: Accounting for Violence in Developing Countries* (London: Hurst & Company, 2006).

17 See Collier et al., *Breaking the Conflict Trap*.

18 See, for example, R. Paris, *At War's End: Building Peace After Civil Conflict* (New York: Cambridge University Press, 2004).

19 See, for example, N. McFarlane and Y. Khong, *Human Security and the UN: A Critical History* (New York: Indiana University Press, 2006).

20 See, for example, the Human Security Network (which has met regularly since 1999): http://www.mzz.gov.si/en/foreign_policy/human_security_network_hsn/.

21 See, for example, USIP Briefing 'Post-Conflict Stabilisation and Reconstruction: What have we learned from Iraq and Afghanistan?' (Washington DC: the US Institute for Peace, 2005); Bensahel et al., *Principles for Stabilisation and Reconstruction* (The Rand Cooperation: 2009). These, and other texts, are shaping doctrine in Canada, the UK and the US.

22 See, for example, www.guardian. co.uk/world/2009/aug/31/general-mcchrystal-afghanistan.com.

23 That said, the UK has also given greater weight to the tension between politics and ostensibly neutral humanitarian assistance. See, for example, DfID, *Why We Need to Work More Effectively in Fragile States* (London: DfID, 2005): available at http://webarchive.nationalarchives. gov.uk/+/http://www.dfid.gov.uk/ Documents/publications/fragilestates-paper.pdf.

24 It is worth noting, however, that the UN has yet to fully take on the language of fragility. According to senior figures in the UNDP and UNDPKO, there is sufficient apprehension among G77 (group of 77 developing) member states with the concept of fragility as to limit its use in the wider UN system.

25 See, for example, UNDPKO, *United Nations Peacekeeping Operations: Guidelines and Principles* (New York: DPKO, 2008): available at http://www. peacekeepingbestpractices.unlb.org/ Pbps/Library/Capstone_Doctrine_ ENG.pdf. Accessed 20 April 2010; see also A. Le Roy and S. Malcorra, 'A New Partnership Agenda: Charting A New Horizon for UN Peacekeeping', United Nations Department of Peacekeeping Operations and UN Department for Field Support, New York, July 2009; available at http://www.

un.org/en/peacekeeping/documents/ newhorizon.pdf.

26 See, for example, OECD, *Concepts and Dilemmas of State Building in Fragile Situations*, 2008: http://www. oecd.org/dataoecd/59/51/41100930. pdf; OECD, *Service Delivery in Fragile Situations*, 2008: http://www. oecd.org/dataoecd/17/54/40886707. pdf; OECD, *State Building in Fragile Situations*, 2008: http://www.oecd. org/dataoecd/62/9/41212290.pdf; and OECD, *Ensuring Fragile States are Not Left Behind, Factsheet*, 2007: http://www. oecd.org/dataoecd/34/24/40090369.pdf

27 See Zoellick, 2008.

28 There are 23 countries classified as fragile in Africa, six in Asia, six in Central Asia, five in the Americas and three in the Middle East.

29 According to the OECD, aid to fragile states was approximately $34.6bn in 2008. See also https://community. oecd.org/community/factblog/ blog/2010/04/16/aid-for-fragile-states.

30 See, for example, www.jfcom.mil/ newslink/storyarchive/2010/pa031510. html.

31 See, for example, R. Muggah and S. de Carvalho, *The Southern Effect: Brazil's Engagement in Fragile States,* (Paris: OECD, 2009); and S. Elharawy, *Stabilisation and Humanitarian Action in Colombia: Background Paper* (London: ODI, 2010).

32 See, for example, M. Duffield, *Development, Security and Unending war: Governing the World of Peoples,* (Cambridge: Polity, 2007).

33 See, for example, M. McNerney, 'Stabilisation and Reconstruction in Afghanistan: Are PRTs a Model or a Muddle?', Carlisle Defence Academy, 2006.

34 See, for example, A. Zwitter, 'Humanitarian Action on the Battlefields of

the Global War on Terror', *Journal of Humanitarian Assistance*, 25 October, 2008.

35 See N. De Torrent, 'Humanitarianism Sacrificed: Integration's False Promise', *Ethics and International Affairs* vol. 18 no. 2, 2004, pp. 3–12.

36 N. Leader, *The Politics of Principle: The Principles of Humanitarian Action in Practice*, HPG Report 2 (London: ODI, 2000).

37 See OECD, *Armed Violence Reduction: Enabling Development* (Paris: OECD, 2009).

38 See, for example, M. Barnett and T.G. Weiss, 'Humanitarianism: a brief history of the present', in Barnett and Weiss (eds.), *Humanitarianism in Question: Politics, Power, Ethics* (London: Cornell University Press, 2008).

39 See S. Collinson, S. Elhawary and R. Muggah, 'States of fragility: stabilisation and its implications for humanitarian action', HPG Working Papers published by ODI, May 2010, available at http://www.odi.org.uk/resources/ details.asp?id=4881&title=states-fragility-stabilisation-its-implications-humanitarian-action.

40 See H. Rittel and W. Webber, 'Dilemmas in a General Theory of Planning', *Policy Sciences*, vol. 4, 1973: pp. 155–69.

41 See, for example, M. Barnett and D. Zurcher, 'Peacebuilders Contract: Why Peacebuilding Recreate Weak States', in Paris and Sisk (eds), *Dilemmas of Statebuilding: Confronting the Contradictions of Post-War Peace Operations*, (New York: Routledge, 2008).

42 See, for example, Muggah and Krause, 'Closing the Gap Between Peace Operations and Post-Conflict Insecurity: Towards a Violence Reduction Agenda', pp. 136–150.

43 See, for example, A. Stoddard, A. Harmer and V. DiDomenico, 'Providing Aid in Insecure Environments: 2009 Update', HPG Policy Brief 34, April, 2009, at http://www.odi.org.uk/resources/download/3250.pdf. Accessed 20 April 2010.

Chapter Three

1 'Whole-of-government' approaches in this context refer to the coordination of policy input across various government departments dealing with fragile or conflict countries, with the aim of increasing cost effectiveness and legitimacy, and strengthening implementation. See Organization for Economic Cooperation and Development (OECD), *Whole of Government Approaches to Fragile States* (Paris: OECD, 2006), p. 18.

2 S. Patrick and K. Brown, *Greater than the Sum of its Parts: Assessing 'Whole of Government' Approaches to Fragile States*, Center for Global Development brief, 2007, p. 6, available at http://www.cgdev.org/doc/weakstates/Fragile_States.pdf

3 L. van der Goor and M. van Beijnum, *The Netherlands and its Whole of Government Approaches on Fragile States: Case Study Sudan* (The Hague: Clingendael Institute/OECD 2006), p. 39.

4 UNDG and World Bank, *Joint Guidance Note on Integrated Recovery Planning*

using Post Conflict Needs Assessments and Transitional Results Frameworks (Working Draft, September 2007, p. 3), available at http://www.undg.org/?P=147.

5 See Stephen John Stedman, 'Spoiler Problems in Peace Processes', in Paul C. Stern and Daniel Druckman (eds), *International Conflict Resolution After the Cold War* (Washington DC: National Academies Press, 2000).

6 The longer version of this paper goes into greater detail for these country case studies and additionally includes analysis of Haiti, Kosovo and South Sudan.

7 This process culminated in the Berlin Conference of 31 March to 1 April 2004 (which resulted in pledges of $8.2 billion over three years) and the London conference the following year.

8 See for example, the International Political Institute, *A Review of Peace Operations: a Case for Change* (London: King's College London, University of London, 2003).

9 This applies, of course, across the spectrum of governmental actors in these contexts, not just diplomacy and development actors. Cooperation with the military is particularly important to ensure complementarity of thought and action.

10 See International Dialogue on Peacebuilding and Statebuilding, *Dili Declaration: A New Vision for Peacebuilding and Statebuilding,* available at http://www.oecd.org/dataoecd/12/30/44927821.pdf. See also Swiss Agency for Development and Cooperation, *3C Conference Report,* (Bern: SDC, 2009).

Chapter Four

1 See *In Larger Freedom: Towards Development, Security and Human Rights for All* (New York: Report of the Secretary-General to the General Assembly, A/59/2005, 21 March 2005). See also, Robert B. Zoellick, 'Securing Development' (Washington DC: United States Institute of Peace, 8 January 2009), available at http://siteresources.worldbank.org/NEWS/Resources/RBZUSIPSpeech010809.pdf.

2 For information on the mandates and framework of cooperation between these two institutions, as well as on the specific financing instruments (i.e., trust funds, SPF, PRGF, etc.), see http://www.imf.org/external/about.htm and http://web.worldbank.org/WBSITE/

EXTERNAL/EXTABOUTUS/0,,page PK:50004410~piPK:36602~theSitePK:29708,00.html.

3 Afghanistan, for example, a country at the top of the international peace and security agenda, and the top of the US foreign-policy agenda, contributes only 0.02% of global output and even less to global exports. In contrast to its tiny economy, with GDP estimated at $15 billion in 2010, the Afghan war will cost the United States about $100bn in 2010 – twice what the US allocated to social and development aid across the world.

4 Some of the criticism continued even after enough evidence to refute was provided. See, for example, Graciana del Castillo, 'Post-Conflict

Reconstruction and the Challenge to the International Organizations: The Case of El Salvador', *World Development*, vol. 29, no. 12, 2001, pp. 1969 and 1978–79.

5   For example, Mozambique signed its peace agreement in 1992 and ODA peaked at 80% of GNI. Ten years later, aid was still 55% of GNI, and in 2005–08 the country still relied on aid levels of about a quarter of its GNI.

6   John M. Keynes, *The Economic Consequences of the Peace* (New York: Harcourt, Brace and Howe, Inc., 1920).

7   For an overview of the non-economic aspects of the transition to peace, see Mats Berdal, *Building Peace After War* (London: Routledge for the IISS, 2009).

8   This is slowly changing. See, for example, Tony Addison and Tilman Brück, *Making Peace Work: The Challenges of Social and Economic Reconstruction* (London: Palgrave Macmillan, 2008); Ashraf Ghani and Clare Lockhart, *Fixing Failed Sates* (Oxford: Oxford University Press, 2008); and James K. Boyce and Madalene O'Donnell (eds), *Peace and the Public Purse: Economic Policies for Postwar State-Building* (Boulder, CO: Lynne Rienner Publishers, 2007).

9   As a general rule, both groups of countries have devastated or significantly distorted economies, their human and physical infrastructure are in shambles and major macroeconomic imbalances.

10 See Graciana del Castillo, *Rebuilding War-Torn States: The Challenge of Post-Conflict Economic Reconstruction* (Oxford: Oxford University Press, 2008), p. 40 and del Castillo, 'Auferstehen aus Ruinen: Die Besonderen Bedingungen des Wirtschaftlichen Wiederaufbaus nach Konflikten', *der Überblick* (Germany's *Foreign Affairs*), vol. 4, December 2006.

11 See Alvaro de Soto and Graciana del Castillo, 'Obstacles to Peacebuilding', *Foreign Policy*, vol. 94, Spring 1994, pp. 69–83 and del Castillo, 'Peace Through Reconstruction', *Brown Journal of World Affairs*, vol. VXI, issue II, Spring/Summer 2010.

12 See Graciana del Castillo, *Rebuilding War-Torn States*, pp. 33–35.

13 This argument was not at all accepted by the BWI when it was first raised in the early 1990s (see del Castillo, 'Post-Conflict Peacebuilding: The Challenge to the UN', *CEPAL Review*, vol. 55, October 1995, pp. 29–30; See, also del Castillo, 'Post-Conflict Reconstruction and the Challenge to the International Organizations', p. 1968; and del Castillo, *Rebuilding War-Torn States*, pp. 4, 20, 30, 133–4, 215 and 232). As Zoellick's statement shows, the Bank has now accepted this at the highest level, and the IMF has come to accept it in some cases. See Sanjeev Gupta, Tareq Shamsuddin, Benedict J. Clements, Alex Segura-Ubiergo, Rina Bhattacharya and Todd D. Mattina, 'Rebuilding Fiscal Institutions in Postconflict Countries', Occasional Paper no. 247 (Washington DC: IMF, 2005), for a discussion of how tax policy in post-conflict situations may require adopting policies that are not optimally efficient. Available at http://www.imf.org/External/Pubs/NFT/Op/247/op247.pdf.

14 See del Castillo, *Rebuilding War-Torn States*, p. 30.

15 For a comprehensive analysis of the role that the UN Security Council gives the BWI in peace and security, see Kristen E. Boon, 'Coining a New Jurisdiction: The Security Council as Economic Peacekeeper', *Vanderbilt Journal of Transnational Law*, vol. 41,

no. 4, October 2008; and Boon, 'Open for Business: International Financial Institutions, Post-Conflict Economic Reform and the Rule of Law', *New York University Journal of International Law and Politics*, vol. 39, no. 3, 2007, pp. 513–81.

16 See del Castillo, *Rebuilding War-Torn States*, pp. 66–93 and pp. 103–221. For the evolution of this assistance up to 2008, see del Castillo, 'Economic Reconstruction of War-Torn Countries: The Role of the International Financial Institutions', *Seton Hall Law Review*, vol. 38, no. 4, pp. 1280–1295.

17 For changes in conditionality at the Fund, see IMF, 'Creating Policy Space – Responsive Design and Streamlined Conditionality in Recent Low-Income Country Programs', 10 September 2009, p. 5, available at http://www.imf. org/external/np/pp/eng/2009/091009a. pdf. See also, 'Review of World Bank Conditionality', September 2005, available at http://siteresources. worldbank.org/PROJECTS/ Resources/40940-1114615847489/ webConditionalitysept05.pdf .

18 See Zoellick, 'Securing Development'.

19 *Ibid.*

20 The 'integrated approach to human security', was a concept developed by former UN Secretary-General Boutros Boutros-Ghali in his *Agenda for Peace* in 1992. Under such an approach, military, political, economic, social, and environmental problems should be addressed jointly and coherently rather than separately as had traditionally been the case. That is the approach we advocated for El Salvador at a time when the peace process and the economic programme clearly clashed. See de Soto and del Castillo, 'Obstacles to Peacebuilding', p. 71.

21 For all information concerning World Development Report, including Concept Note, go to http://search. worldbank.org/all?qterm=WDR%20 2011.

22 The other parts of the World Bank Group also play an important role in supporting countries coming out of war. While the International Finance Corporation (IFC) supports economic recovery by helping to improve the investment climate and the financial sector, it also supports private participation in infrastructure, agribusiness and mining. The Multilateral Investment Guarantee Agency (MIGA) promotes foreign direct investment through the provision of political risk insurance, or guarantees, to investors and lenders against losses by noncommercial risks.

23 The IDA lends money (known as credits) on concessional terms (no interest charge, 35 to 40 years repayment and ten-year grace period). The IDA also provides grants to countries at risk of debt distress. The SPF replaced the Post-Conflict Fund (PCF) and the Low Income Countries Under Stress Trust Fund (LICUS TF) which had been in operation since 1998 and 2004, respectively. By going through a single fund, the Bank aimed to adopt a more unified approach in its support for these countries.

24 See IMF, 'IMF Managing Director Dominique Strauss-Kahn Says Economic Recovery Linked to Global Stability and Peace', Press Release no. 10/22, 31 January 2010, available at http://www.imf.org/external/np/sec/ pr/2010/pr1022.htm.

25 See *IMF Survey Online*, 'IMF Chief Emphasizes Support for Haiti', 1 April 2010, at http://www.imf.org/external/

pubs/ft/survey/so/2010/car040110a.htm.

26 See Giovanni Andrea Cornia, Richard Jolly and Frances Stewart, *Adjustment with a Human Face* (New York: Oxford University Press, 1987). The area of adjustment with a human face can now be added to those in which theoretical and practical research by the UN eventually spilled over to the BWI. See Richard Jolly, Louis Emmerij, Dharam Ghai and Frédéric Lapeyre, *UN Contributions to Development Thinking and Practice* (Bloomington, Indiana: Indiana University Press, 2004).

27 See http://www.changes-challenges.org/story/dominique-strauss-kahn-successful-partnerships-africa's-growth-challenge.

28 The PRGT replaced the Poverty Reduction and Growth Facility-Exogenous Shock Facility (PRGF-ESF) Trust. The facilities are distinguished primarily by the duration of the financing and adjustment needs, and the conditionality standard. For the details see 'A New Architecture of Facilities for Low-Income Countries,' (Washington DC: IMF, 26 June 2009), available at http://www.imf.org/external/np/pp/eng/2009/062609.pdf. The reform became effective and operational in January 2010, when all lenders and subsidy contributors approved it. Most of the subsidy resources will come from IMF limited sales of gold reserves.

29 See 'Eligibility to Use the Fund's Facilities for Concessional Financing', Washington DC: IMF, 11 January 2010), available at http://www.imf.org/external/np/pp/eng/2010/011110.pdf.

30 See del Castillo, 'Economic Reconstruction of War-Torn Countries: The Role of the International Financial Institutions', p. 1288, for the constraining requirements to qualify for EPCA. Because of this, the last middle-income country to use it was Lebanon in 2008, and the facility was only used once in 2009 by Guinea-Bissau.

31 See, 'IMF Executive Board Approves US$114 Million in Aid to Haiti', Press Release no. 10/17, 27 January 2010, at http://www.imf.org/external/np/sec/pr/2010/pr1017.htm.

32 Bosnia was removed from the PRGT list for concessional financing in 2003, but remained on the IDA list, and rightly so. In July 2009, shortly after joining the World Bank, Kosovo became IDA eligible but it is not included in the PRGT. So the PRGT and IDA lists differ in that the IDA includes Albania, Bosnia and Kosovo.

33 The Stand-By Arrangement (SBA) is a widely used facility that lends at market rates, after the country complies with specified conditionality. The length of a SBA is flexible, and typically covers a period of 12–24 months, but no more than 36 months, consistent with addressing short-term balance-of-payments problems.

34 Recent SBAs for post-conflict countries are of much longer duration than the ones in El Salvador and Bosnia in the early 1990s which were for 12–18 months. For example, Iraq has an SBA for two years, Angola for 27 months, and Bosnia for 36 months.

35 See Graciana del Castillo and Edmund S. Phelps, 'The Right Way to Rebuild Georgia', Project Syndicate, November 2008, available at http://www.project-syndicate.org/commentary/delcastillo6/English.

36 In 2007 the World Bank included post-conflict countries with other

fragile states in the LICUS Initiative. In 2010, the IMF included post-conflict countries with other low-income countries. Although efforts to make assistance more effective for these more vulnerable countries are welcome, the lumping together of these countries is unfortunate since it leads to a 'development as usual' approach.

37 See del Castillo, *Rebuilding War-Torn States*, p. 47.

38 This rule in facts eliminates the possibility that the government runs a budget deficit and finances it through money creation. See del Castillo, *Rebuilding War-Torn States*, Chapter 9, pp. 166–190.

39 For more on aid channelled outside the government budget, see IMF, 'Islamic Republic of Afghanistan: Sixth Review Under the Arrangement Under the Poverty Reduction and Growth Facility (PRGF)', 21 January, 2010, available at http://imf.org/external/pubs/ft/scr/2010/cr1022.pdf.

40 Since 2004 the IMF has been increasingly involved in a public debate on its policies. See, for example, IMF: 'Response to ActionAid International', 17 May 2007, available at http://www.imf.org/external/np/vc/2007/051707.htm. Revisions concerning conditionality also represent a major change from earlier policy (see chapter four, endnote 24). In 2004, the organisation also engaged in a debate with ActionAid International on the impact of the IMF programmes on HIV/AIDS and other social programmes. This debate is indicative of the tradeoffs involved with regard to expenditure following crises: http://www.imf.org/external/np/vc/2004/093004.htm.

41 In fact, the Fund reinforces the linkage between the programmes it supports and the goal of poverty alleviation and growth, and acknowledges the importance of taking exceptional measures to protect the poor during the current crisis.

42 It is no exaggeration to argue that aid information has been, and remains, one of the most chaotic aspects of reconstruction. Without this information, governments will not be able to design their policies effectively. Not much change has taken place since the problem was first identified. See Susan Woodward, 'Economic priorities for successful peace implementation', in Stephen J. Stedman, Donald Rothchild and Elizabeth M. Cousens, *Ending Civil Wars: The Implementation of Peace Agreements* (Boulder, CO: Lynne Rienner, 2002), chapter 7, p. 200.

43 See http://www.haiticonference.org/story.html.

44 The problem of lack of integration in rural development programmes is certainly not new, nor is it restricted to conflict countries. In 2007, the Independent Evaluation Group of the World Bank concluded that Bank policies were pushing African governments to cut or eliminate fertiliser subsidies, decontrol prices and privatise. Although they may have improved fiscal discipline, they had failed to achieve food security. The findings led Robert Zoellick to declare a Green Revolution for Africa as one of his top priorities on his appointment as president. The report is discussed in: http://www.brettonwoodsproject.org/art-558763. See also Celia W. Dugger, 'World Bank Neglects African Agriculture', *New York Times*, 15 October, 2007; and 'Malawi: Can it Feed Itself?', *The Economist*, 3 May 2008.

45 A notable exception to the fragmented approach to rural development is the Millennium Villages Project in Africa, which has produced important positive results after only three years of operation. See Earth Institute at Columbia University, Millennium Promise and UNDP, *Harvest of Development in Rural Africa: The Millennium Villages After Three Years*, 2010, available at http://www.millenniumvillages.org/docs/MVP_Report_2010FINAL.pdf.

46 See IMF, 'Creating Policy Space', p. 4, in which the Fund has accepted the need for improvements in targeting subsidies to the most needy low-income countries to ensure social protection during crises.

47 Fertiliser and seed subsidies in Malawi (a non-conflict country) adopted in 2004 amounted to 6% of current expenditure (close to 2% of GDP). In two years they increased to close to 9% of current expenditure and 2.5% of GDP (calculated with IMF data). Three years later, the IMF recognised that 'recent robust economic growth has enabled one of Africa's poorest countries to make real strides in reducing chronic food insecurity and progress toward poverty reduction and development targets'; see IMF Survey Online, *'Malawi New IMF Loan Boosts Prospects for Sustained Growth'*, 1 April 2010, available at http://www.imf.org/external/pubs/ft/survey/so/2010/car033110a.htm.

48 In the mid-1990s, with the support of the BWI and the US, Haiti reduced tariffs on rice production from 35% to 3% as part of sweeping trade liberalisation reforms; as a result, a country that once produced all the rice it consumed has now become dependent on rice imports to support its population. See Josiane Georges, 'Trade and the Disappearance of Rice', TED Case Studies, no. 725, June 2004, at http://www1.american.edu/TED/haitirice.htm.

49 Quoted in Andrew Martin, 'So Much Food, So Much Hunger', *New York Times*, 20 September 2009.

50 In Vietnam, the combination of a relatively educated but cheap labour force, and untapped natural resources (oil and gas, gold, gemstones and tungsten), made the country attractive to foreign investment early on in its reconstruction. Although countries like the DRC, Angola and Afghanistan are rich in natural resources, they largely lack the security and human resources needed. Although these countries always find investors greedy for these resources that are willing to take increased risk, improved labour skills could make the countries more attractive to investment and would create more links to the national economy. Otherwise, particularly when foreign labour is necessary, it may lead to enclaves, without much impact on the local economy.

51 The latter two are problems to be addressed in Afghanistan, where the Aynak contract contemplates the employment of local labour but the required skills are not easily available in the country, and where water is a scarce commodity.

52 The last two are key areas to be addressed in Timor Leste.

53 See del Castillo, 'Economic Reconstruction of War-Torn Countries, pp. 1285–87.

Chapter Five

1   Paul Smoke and Robert R. Taliercio Jr., 'Aid, Public Finance, and Accountability: Cambodian Dilemmas', in James Boyce and Madalene O'Donnell (eds), *Peace and the Public Purse: Economic Policies for Postwar Statebuilding* (Boulder, CO: Lynne Rienner, 2007), pp. 85–118.

2   For more on this, see Ashraf Ghani, Clare Lockhart, Nargis Nehan and Baqer Massoud, 'The Budget as the Linchpin of the State: Lessons from Afghanistan', in Boyce and O'Donnell, eds, *Peace and the Public Purse*, pp. 153–84.

3   Sanjeev Gupta, Benedict Clements, Rina Bhattacharya and Shamit Chakravarti find a negative relationship between government revenue and conflict in a sample of low- and middle-income countries; see Gupta et al, 'Fiscal Consequences of Armed Conflict and Terrorism in Low- and Middle-income Countries', *European Journal of Political Economy*, vol. 20 no. 2, 2004, pp. 403–421. The intensity of conflict, as well as its presence, also negatively affects the tax/GDP ratio; see Tony Addison, Abdur R. Chowdhury and S. Mansoob Murshed, 'The Fiscal Dimensions of Conflict and Reconstruction,' in Tony Addison and Alan Roe (eds), *Fiscal Policy for Development: Poverty, Reconstruction and Growth* (Basingstoke: Palgrave Macmillan, 2004), pp. 260–73.

4   Emilia Pires and Michael Francino, 'National Ownership and International Trusteeship: The Case of Timor-Leste', in Boyce and O'Donnell, eds, *Peace and the Public Purse*, pp. 147.

5   See Boyce *Investing in Peace: Aid and Conditionality after Civil Wars*, (Oxford: Oxford University Press, 2002), pp. 41–2; and Susanne Jonas, *Of Centaurs and Dove: Guatemala's Peace Process*, (Boulder, CO: Westview, 2000), pp. 185–186.

6   Among dozens of examples of EU budget-support conditionality listed in a report by the European Commission (2005), the Mozambique case is the sole example of revenue-side conditionality.

7   'The Afghanistan Compact', London Conference on Afghanistan, 31 January–1 February 2006, p. 12. Available at http://www.unama-afg.org/news/_londonConf/_docs/06jan30-AfghanistanCompact-Final.pdf.

8   For further discussion of revenue conditionality, see Michael Carnahan, 'Options for Revenue Generation in Post-Conflict Environments,' Political Economy Research Institute, Policy Paper Series on Post-Conflict Public Finance (Amherst, MA and New York: Center on International Cooperation: May 2007).

9   Quoted in Sanjeev Gupta, Shamsuddin Tareq, Benedict Clemens, Alex Segura-Ubiergo and Rina Bhattacharya, 'Rebuilding Fiscal Institutions in Postconflict Countries' Occasional Paper no. 247 (Washington DC: IMF, December, 2005), p. 12, available at http://www.imf.org/External/Pubs/NFT/Op/247/op247.pdf.

10 Ghani et al, in Boyce and O'Donnell eds, *Peace and the Public Purse*, p. 174.

11 *Ibid.*, p. 136.

12 *Ibid.*, p.136.

13 Quoted in Paul Collier, Lani Elliott, Havard Hegre, Anke Hoeffler, Marta Reynal-Querol and Nicholas Sambanis, *Breaking the Conflict Trap: Civil War and Development Policy* (New York: Oxford University Press, 2003), p.166.

14 Mansoob S. Murshed and Mohammad Zulfan Tadjoeddin, 'Reappraising the Greed and Grievance Explanations for Violent Internal Conflict', Micro-Level Analysis of Violent Conflict, Research Working Paper No. 2 (Brighton: Institute of Development Studies, 2007) p. 35.

15 The World Bank, 2002; UK Department for International Development (DfID), 2003; the US Agency for International Development (USAID), 2005; and the Swedish International Development Cooperation Agency (SIDA), 2006.

16 See Frances Stewart, Graham Brown and Alex Cobham, 'Promoting Group Justice: Fiscal Policies in Post-Conflict Countries', Policy Paper Series on Post-Conflict Public Finance, November 2007, available at http://www. cic.nyu.edu/peacebuilding/docs/ Promoting%20Group%20Justice.pdf.

17 Ghani et al, in Boyce and O'Donnell (eds), *Peace and the Public Purse*, p. 179.

18 See, for example, Joan Esteban and Debraj Ray, 'Conflict and Distribution,' *Journal of Economic Theory* 87, 1999, pp. 379–415.; and José G. Montalvo and Marta Reynal-Querol, 'Ethnic Polarization, Potential Conflict, and Civil Wars,' *American Economic Review* 95(3), 2005, pp. 796–816.

19 Ravi Kanbur, 'Poverty and Conflict: The Inequality Link.' New York: International Peace Academy, 'Coping with Crisis' Working Paper Series, June 2007, p. 3.

20 Robert Putnam, *Bowling Alone: The Collapse and Revival of American Community* (New York: Simon & Schuster, 2000), p. 362.

21 Kanbur, 'Poverty and Conflict', p.6.22 For a review of the rather sparse literature on the distributional impacts of taxation in developing countries, see N. Gemmell and O. Morrissey,

'Distribution and Poverty Impacts of Tax Structure Reform in Developing Countries: How Little We Know', *Development Policy Review vol.* 23 no. 2, 2005, pp. 131-144.

23 P. Rodas-Martini, 'Building Fiscal Provisions into Peace Agreements: Cautionary Tales from Guatemala' in Boyce and O'Donnell (eds), *Peace and The Public Purse*, p. 90; Jonas, *Of Centaurs and Dove*, pp. 171–72.

24 This figure excludes counter-narcotics expenditures, which would push the ratio closer to 600%. Figures from World Bank, *Afghanistan: Managing Public Finances for Development. Volume V: Improving Public Finance Management in the Security Sector*, report no. 34582-AF, (Washington DC: World Bank, December 22, 2005), p.42. Available at http://www-wds.worldbank.org/ servlet/WDSContentServer/WDSP/IB/ 2006/01/11/000160016_20060111123047 /Rendered/PDF/345821vol051AF.pdf.

25 *Ibid*, p. 47.

26 World Bank and IMF, *Global Monitoring Report 2005: Millennium Development Goals: From Consensus to Momentum.* Washington DC: World Bank and IMF, 2005, p.4.. Available at http://siteresources.worldbank. org/GLOBALMONITORINGEXT/ Resources/complete.pdf.

27 Rex Brynen, 'Managing Public Resources: The Experience of the Palestinian "Proto-State"', in Boyce and O'Donnell, eds, *Peace and The Public Purse*, p. 199.

28 The supposed efficiency advantages of foreign sourcing can be illusory. In Afghanistan, for example, where USAID funds for rebuilding schools and health clinics were routed through a New Jersey-based private contractor, press reports have revealed inordinate

delays, shoddy construction and costs exceeding expectations.

29 Pires and Francino in Boyce and O'Donnell (eds), *Peace and The Public Purse*, pp. 141–42.

30 See Boyce, *Investing in Peace: Aid and Conditionality after Civil Wars*, *Adelphi* Paper No. 351 (Oxford: Oxford University Press, 2002); and 'Post-Conflict Recovery: Resource Mobilization and Peacebuilding', Working Paper no. 159 (Amherst, MA: Political Economy Research Institute, February 2008), available at http://www.un.org/esa/policy/wess/wess2008files/boyce_postconflict.pdf.

Chapter Six

1 Data from IMF country reports and the Peace Research Institute Oslo (PRIO). On post-conflict revenue management, see P. Le Billon 'Resources for Peace? Managing Revenues from Extractive Industries in Post-Conflict Environments' (New York and Amherst, MA: Center on InternationalCooperation and Political Economy Research Institute, 2008).

2 For the purpose of this chapter we will concentrate on internal conflicts (armed civil conflict) which make up the lion's share of recent armed conflicts. Although those cases discussed here highlight resource revenues have been an – or even the most – important source of financing, most rebel groups rely on multiple financing sources of which natural resources may be one. See A. Wennmann, 'The Political Economy of Conflict Financing: A Comprehensive Approach Beyond Natural Resources', *Global Governance* vol. 13, 2007, pp. 427–444.

3 According to *Global Witness* the contract awarded in 2005 to Mittal Steel by the Liberian transition government ceded to the company 'important sovereign powers' and an ability 'to set the price of iron ore, and therefore the basis of the royalty rate' payable to the government, see www.globalwitness.org/media_library_detail.php/156/en/heavy_mittal.

4 For further reading, see for example, P. Collier and A. Hoeffler, 'Greed and Grievance in Civil War', *Oxford Economic Papers*, vol. 56 no. 4, 2004, pp. 563–596; I. de Soysa and E. Neumayer, 'Resource Wealth and the Risk of Civil War Onset: Results From a New Dataset on Natural Resource Rents, 1970–99', *Conflict Management and Peace Science*, vol. 24 no. 3, 2007, pp. 201–218.

5 For further reading, see for example, M. Basedau and J. Lay, 'Resource Curse or Rentier Peace? The Ambiguous Effects of Oil Wealth and Oil Dependence on Violent Conflict', *Journal of Peace Research*, vol. 46 no. 6, 2009, pp. 757–776; M. Humphreys, 'Natural Resources, Conflict, and Conflict Resolution'. *Journal of Conflict Resolution*, vol. 49 no. 4, 2005, pp. 508–537.

6 See P. Le Billon, 'Natural resource types and conflict termination initiatives', *Colombia Internacional*, vol. 70, 2009, pp. 9–34.

7 This is the case for alluvial diamonds. On the case of Sierra Leone, see P. Le Billon & A. Levine, 'Building Peace with Conflict Diamonds? Merging

Security and Development in Sierra Leone's Diamond Sector', *Development and Change*, vol. 40 no. 4, 2009, pp. 693–715.

8   Namely Cuba and the Soviet Union for the government, and the US and South Africa for the rebellion. On the transition, see Le Billon, *Fuelling War: Natural Resources and Armed Conflicts*, Adelphi Paper 373, (London: Routledge for IISS, 2005).

9   *Ibid*.

10 Even if this represents only about $400 per person per year, far below the revenues generated in Gulf Emirates or even Gabon. Standard Bank figure updated from 'Nigeria's Oil Wealth Fails to Benefit Poor', Reuters, 20 July 2008.

11 See K. Lambrechts, 'Breaking the Curse: How Transparent Taxation and Fair Taxed Can Turn Africa's Mineral Wealth into Development' (Johannesburg: Open Society Institute of Southern Africa, 2009), available at http://news.bbc.co.uk/2/shared/bsp/hi/pdfs/25_03_09_breaking_the_curse.pdf. Accessed May 9, 2010..

12 See S. Altman, S. Nichols and J. Woods, 'Leveraging High Value Natural Resources to Engage Stakeholders in Industry Reform: The Liberia Forestry Initiative's Role in Liberia's Transition to Stability', in *High-Value Natural Resources and Post-Conflict Peacebuilding*, P. Lujala and S. Rustad (eds), forthcoming, Earthscan.

13 See 'Diamonds and Human Security, Annual Review 2009', by Partnership Africa Canada, available at www.pacweb.org/Documents/annual-reviews-diamonds/AR_diamonds_2009_eng.pdf.

14 On the example of De Beers, see I. Smillie, 'Dirty Diamonds: Armed Conflict and the Trade in Rough Dia-

monds', Report no. 377 (Oslo: Institute for Applied Social Science, Programme for International Co-operation and Conflict Resolution, 2002), p. 58.

15 From an estimated 25% to about 10%, (personal communication with Ian Smillie at Partnership Africa Canada).

16 See N. Garrett, S. Van Bockstael and K. Vlassenroot, 'The Right Interventions? Donors in the DRC Mining', in Lujala and Rustad (eds), *High-Value Natural Resources*.

17 For more on the ITRI initiative, refer to www.thestreet.com/print/story/10716904.html and www.itri.co.uk/POOLED/ARTICLES/BF_PARTART/VIEW.ASP?Q=BF_PARTART_310250.

18 N. Haysom and S. Kane, 'Negotiating natural resources for peace: Ownership, control and wealth-sharing', Briefing Paper, 3 November, (Geneva: The Centre for Humanitarian Dialogue 2009), Available at www.hdcentre.org/files/Negotiating%20natural%20resources%20for%20peace.pdf (accessed May, 2010).

19 M. Sandbu, 'Direct Distribution of Natural Resource Revenues as a Policy for Conflict Resolution and Prevention', in Lujala and Rustad (eds), *High-Value Natural Resources*.

20 M. Al Moumin, 'The Legal Framework for Managing Oil In Post-Conflict Iraq', see *ibid*.

21 Using average world price between 1970 and 2009 of $35 per barrel, in constant 2008 dollars.

22 For example the Natural Resource Charter lists this type of general transparency as one of its core 12 precepts (http://www.naturalresourcecharter.org/).

23 See M. Lundahl & F. Sjöholm, 'The Oil Resources of Timor-Leste: Cure or

Blessing?', *Pacific Review* vol. 21 no. 1, 2008, pp. 67–86.

24 See Altman, Nichols and Woods, 'Leveraging High Value Natural Resources', in Lujala and Rustad (eds), *High-Value Natural Resources*.

25 The Liberia Governance and Economic Management Assistance Program (GEMAP) is a joint effort between the government of Liberia and the international community that seeks to promote good governance through accountability and transparency. Among other things it seeks to reform key institutions. For more details, see www.gemapliberia.org/.

Chapter Seven

1 UNCTAD, *World Investment Report*, (New York and Geneva: UNCTAD, 2005, 2006, 2008, 2009).

2 See, for instance, Pieter Bouwen, 'Corporate Lobbying in the European Union: The Logic of Access', *Journal of European Public Policy*, vol. 9, no. 3, 2002, pp. 365–90.

3 See, for instance, Paul Collier and Anke Hoeffler, 'Greed and Grievance in Civil War', *Oxford Economic Papers*, vol. 56, no.4, 2004, pp.563–95; Nils Petter Gleditsch and Ranveig Gissinger, 'Globalization and Conflict: Welfare, Distribution, and Political Unrest', *Journal of World Systems Research*, vol. 5, no. 2, 1999, pp. 247–300.

4 See, for instance, Laura Alfaro, 'Foreign Direct Investment and Growth: Does the Sector Matter?', unpublished manuscript (Boston, MA: Harvard Business School, 2003); Andreea Mihalache and Quan Li, 'Modernization vs. Dependency Revisited: Effects of Foreign Direct Investments on Food Security in Less Developed Countries', *International Studies Quarterly*, forthcoming.

5 A foreign affiliate is a company located in country A (host country) and owned by a parent located in country B (home country).

6 Between 1980 and 2004, in developing countries, primary FDI flows as a percentage of GDP range from -11% (Namibia in 1993) to 74% (Solomon Islands in 1994), with a mean of 1.4 and a standard deviation of 5. Manufacturing FDI flows as a percentage of GDP range from -1% (Venezuela in 1984) to 21% (Cambodia in 2001), with a mean of 1.4 (e.g., Mexico in the 1990s, Thailand in 1990, Cape Verde in 1994) and a standard deviation of 3. Service-sector FDI flows as percentage of GDP range from -1% (Argentina in 2002) to 60% (Cambodia in 1995), with a mean of 1.9 (Honduras in 2001 and 2002, Bulgaria in 1998, Uganda in 2000) and a standard deviation of 5.

7 Overseas Private Investment Corporation (OPIC), *Annual Report* (Washington DC: US Government Printing Office, 2004), see http://www.opic.gov/publications/reports-handbooks/annual.

8 OPIC, *Annual Report*, 1999, *ibid*.

9 OPIC, *Annual Report*, 1992, *ibid*.

10 OPIC, *Annual Report*, 2005, *ibid*.

11 Nils Petter Gleditsch et al., 'Armed Conflict 1946–2001'.

[12] For more information on OPIC, see www.opic.gov.

[13] OPIC was actually established in 1971, when, through Executive Order 11579, it was deemed the successor of the Agency for International Development (AID), created in 1961. Since 1961, AID, then OPIC, have provided support and political-risk insurance to US investors in developing countries.

[14] Theodore H. Moran and Gerald T. West (eds), *International Political Risk Management, Volume 3: Looking to the Future* (Washington DC: the World Bank, 2005).

[15] Paul Collier, 'On the Economic Consequences of Civil War', *Oxford Economic Papers*, vol. 51, no. 1, 1999, p. 170.

[16] Andrew R. Morrison, 'Violence or Economics: What Drives Internal Migration in Guatemala', *Economic Development and Cultural Change*, vol. 41, no. 4, 1993.

[17] Bruno S. Frey, Simon Luechinger and Alois Stutzer, 'Calculating Tragedy: Assessing the Costs of Terrorism', *Journal of Economic Surveys*, vol. 21, no. 1, 2007. See also, Collier, 'On the Economic Consequences of Civil War'.

[18] Alfredo Rangel, 'Parasites and Predators: Guerrillas and the Insurrection Economy of Colombia', *Journal of International Affairs*, vol. 53, no. 2, Spring, 2000.

[19] UNCTAD, *Development and Globalization: Facts and Figures*, UNCTAD/GDS/CSIR/2004/1, (New York and Geneva: UNCTAD, 2004), p. 44, available at http://www.unctad.org/en/docs/gdscsir20041_en.pdf.

[20] *Ibid.*, p. 44.

[21] Nils Petter Gleditsch et al., 'Armed Conflict 1946–2001'.

[22] Data on FDI flows reported by the United Nations Committee on Trade and Development are on a net basis — 'capital transactions credits less debits between direct investors and their foreign affiliates'. For more information, see http://www.unctad.org/Templates/Page.asp?intItemID=3153.

[23] FDI data come from the World Development Indicators (WDI), a dataset collected by the World Bank. For more information, see http://data.worldbank.org/data-catalog/world-development-indicators.

[24] Based on data from the WDI.

[25] Colombia face civil war in 1998-1990, 1992-1993, 1998-2002, and again in 2004 (UCDP/PRIO Armed Conflicts Dataset, v. 3-2005b; Gleditsch et al., 'Armed Conflict 1946–2001').

[26] Based on data from the WDI.

[27] For more information about MIGA, see http://www.miga.org/. Information about the investment projects insured through MIGA is available at http://www.miga.org/projects/index_sv.cfm. Information about the investment projects insured through OPIC is available in the agency's Annual Reports. The most recent reports can be accessed online at http://www.opic.gov/publications/reports-handbooks/annual. Reports released prior to 2000 are available upon request.

[28] This paper focuses on the interaction between investors and governments and the respective behaviour of each. Another explanation for continued FDI flows to countries with political violence takes into account the characteristics of conflict: when conflict is contained in a small area of the country, investments may continue to unaffected regions.

[29] Robert C. O'Sullivan, 'Learning from OPIC's Experience with Claims and Arbitrations', in Theodore Moran and

Gerald West (eds), *International Political Risk Management, Volume 3: Looking to the Future*, (Washington DC: The World Bank, 2005), pp. 30–74, p. 34.

30 See Achim Wennmann, 'Guidelines for Mediators: Private Sector Investment', *CCDP* Issue Brief, no. 3, March 2010, pp. 1–8; OECD, 'Resource Flows to Fragile and Conflict-Affected Countries' (Paris: OECD, 2009), available at http://www.oecd.org/dataoecd/14/14/43293581.pdf.

31 More information about the survey, implemented by EIU, ACE, IBM and KPMG in October 2006, is available at http://a330.g.akamai.net/7/330/25828/20070329204830/graphics.eiu.com/files/ad_pdfs/eiu_Operating_Risk_wp.pdf.

32 Andreea Mihalache, 'Gambling on Conflict: Profiling Investors in Conflict Countries', unpublished paper, September 2009.

33 The analyses that lead us to this conclusion are available upon request. Our models control for lagged FDI, economic growth, development, market size, capital openness, democracy and country fixed effects. FDI data were collected from UNCTAD records (Mihalache and Li, 'Modernization vs. Dependency Revisited').

34 F. Kydland and E. Prescott, 'Rules Rather Than Discretion: The Inconsistency of Optimal Plans', *Journal of Political Economy*, vol. 85, 1977, pp. 473–90; F. Kydland and E. Prescott, 'Time to Build and Aggregate Fluctuations', *Econometrica*, vol. 50, 1982, pp. 1345–71.)

35 Andrew T. Guzman, 'Why LDC's Sign Treaties That Hurt Them: Explaining the Popularity of Bilateral Investment Treaties', *Virginia Journal of International Law*, vol. 38, pp. 639–88, 659.

36 Customary law represents the general and consistent practices of states that they follow from a sense of legal obligation; Jack L. Goldsmith and Eric A. Posner, *The Limits of International Law* (New York: Oxford University Press, 2005), p. 23.

37 Guzman, 'Why LDC's Sign Treaties That Hurt Them', p. 659.

38 *Ibid.*, p. 681.

39 UNCTAD, *World Investment Report (WIR): FDI Policies for Development: National and International Perspectives* (New York and Geneva: UNCTAD, 2003), p. 171.

40 Some double-taxation treaties and free trade agreements also have investment clauses.

41 Mary Hallward-Driemeier, 'Do bilateral Investment Treaties Attract foreign Direct Investment? Only a Bit… and They Could Bite', *Policy Research Working Paper no. 3121* (Washington DC: World Bank, 2003); Tim Büthe and Helen V. Milner, 'The Politics of Foreign Direct Investment into Developing Countries: Increasing FDI through International Trade Agreements?', *American Journal of Political Science*, vol. 52, no. 4, October 2008, pp. 741–62.

42 Zachary Elkins, Andrew T. Guzman, and Beth A. Simmons, 'Competing for Capital: The Diffusion of Bilateral Investment Treaties, 1960–2000', *International Organization*, vol. 60, no. 4, Fall 2006, pp.811–46.

43 Ravi Ramamurti, 'The Obsolescing Bargaining Model: MNC-Host Developing Country Relations Revisited', *Journal of International Business Studies*, vol. 32, no. 1, 2001.

44 Our sample includes 184 non-OECD countries, observed between 1975 and 2004. We excluded OECD countries

from this analysis because their disproportionately large economies and higher economic integration makes them more likely to sign BITs.

45 We estimated cross-sectional linear models of FDI flows and BITs, controlling for economic development, which is the foremost determinant of FDI flows. We also compared average FDI across subsamples of the data.

46 Laura Alfaro, 'Foreign Direct Investment and Growth'; Mihalache and Li, 'Modernization vs. Dependency Revisited'.

47 Also see Wennmann, 'Guidelines for Mediators', p. 5.

Chapter Eight

1 This chapter focuses on intrastate conflicts, defined as those that 'occur between the government of a state and internal opposition groups.' Lotta Harbom, Stina Hogbladh and Peter Wallensteen, 'Armed Conflict and Peace Agreements', *Journal of Peace Research*, vol. 43, no. 5, September 2006, p. 626.

2 While debate remains over the rate of risk of a return to civil war, datasets do illustrate that many civil wars require more than one agreement to end the war and that relapses into war are not uncommon. See Stina Hogbladh, 'Patterns of Peace Agreements: Presenting new data on peace processes and peace agreements,' Paper presented at annual International Studies Association conference, San Diego, 2006, p. 19; Joakim Kreutz, 'How and when armed conflicts end: Introducing the UCDP Conflict Termination dataset', *Journal of Peace Research*, vol. 47, no. 2, 2010, p. 246.

3 For examples see Harbom, Hogbladh and Wallensteen, 'Armed Conflict and Peace Agreements', pp. 619–621.

4 Stewart Patrick, 'Weak States and Global Threats: Fact or Fiction?', *The Washington Quarterly*, vol. 29, no. 2, Spring 2006, p. 29.

5 Patrick, 'Weak States and Global Threats', pp. 34–40; James Cockayne and Adam Lupel, 'Introduction: Rethinking the Relationship between Peace Operations and Organized Crime', *International Peacekeeping*, vol. 16, no. 1, February 2009, pp. 4–19.

6 Edward Newman, 'Failed States and International Order: Constructing a Post-Westphalian World', *Contemporary Security Policy*, vol. 30, no. 3, December 2009, pp. 429–33.

7 Between 1989 and 2005, only 46% of peace agreements in intrastate conflicts over government, and 41% of peace agreements in intrastate conflicts over territory, contained provisions about disarmament. Harbom, Hogbladh and Wallensteen, 'Armed Conflict and Peace Agreements,' p. 624.

8 For a discussion, see Jeremy Ginifer, with Mike Bourne and Owen Greene, *Considering armed violence in the post conflict transition: DDR and small arms and light weapons reduction initiatives*, CICS briefing paper, University of Bradford, UK, September 2004.

9 See *Global Burden of Armed Violence* (Geneva: Geneva Declaration Secretariat, 2008), chapter 3; Hazem Adam Ghobarah, Paul Huth and Bruce

Russett, 'Civil Wars Kill and Maim People – Long After the Shooting Stops', *American Political Science Review*, vol. 97, no. 2, May 2003, p. 200.

10 *Global Burden of Armed Violence*, pp. 53–7.

11 See Patrick, 'Weak States and Global Threats', p. 34–40.

12 This chapter focuses on the domestic emergence of armed groups. In some cases external military actors have imported external criminal networks into post conflict settings, leading to violence and crime. See Cockayne and Lupel, 'Introduction', p. 12. But international interventions have also enabled the emergence and solidification of local actors in criminal endeavours. See James Cockayne, 'Winning Haiti's Protection Competition: Organized Crime and Peace Operations Past, Present and Future', *International Peacekeeping*, vol. 16, no. 1, 2009, pp. 77–99.

13 It remains difficult to mark the end of a war with a ceasefire or peace agreement because many civil wars involve numerous efforts at conflict termination. The latest UCDP dataset on conflict termination 1989–2007 (http://www.pcr.uu.se/database), the most comprehensive at this point, and used as a basis for selecting cases in this chapter. Twelve cases of terminated conflicts (no return to war within five years) were reviewed: Algeria, Angola, Burundi, El Salvador, Guatemala, Liberia, Mozambique, Nicaragua, Peru, Rwanda, Sierra Leone, and Tajikistan (see Appendix 1).

14 For a typology of armed groups active in post-conflict settings see Schneckener, 'Fragile Statehood, Armed Non-State Actors and Security Governance', in Alan Bryden and Marina Caparini

(eds), *Private Actors and Security Governance* (Berlin: Berlin Lit-Verlag, 2006), pp. 25–28.

15 For a number of case studies on such transitions see: Jeroen de Zeeuw, ed., *From Soldiers to Politicians: Transforming Rebel Movements after Civil Wars* (Boulder, CO: Lynne Rienner, 2008).

16 Dennis Rodgers, 'Youth Gangs in Colombia and Nicaragua: New Forms of Violence, New Theoretical Directions?' in A. Rudqvist (ed.) *Breeding Inequality/Reaping violence: Exploring linkages and causality in Colombia and beyond* (Uppsala: Uppsala University, 2002), pp. 126–27.

17 Arthur Brice, 'Gangs tied to paramilitaries cited in Colombia violence', CNN, 3 February 2010, http://edition.cnn.com/2010/WORLD/americas/02/03/colombia.violence/index.html; Jennifer Hazen, 'Force Multiplier: Pro-Government Armed Groups' in Small Arms Survey (ed.) *Small Arms Survey 2010* (Cambridge, MA: Cambridge University, 2010), p. 271.

18 See Maya M. Christensen and Mats Utas, 'Mercenaries of democracy: The "Politricks" of remobilized combatants in the 2007 general elections, Sierra Leone,' *African Affairs*, vol. 107, no. 429, pp. 515–39.

19 Cockayne and Lupel, 'Introduction', p. 11.

20 Jennifer Hazen, *Small Arms, Armed Violence, and Insecurity in Nigeria: The Niger Delta in Perspective*, Occasional Paper No. 20 (Geneva: Small Arms Survey, 2007), pp. 77–79.

21 For a discussion of organised crime in post-conflict settings see Cockayne and Lupel, 'Introduction', pp. 6–8.

22 Ana Kantor and Miriam Persson, *Understanding Vigilantism: Informal*

Security Providers and Security Sector Reform in Liberia (Stockholm, Sweden: Folke Bernadotte Academy, June 2010).

23 Jennifer Hazen, 'Gangs, Groups, and Guns: An Overview', in *Small Arms Survey 2010* (Cambridge: Cambridge University, 2010), pp. 88–89.

24 Jennifer Hazen and Chris Stevenson, 'Targeting Armed Violence: Public Health Interventions', in *Small Arms Survey 2008* (Cambridge: Cambridge University Press, 2008), pp. 289, 293; Oliver Jutersonke, Robert Muggah and Dennis Rodgers, 'Urban Violence and Security Promotion in Central America', *Security Dialogue*, vol. 40, 2009, pp. 382–85.

25 Benjamin Lessing, 'The Danger of Dungeons: Prison Gangs and Incarcerated Militant Groups', in *Small Arms Survey 2010* (Cambridge: Cambridge University, 2010).

26 Some have raised concerns about negotiating with armed groups. See Denis M. Tull and Andreas Mehler, 'The Hidden Costs of Power-Sharing: Reproducing Insurgent Violence in Africa', *African Affairs*, Vol. 104, no. 416, 2005, pp. 375–98.

Chapter Nine

1 Robert Kaplan, 'The Coming Anarchy', *The Atlantic Monthly* vol. 273, no. 4, February 1994, pp. 44–76.

2 Bernard Finel, 'What is Security? Why the Debate Matters', *National Security Studies Quarterly*, vol. 4, no. 4, Autumn 1998, pp. 2–7.

3 The 'Responsibility to Protect' doctrine arose out of international discussions in the 1990s over how to reconcile the tension between the principle of state sovereignty and the right of humanitarian intervention. The International Commission on Intervention and State Sovereignty (ICISS) produced a report articulating the new norm: 'The Responsibility to Protect' (Ottawa: IDRC, December 2001), http://www.iciss.ca/pdf/Commission-Report.pdf. The 'R2P' doctrine challenges state sovereignty as an absolute principle and argues that: 'where a population is suffering serious harm, as a result of internal war, insurgency, repression, or state failure, and the state in question is unwilling or unable to halt or avert it, the principle of non-intervention yields to the international responsibility to protect.' (p. xi).

4 Robert Gates, 'Helping Others Defend Themselves', *Foreign Affairs*, vol. 89, no. 3, May–June 2010, pp. 2–6.

5 This section of the chapter is adapted from a portion of the author's 'State Fragility as Wicked Problem', *PRISM*, vol. 1, no. 2, March 2010, pp. 85–100.

6 The International Crisis Group's 'Crisis Watch' can be accessed at: http://www.crisisgroup.org/home/index.cfm.

7 Political Instability Task Force, George Mason University http://globalpolicy.gmu.edu/pitf/index.htm. The PITF received funding from the Central Intelligence Agency beginning in 1994, one of several academic research projects supported by the CIA in that era to identify predictors of state failure or civil war.

8   World Bank, 'Governance Matters, Worldwide Governance Indicators', accessible at: http://info.worldbank.org/governance/wgi/index.asp.

9   The Fund for Peace, 'Failed States Index', accessible at: http://www.fundforpeace.org/web/index.php?option=com_content&task=view&id=99&Itemid=140. The Index was launched in 2005 and provides the basis for an annual set of articles on state failure in the journal *Foreign Policy.*

10   Brookings Institution, 'Index of State Weakness', accessible at: http://www.brookings.edu/reports/2008/02_weak_states_index.aspx

11   Mo Ibrahim Foundation, 'Index of African Governance', accessible at: http://www.moibrahimfoundation.org/en/section/the-ibrahim-index.

12   Transparency International, 'Corruption Perceptions Index', http://www.transparency.org/policy_research/surveys_indices/cpi.

13   Christiane Arndt and Charles Oman, 'Uses and Abuses of Governance Indicators', OECD Development Center, 2006. Another useful review of different indices of state fragility is the German Development Institute (DIE) and UN Development Programme (UNDP), 'Users' Guide on Measuring Fragility', Bonn: DIE, 2009.

14   See Fund for Peace, http://www.fundforpeace.org/web/index.php?option=com_content&task=view&id=391&Itemid=549; for an interactive map of these data, see *Foreign Policy*, http://www.foreignpolicy.com/articles/2009/06/22/2009_failed_states_index_interactive_map_and_rankings.

15   Stewart Patrick, 'US Policy Towards Fragile States: An Integrated Approach to Security and Development', in Nancy Birdsall (ed.), *The White House and the World* (Washington DC: Center for Global Development, 2008), p. 329. http://www.cgdev.org/content/publications/detail/16560.

16   For a recent review and critique of this literature, including efforts to measure state fragility and failure, see Achim Wennmann, 'Grasping the Strengths of Fragile States: Aid Effectiveness between "Top-down" and "Bottom-Up" Statebuilding' (Geneva: CCDP Working Paper, 2010), pp. 15–27, available at http://graduateinstitute.ch/webdav/site/ccdp/shared/6305/Broch_6_BD.pdf.

17   Jack Goldstone et al., 'A Global Forecasting Model of Political Instability', Paper delivered at the American Political Science Association Conference, Washington DC, 2005.

18   *Ibid.,* p. 11.

19   Will Reno, *Warlord Politics and African States* (Boulder, CO: Lynne Rienner, 2000).

20   Stephen John Stedman, 'The Spoiler Problem in Peace Processes', *International Security*, vol. 22, no. 2, Autumn 1997, pp. 5–53.

21   Charles King, *Ending Civil Wars, Adelphi Paper* 308 (Oxford: Oxford University Press for the IISS, 1997).

22   Ken Menkhaus, *Somalia: State Collapse and the Threat of Terrorism, Adelphi Paper* 364 (Oxford: Oxford University Press for the IISS, 2004), pp. 37–48.

23   Jeffrey Herbst, *States and Power in Africa* (Princeton: Princeton University Press, 2000).

24   See, for instance, the articles in the special issue of *Afrika Focus* 'Dossier; Governance without Government in African Crises' vol. 21, no. 2, 2008; Louise Andresen, Bjorn Moller and

Finn Stepputat (eds), *Fragile States and Insecure People? Violence, Security, and Statehood in the Twenty-First Century* (New York: Palgrave MacMillan, 2007); Ken Menkhaus, 'Governance without Government in Somalia', *International Security*, vol. 31, no. 3, Winter 2006-07, pp. 74–106.

[25] Koen Vlassenroot and Timothy Raeymaekers, 'The Politics of Rebellion and Intervention in Ituri: The Emergence of a New Political Complex?' *African Affairs* Vol.103, No. 412, July 2004, pp. 359–83.

[26] Ken Menkhaus, 'The Rise of a Mediated State in Northern Kenya: The Wajir Story and its Implications for Statebuilding,' *Afrika Focus* vol. 21, no. 2, 2008, pp. 23–38.

[27] Combating Terrorism Center at West Point, 'Al-Qa'ida's (Mis)Adventures in the Horn of Africa' (West Point, NY: US Military Academy, 2007), pp. 29–46. http://www.ctc.usma.edu/aqII.asp.

Chapter Ten

[1] See, for example, Vadim Volkov, *Violent entrepreneurs: The use of force in the making of Russian capitalism* (Cornell, NY: Cornell University Press, 2002).

[2] Roy Godson, *Menace to society: political-criminal collaboration around the world* (Washington DC: National Strategy Information Center, 2003).

[3] R. T. Naylor, 'The Insurgent Economy: Black Market Operations of Guerrilla Organizations', *Crime, Law and Social Change*, vol. 20, no. 1, 1993, pp. 13–51. See also A. Wennmann, *The Political Economy of Peacemaking* (London: Routledge, forthcoming 2011), especially chapter six.

[4] Naylor, 'The Insurgent Economy'.

[5] Alfredo Rangel Suárez, 'Parasites and predators: guerrillas and the insurrection economy of Colombia', *Journal of International Affairs*, vol. 53, no. 2, Spring 2000, pp. 577–601.

[6] See Richard Snyder, 'Does Lootable Wealth Breed Disorder? A Political Economy of Extraction Framework', in *Comparative Political Studies*, vol. 39, no. 8, October 2006, pp. 943–68.

[7] See John Rollins, Liana Sun Wyler and Seth Rosen, 'International Terrorism and Transnational Crime: Security Threats, U.S. Policy, and Considerations for Congress', Congressional Research Service Report R41004, Washington DC, 5 January 2010.

[8] Matthew Levitt and Michael Jacobson, *The Money Trail: Finding, Following, and Freezing Terrorist Finances*, Policy Focus no. 89 (Washington DC: The Washington Institute for Near East Policy, November 2008), p. 9.

[9] Financial Action Task Force, *Terrorist Financing* (Paris, France: FATF Secretariat, OECD, 2008), pp. 9, 18.

[10] Rangel Suárez, 'Parasites and Predators'.

[11] Naylor, 'The Insurgent Economy', pp. 24–25

[12] William Billingslea, 'Illicit Cigarette Trafficking and the Funding of Terrorism', *The Police Chief*, vol. 71, no. 2, February 2004.

[13] Aamir Latif and Kate Wilson, *The Taliban and Tobacco: Smuggled Cigarettes Give Boost To Pakistani Militants*

(Washington DC: Center for Public Integrity, 28 June 2009).

14 Kate Wilson, *Terrorism and Tobacco: Extremists, Insurgents Turn to Cigarette Smuggling* (Washington DC: Center for Public Integrity, 2009).

15 See Peter Andreas, *Blue Helmets and Black Markets: The Business of Survival in the Siege of Sarajevo* (Cornell, NY: Cornell University Press, 2008).

16 *Ibid.*

17 *Ibid.*, p. 25.

18 Naylor, 'The Insurgent Economy', p. 42.

19 Achim Wennmann, 'Grasping the Financing and Mobilization Cost of Armed Groups: A New Perspective on Conflict Dynamics', in *Contemporary Security Policy*, vol. 30, no. 2, August 2009, pp. 265–280.

20 Vanda Felbab-Brown, *Shooting Up: Counterinsurgency and the War on Drugs* (Washington DC: The Brookings Institution, 2010).

21 See Svante Cornell, 'Narcotics and Armed Conflict: Interaction and Implications', in *Studies in Conflict & Terrorism*, vol. 30, 2007, pp. 207–227.

22 Florian P. Kühn, 'Aid, Opium, and the State of Rents in Afghanistan: Competition, Cooperation or Cohabitation?', *Journal of Intervention and Statebuilding*, vol. 2 no. 3, 2008, pp. 309–327.

23 James Cockayne and Phil Williams, *The Invisible Tide: Towards an International Strategy to Deal with Drug Trafficking Through West Africa*, policy paper (New York: International Peace Institute, 2009).

24 Peter Leonard, 'Heroin Trade a Backdrop to Kyrgyz Violence', *Associated Press*, 24 June 2010.

25 James Cockayne and Adam Lupel, 'Introduction: Rethinking the Relationship between Peace Operations and Organized Crime', *International Peacekeeping*, vol. 16, no. 1, 2009, pp. 4–19.

26 Peter Andreas, 'Symbiosis Between Peace Operations and Illicit Business in Bosnia', in *International Peacekeeping*, vol. 16, no. 1, February 2009, pp. 33–46.

27 See Mike Pugh, 'The Political Economy of Peacebuilding: A Critical Theory Perspective', *International Journal of Peace Studies*, vol. 10, no. 2, 2005, pp. 23–42.

28 Mike Pugh, 'Postwar Political Economy in Bosnia and Herzegovina: the Spoils of Peace', *Global Governance*, vol. 8, no. 4, 2002, pp. 467–82.

29 See Ken Menkhaus, 'The rise of a mediated state in northern Kenya: the Wajir story and its implications for state-building', *Afrika focus*, vol. 21, no. 2, 2008, pp. 23–38.

30 William Reno, 'Understanding Criminality in West African Contexts', *International Peacekeeping*, vol. 16, no. 1 February 2009 , pp. 47–61.

31 See for example Sarah E. Mendelson, *Barracks and Brothels: Peacekeepers and Human Trafficking in the Balkans* (Washington DC, Center for Strategic and International Studies Press, 2005).

32 James Cockayne and Adam Lupel, 'Conclusion: From Iron Fist to Invisible Hand – Peace Operations, Organized Crime and Intelligent International Law Enforcement', *International Peacekeeping*, vol. 16, no. 1, February 2009, pp. 154–55.

33 William Reno, 'Protectors and Predators: Why Is There a Difference Among West African Militias?', in Louise Andersen, Bjørn Moller and Finn Stepputat (eds), *Fragile States and*

Insecure People? Violence, Security, and Statehood in the Twenty-First Century (New York: Palgrave Macmillan, 2007), pp. 99–122.

34 Thom Shanker and Eric Schmitt, 'U.S. Intelligence Puts New Focus on Afghan Graft', *New York Times*, 12 June 2010.

35 UN docs, S/PRST/2009/32, 8 December 2009, available at http://www.un.org/Docs/sc/unsc_pres_statements09.htm and S/PRST/2010/4, 24 February 2010, at http://www.un.org/Docs/sc/unsc_pres_statements10.htm.

36 Victoria K. Holt and Alix J. Boucher, 'Framing the Issue: UN Responses to Corruption and Criminal Networks in Post-Conflict Settings', in *International Peacekeeping*, vol. 16, no. 1, February 2009, pp. 20–32.

37 See further Cockayne and Lupel, 'Conclusion: From Iron Fist', pp. 164–65.

38 Andrew Hudson and Alexandra W. Taylor, 'The International Commission against Impunity in Guatemala: A New Model for International Criminal Justice Mechanisms', *Journal of International Criminal Justice*, vol. 8, no. 1, 2010, pp. 53–74.

39 On the Liberian example see James Cockayne, 'Wrestling with Shadows: Principled Engagement with Violent Economies and the Repressive Regimes that Rule Them' forthcoming in Morten Pedersen and David Kinley, eds, *Principled Engagement* (United Nations University Press, forthcoming 2010).

40 Cockayne and Lupel, 'Conclusion: From Iron Fist'.

41 Global Witness report, *Lessons UNlearned*, 2010 (available at http://www.globalwitness.org).

42 United Nations, *Final report of the Group of Experts on the DRC submitted in accordance with paragraph 8 of Security Council resolution 1857 (2008)*. UN Doc. S/2009/603, 23 November 2009, available at http://www.un.org/sc/committees/1533/egroup.shtml.

43 Bruce Broomhall, *Illicit Conflict Economies: Enhancing the Role of Law Enforcement and Financial Machinery*, (Montreal: University of Quebec, 2010).

44 Jonathan Winer, 'Tracking Conflict Commodities and Financing', in Karen Ballentine and Heiko Nitzschke, eds, *Profiting from Peace: Managing the Resource Dimensions of Civil War*, (Boulder, CO: International Peace Academy and Lynne Rienner publishers, 2005), pp. 69–93.

45 See generally John Ruggie, *Protect, Respect and Remedy: A Framework for Business and Human Rights*. Report of the Special Representative of the Secretary-General on the Issue of Human Rights and Transnational Corporations and other Business Enterprises. UN Doc. A/HRC/85, 7 April 2008, available at http://www.unglobalcompact.org/docs/issues_doc/human_rights/Human_Rights_Working_Group/29Apr08_7_Report_of_SRSG_to_HRC.pdf.

46 See Cockayne, 'Wrestling with Shadows', forthcoming.

47 Cockayne and Lupel, 'Introduction', p. 7.

48 US Supreme Court, *Holder, Attorney General, et al. v. Humanitarian Law Project et al.*, No. 08-1498, Judgment of 21 June 2010.

49 See Felbab-Brown, *Shooting Up*.

Conclusion

1   A. De Soto and G. Del Castillo, 'Obstacles to Peacebuidling', *Foreign Policy*, vol. 94, 1994, pp. 69–83, at p. 76.

2   See also K. Papagianni and A. Wennmann, 'Improved International Support to Peace Processes to Peace Processes', Approach Paper for the International Network on Conflict and Fragility, 11 June 2010.

3   See for example the 2005 *Paris Declaration on Aid Effectiveness*, the 2007 *Principles for Good International Engagement in Fragile States and Situations*, and the 2010 *Dili Declaration: A New Vision for Peacebuilding and Statebuilding*.

4   Comment by Graeme Simpson at the conference *Connecting the Dots: Linking Peacemaking to Peacebuidling to Development*, Geneva, 8 June 2010.

5   S. L. Woodward, 'Economic Priorities for Successful Peace Implementation' in S. J. Stedman, D. Rothchild and E. M. Cousens (eds), *Ending Civil Wars: The Implementation of Peace Agreements* (Boulder, CO: Lynne Rienner, 2002) pp. 183–214.

6   See S. Raine, *China's African Challenges* (London: Routledge for the International Institute for Strategic Studies, 2009), pp. 105–37.

7   See International Dialogue on Peacebuilding and Statebuilding, *Dili Declaration: A New Vision for Peacebuilding and Statebuilding*, Dili, 10 April 2010, available at http://www.oecd.org/dataoecd/12/30/44927821.pdf.